THE WALL STREET JOURNAL

Guide to Wine

New and Improved

How to

Buy, Drink, and

Enjoy Wine

Broadway Books / New York

THE WALL STREET JOURNAL

Guide to Wine

New and Improved

Dorothy J. Gaiter
&
John Brecher

authors of the popular "Tastings" column

BROADWAY

THE WALL STREET JOURNAL GUIDE TO WINE, NEW AND IMPROVED
Copyright © 2002 by Dorothy J. Gaiter and John Brecher.
All rights reserved. No part of this book may be reproduced or transmitted
in any form or by any means, electronic or mechanical, including
photocopying, recording, or by any information storage and retrieval
system, without written permission from the publisher. For information,
address Broadway Books, a division of Random House, Inc.,
1540 Broadway, New York, NY 10036.

Broadway Books titles may be purchased for business or promotional use or
for special sales. For information, please write to: Special Markets
Department, Random House, Inc., 1540 Broadway, New York, NY 10036.

PRINTED IN THE UNITED STATES OF AMERICA.

BROADWAY BOOKS and its logo, a letter B bisected on the diagonal, are
trademarks of Broadway Books, a division of Random House, Inc.

THE WALL STREET JOURNAL© is a trademark and service mark of
Dow Jones & Company, Inc.

Visit our website at www.broadwaybooks.com

The Cataloging-in-Publication Data is on file with the Library of Congress.

SECOND EDITION

Designed by Donna Sinisgalli

ISBN 0-7679-0814-7

3 5 7 9 10 8 6 4 2

To Media and Zoë

Contents

Red Wine

This 'n' That

Sparkling Wine

Introduction

*"You take the mystery out of wine
without taking the magic out of it."*
—WINEMAKER DANIEL GEHRS, OF DANIEL GEHRS WINES

Too many books about wine read like textbooks to us. Some are textbooks for first-graders and some are textbooks for graduate students, but they're textbooks nonetheless. There's certainly a place for them, and great value in them, but we worry sometimes that there's too much emphasis on learning about wine and not enough on enjoying it. We don't understand why people are told that they have to become experts on wine before they can appreciate it. Imagine if people were told they had to understand all of the intricacies of baseball before they could bask in the simple beauty of the game, or if they were told they had to make a study of art before they could be astonished by a Rembrandt. Do we have to know why the sky turns purple and gold and orange before we can love a magnificent sunset?

To us, wine is like art, or a sunset, or even the green grass of the outfield on a sunny day. It can be appreciated, reveled in, for no reason other than the way it touches our senses and makes us feel. We believe people should simply enjoy wine. If they do, they might want to learn more about it, which will increase their appreciation and joy as time goes on. That's certainly what happened to us. We met and fell in love on June 4, 1973, the day both of us began working as reporters at the *Miami Herald*. We'd both just finished college—Dorothy at the University of Missouri, John at Columbia—and we were both twenty-one years old. We fell in love with wine soon after that. Neither of us grew up in families where wine was served at meals, so we started at the bottom, learning by drinking inexpensive wine and reading books. In the late 1970s, we began taking notes on our wines and saving labels so we could relive some of our experiences ("Oh, yeah, remember *that* Chardonnay?").

Wine, for us, has never been an end in itself, but just one part of a good life. We remember good times and bad through the wines we were sharing during that period. Ask us about almost any moment in our lives, even just a restaurant meal, and we'll tell you how the wine was. We've been serious, hardworking journalists our whole lives. John was City Editor of the *Miami Herald,* a foreign writer for *Newsweek,* and Page One Editor of the *Wall Street Journal* for seven years. Dottie was an editorial writer and columnist for the *Miami Herald,* a reporter for the *New York Times,* and a national reporter and editor covering issues of race for the *Wall Street Journal* for a decade. Through all of that, through more than twenty years of marriage, and through the births of our two daughters, wine has always been a part of our lives.

But it was always an intimate pleasure. We had never written about wine, nor intended to, until early 1998, when the *Wall Street Journal* began its Weekend edition, which is published as part of the newspaper every Friday. Because the Weekend section's editor, Joanne Lipman, knew of our interest in wine, she asked us to write a weekly column. The column, called "Tastings," was an immediate success. We've received thousands of warm, delightful, and instructive letters from readers all over the world, which has given us a unique insight into the real questions and concerns people have about wine. Wine merchants everywhere report that customers, many of them new customers, rush in to buy our recommendations every Friday morning. We have appeared often on Martha Stewart's television show to discuss wine (she has an excellent palate), on *Today* to discuss Champagne (Matt liked the most expensive one and Katie liked the cheapest), and on many radio shows. This has brought more people to our column, people who, most important to us, say that our column helps make wine more approachable and more enjoyable, which in turn makes their lives fuller and richer.

I'm a 24-year-old budding wine lover and I've lived in San Francisco for three years. I've really enjoyed living in close proximity to Napa Valley and also enjoyed the wines of the region. My dad is 62 and lives

in Pennsylvania and we don't see each other often. But, every Friday,
we read your column and buy some wines from your recommended lists
and talk about what we like and don't like, among other things. It's
been a way for us to remain close and get even closer. Just wanted to
say thanks for writing a truly world-class wine column.

—MARK WILLIAMS

This book is an outgrowth of our columns, and borrows liberally from them. In this book, we aren't writing for aficionados. Although we hope aficionados enjoy our writing, there are many books and magazines for them on the market. We're also not trying to convince people who don't like wine that they should. Everyone's taste is different. John doesn't like sushi. Dottie doesn't like hamburgers. Some people don't like wine. So what? Instead, this book is intended for a frustrated majority: people who can afford more and better wine, who want to enjoy wine more but who don't know where to begin. Our purpose is not to educate you but rather to share our passion, give you some smiles, and maybe offer a little insight into the world of wine. What we've found, in general, is that people don't want to become wine experts. They just want to know what to pick up on the way home to sip with dinner. If your interest grows, you can read other books. More important, you can educate yourself by trying new wines. That, in the end, is the only way you'll truly learn anything really worth knowing about wine.

We're not know-it-alls. Wine, to us, is one of those things that the more you know, the more you realize you don't know. After all, there are thousands of different wines; new wineries, and promising new wine regions, appear all the time; there's a whole new vintage every year; and, most daunting, every wine from every previous vintage changes in the bottle over the years. The fun isn't in mastering all that, it's simply trying to keep up. We learn something new about wine every day. Indeed, we feel we know so much more than we did when we wrote the first edition of this book in 1999. If we write a third edition, we'll surely know much more than we know today. We're not embarrassed to admit that. It's a process, and a fun one at that.

We don't really write a wine column. We write a lifestyle column that happens to focus on wine. Our readers understand that. Of all of the thousands of notes we've received, only one of them hangs on our wall at work. It is from Debra Rensing of Tecumseh, Kansas:

When I was younger, I worked for a very educated, successful and worldly couple. They took me under their wing with business and social situations. The business and most of the social was very easy for me to pick up, but when it came to my wine education, that was very frustrating.

They both had very educated palates about wine. I listened to what they said to look for, taste for and pay for. They explained how to buy by the case, how to store it in a proper wine cellar and how to open it to breathe and serve it.

But they didn't tell me how to enjoy it—or that I was supposed to enjoy it. Now, 25-plus years later, I have found you two and I have learned about enjoying wine. For that, thank you! Thank you! Thank you!

How to Use This Book

This book is not a comprehensive look at the wine world. Instead, we've focused on some wines we like and think you'd like. We've also added additional information on topics such as chilling wine, choosing a wine store, and ordering wine in a restaurant. In many cases, these reflect the questions posed to us by readers.

At the end of each chapter, there are notes about the wines that emerged from our tastings as our favorites. We've rated them on a scale that, from worst to best, goes like this: Yech, OK, Good, Very Good, Delicious, and the rare Delicious! This has been our personal scorekeeping system since we began taking notes a quarter century ago. We cannot emphasize this too strongly: The list of specific wines is just a guide. Don't get obsessed with these. We list specific wines only to give you a point of reference, a kind of road map of what this particular kind of wine should taste like. We don't even try to find the "best" of each type. There are far too many wines out there, from too many years, stored under too many different conditions, to ever declare a "best." Instead, we've listed a few wines that we enjoyed in our tastings, with descriptions that should give you an idea of why we liked these best among the many wines we tried. In most cases, we have noted the vintage we tasted in parentheses at the end of the notes.

Several factors will conspire against your finding these specific wines. Most very good wines aren't made in huge quantities, they don't often stay in stores for very long, and wine distribution is so screwy that it's hard to say what wines are available in any state. Instead, focus on our more general advice: For instance, we think Merlot around $20 is much better than Merlot that costs just a few dollars less; we think Muscadet and Beaujolais are two of the world's great wine bargains; and we think—and we were surprised to find this—that it's hard to go wrong with California Pinot Noir.

You shouldn't take any wine ratings, including ours, too seriously. We can tell you what we like, but we can't tell you what you'll like. Everybody's taste is different. Dottie prefers her steak virtually raw, while John likes his medium. In the long run, the only rating that matters is your own. If you don't like a wine that experts have recommended, don't think there's something wrong with you. Instead, celebrate your independent palate.

In the General Advice section, we try to give some guidance about how to narrow your search for good wine, including the names of some specific regions, wineries, or shippers. For instance, you might not be able to find the Saintsbury Pinot Noir in the vintage we recommend, but Saintsbury is a reliable name in Pinot Noir, and you might look for that label in a different vintage. Don't take the prices quoted in the Wine Notes literally. They are meant as a very general guide. Prices fluctuate wildly all over the country. But if we say that one wine costs $7 and another costs $40, at least you will have a general idea what kind of money we're talking about and how these wines compare in price with each other. In the Food Pairings notes, we have offered just a few dishes that we enjoy with that kind of wine. These are not meant to be comprehensive lists. Because tastes are so different, it's impossible to know what wine you will like best with various foods, but these suggestions might give you some ideas.

We believe in value, but we believe value and price are very different. Some expensive wines are great values, and some cheap wines are terrible values. That philosophy infuses this book. More broadly, our philosophy is that we cherish our independence. Most of the experiences recounted in this book occurred long before we were wine writers, so we received no special treatment. Nor do we want any now. We do not accept any free wine, free meals, or free trips; we do not meet privately with winemakers when they visit New York; and we do not attend events that are not open to the public or attend press-only events. Our wine is bought under the same circumstances in which you would buy it—at retail stores, except where noted otherwise. It's paid for either by us or by our employer, the *Wall Street Journal*. We taste the wines "blind"—that is, with each bottle wrapped in a paper bag—unless specifically noted otherwise. We do all this because we believe the playing field should be level, and because we believe wines should speak for themselves. We are covered by the same principles of intellectual rigor and conflict of interest as every other journalist at the *Wall Street Journal*. As journalists our whole lives, we have always lived under the strict rules of America's most respected newspapers, and we're not going to change now.

While fairness and impartiality are fundamental to us, we do not claim to be objective. We don't believe there is anything objective about wine. It's simply impossible, as we say again and again in this book, to separate the taste of a wine from the experience you're having when you drink it. The same wine will taste different depending on whether you're having it with the boss at lunch or with a loved one on a terrace overlooking a pond at sunset. It's pointless, and contrary to our whole approach to wine, to pretend otherwise. In other words, we don't believe in dogma. There is no right and no wrong in wine.

In short, wine is supposed to be fun. That's how to use this book: to have fun.

THE WALL STREET JOURNAL

Guide to Wine

New and Improved

White
Wine

Chapter One

Chardonnay

America's Third Ocean

Spring Mountain Chardonnay 1976. *Delicious! Huge, yet crisp, but also soft and very creamy, filling mouth with big creamy taste. Very complex, with contradictory tastes. Lots of pepper. Very much a Chardonnay.*

Cuvaison Chardonnay 1978. *Delicious. Classic Chardonnay nose, very buttery. Green-gold. Half alcohol and half butter, huge and plump. Massive aftertaste comes back up and gets you. Thick yet clean, a little wood but not overwhelming wood. Knocks your socks off.*

Guenoc Chardonnay 1980. *Delicious! Big and rich and creamy, filled with sunshine and butter. Long finish of nutmeg and wood.*

Kistler Chardonnay 1980. *Delicious, but shocking in its bigness. Massive and oaky. Long oak finish. Powerful, chewy, very American.*

Ah, the Chardonnay of our youth. "Powerful, chewy, very American"—those words from our notes back then said it all. Chardonnay has been the world's greatest white-wine grape for centuries. It is, after all, the grape of the famous white Burgundies of France. In the 1970s, California winemakers discovered just what was possible with this grape in the New World. They took the big, superripe grapes provided by California's perfect weather, then fermented and aged them in oak barrels and produced wines that offered a uniquely American taste and, in a sense, a reflection of the American character: bold, unrestrained, and outsized.

We look back on those chewy Chardonnays with the affection of a first crush. As it happens, we fell in love with Chardonnay at about the same time the rest of the country did. Chardonnay became America's sweetheart. Americans now drink about 400 million bottles of Chardonnay a year. It is far and away the country's most popular "varietal" wine—that is, a wine named after its grape. America became a nation of three oceans: the Atlantic, the Pacific, and the Chardonnay.

This is both good and bad. Let's get to the good part first: Chardonnay can be a terrific wine, soul-satisfying and just plain delicious. We—and, we'd guess, most wine lovers—have had more great experiences with Chardonnay-based wines than with any other white. Not only that, but if you enjoy Chardonnay, there's no reason to settle for a simple "glass of white wine." There are excellent, flavorful Chardonnays out there, some of them remarkably inexpensive. And some expensive Chardonnays still have the kind of character, class, breeding, and personality—even the drama—of the Chardonnays we first fell for.

What does a fine California Chardonnay taste like to us? It's big, rich, ripe, and buttery. It's mouthfilling, so you have to take small sips. It has a little bit of toastiness, vanilla, maybe some butterscotch and some cream, and it's almost chewy. Sometimes your nose can pick up hints of fruit—grapefruit or pineapple. Its tastes are broad, rather than focused and sharp, with maybe a hint of oiliness, which doesn't sound so good but adds texture and complexity. The very best Chardonnays have all of this power going on in your mouth, but when you swallow, something miraculous happens. The finish is a clean, light one that lingers for several minutes, like the essence of plump, sweet grapes.

Now *that* is Chardonnay. But now the bad news. As America's affair with Chardonnay grew, wineries began producing a great deal of yucky Chardonnay. ("Yucky" is one of those highly technical wine terms that we will use throughout this book.) The recipe is easy. Get some second-rate vineyard land with plenty of sun. Let the vines grow and grow and don't prune back much, which will leave you with plenty of grapes but little flavor. (Imagine that every vine has only so much flavor in it. The fewer the grapes, the more flavor each grape has.) Let them get overripe, which produces a great deal of sugar—and, later, alcohol—but breaks down acids, leaving the wine simple and flabby. Maybe leave the wine slightly sweet, too, because, as the old saying goes, Americans talk dry but drink sweet.

During fermentation or after, maybe throw in some wood chips for flavor. Now, you can still call that Chardonnay, because it is, indeed, made mostly from Chardonnay grapes. There you have it. Sound good? No, it doesn't sound good to us, either, but America's demand for Chardonnay is so insatiable that bad Chardonnays sell, too.

The other bad thing that happened is that critics began hammering California Chardonnay for being too woody, too buttery, too big. It doesn't go with food, they said, and it won't age well, either. There's even a name for the critics: the ABC Club—Anything But Chardonnay. Ever sensitive to the market, some winemakers began to rein in their Chardonnay. Pretty soon, American winemakers were boasting about their "French-style" Chardonnay, meaning the wine had more restraint, a bit more lemon-acid taste, which made them better with food, and less obvious flavors of wood. And sometimes those can be great, too. You can see the change in our tattered old notebooks:

Chalone 1979. *Delicious! Really fantastic. French in its complexity and terrific finesse. Ripe, full-flavored, complex, fruity, and woody without a wood taste. Long, lemony finish. Yellow, Chardonnay look and a classy lemony nose. No real butter as such, just fruit. Nutmeg, vanilla, and smoke on the nose and in the finish.*

Many of the less-oaky wines were delicious, but all of this created such a split personality for Chardonnay that wine drinkers have a hard time figuring out which is which. We get letters every week from readers who are looking for Chardonnays that have wood or Chardonnays that don't have wood, or just wondering what the fuss is about.

When people talk about wood or oak in good wines, they're talking about wooden barrels. Some wines, especially white wines meant to be fresh and fruity, never see the inside of a barrel. They're treated to stainless steel tanks and they're crisp, fragrant, and delightful. But most Chardonnay, like most good red wine, spends some time in oak barrels, which doesn't just give the wine additional flavors but also extra depth and complexity. Whether the wine is fermented in oak or just aged in oak matters. How long it's in oak matters. The size of the barrels matters. So does the kind of oak itself. We find that American oak imparts more dramatic flavors than French oak, which lends more elegance and finesse. New oak has more power than old oak, whose flavors have been depleted over the years and are mellower. "High-fire" barrels, which have been subject to more fire or charring in the barrel-making process, have more vanilla, toast, and caramel tastes than "low-fire" barrels. How much wood a wine gets—more generally, how a good wine is made—is a reflection of the character and vision of the winemaker.

There's a lot of magic in the process, but there's a lot of method, too. Consider the wine-making notes about a Napa Valley Private Reserve Chardonnay made by Ed Sbragia, winemaker at Beringer Vineyards: "All of the juice went into small French Nevers oak barrels, most of them new, custom-toasted to caramelize the neutral sugars in the wood and contribute a sweet vanilla note to the wine. The wines were fermented and aged in these barrels, and the lees [spent yeast cells] were hand stirred back into the wine every week for about six months. . . . We also put the wines through 100-percent malolactic fermentation to further enhance their dense, creamy mouthfeel. The wines were aged in barrels for over nine months before we made the final assemblage."

You don't need to understand all of that. The point is that winemaking is an art, and a highly personal one. But you know what? In the long run, nothing matters more than the fruit. As Page One editor of the *Wall Street Journal,* John always told reporters: "No matter how good a writer you are, your story won't be great if you don't have great reporting"—the raw data, the facts that go into a story. It's the same way with wine: it all starts with the fruit. Even a great winemaker can't make great wine from so-so fruit. California can produce great Chardonnay fruit—big, plump, rich fruit that can stand up to, and even benefit from, some oak. That's why we tell people that the problem with many Chardonnays isn't that they're overoaked, but that they're underfruited.

Unfortunately, too many people have made peace with the idea that Chardonnay is a simple, inoffensive wine that's slightly comfortable instead of genuinely good. In tastings year after year we have found many substandard Chardonnays that taste vaguely familiar, like "strawberry" soft drinks made entirely of artificial flavors. The wines have little body or mouthfeel. Many have a hot, alcoholic taste and more than a hint of sweetness. Tellingly, Dottie said at one point during a tasting, "They all taste warm," so John made sure the refrigerator was working properly (the bottles had been in there all day). No matter how well chilled, they'd taste too warm. In fact, many Chardonnays taste pretty much the same. Dottie calls them "paint-by-numbers" Chardonnays. They aren't unpleasant, but there's little about them that tastes like grapes. Instead, it's as though they were made in a lab and put together by computer, the way paints are mixed at Home Depot.

You don't have to settle for that! In our most recent tasting of Chardonnays under $20, we found quite a few—some far under $20—that were tasty, well-made wines. Some were woody and some were not, but they had this in common: They tasted as though they were made with ripe, plump grapes with good acids. "Fresh and alive," we wrote about one. "Good fruit left alone." This was Callaway Coastal, which cost just $7.99 at the time. Another fruity, delightful Chardonnay also came from an old favorite, Louis M. Martini Winery. "Quite juicy," we wrote. "Lots of ripe fruit." It was just over $10. About our favorite, we wrote: "It's green-tinged, with lime on the nose. There's some mango taste, a little bit of sour-ness. Quite crisp. More crisp fruit than wood. Classy. Tastes colder than the others! Expensive?" Nope, not expensive at all. In fact, it was just $9.99. What was it? Bogle Vineyards, whose Chardonnay had been our best value the year before.

We should mention one wine that wasn't among our favorites but that rated a solid Good on our scale. It was simple and a bit sweet, but easy to drink and pleasant. We thought that a bottle of this wine, put in a big tub of ice by the pool, would be lovely on a hot day and we wrote: "Everyone would like this." We were certainly right about that: It was Kendall-Jackson 1999, which cost $9.99 at the time and which pretty much everyone does like. In fact, K-J—reliable, widely available, and inexpensive—helped make Chardonnay America's sweetheart.

Of course, in that huge display of Chardonnays at the store there are many over $20, too. What's the difference between a $15 Chardonnay and a $35 Chardonnay? The answer should be something more than "$20." Think about what your everyday Chardonnay tastes like—some creamy, citrus fruit, a little bit of wood, nice mouthfeel that's a bit like meringue. A more expensive Chardonnay should give you that, of course, but much more. It should be a different experience, more than just a pleasant wine. Are American winemakers crossing that bar? We visited several stores and bought the first fifty we could find between $20 and $50 for a blind tasting. For our under-$20 tastings, we focus on wineries that produce enough each year so that their wines are widely distributed and generally available. But for this tasting, we decided not to restrict ourselves that way. Pretty much all more expensive Chardonnays are made in limited quantities, and some high-end wineries specialize in Chardonnay. So we picked up the first fifty, regardless of how big or small the winery was. That meant we picked up well-known names like Mondavi and Beringer, but it also meant we bought less well-known wines and a few that were new even to us. Our selection was inevitably arbitrary. There are hundreds of Chardonnays made in America. We might have found a wholly different fifty at other stores. But, as always, our point wasn't to find the very best Chardonnay in America, but to get an idea of what's out there, and to try to find some general themes.

What should you be looking for in an expensive Chardonnay? A wine that's stretching the bounds a bit. It should be an experience, not just a drink. It should take you places you haven't gone before. It should have enough of a personality that you get some sense of what the winemaker was trying to do. You might not think you could tell, but you could. Is it especially acidic and lemony? Maybe the winemaker was trying to make it a good food wine. Is it especially creamy? Maybe the winemaker really likes oak and felt the fruit was exceptional enough to handle a lot of it. Does the wine have a certain pleasant sourness? Is it austere or is it plump? These characteristics do not develop by accident. They're the winemaker's signature. An expensive wine of any kind should make you notice itself at some point, and often should make you appreciate its elegance. An expensive bottle should at least hold out the hope of a memorable, maybe even transcendent, experience. Extra money is no guarantee of that, but for that kind of money, you have a right to anticipate that the wine will be good enough to recommend to your friends the next day.

How did they fare? Some weren't worth it. The fruit didn't seem particularly ripe and the winemaker's attention to it didn't seem particularly keen. Interestingly, the wines that we favored almost all clustered around the $35 mark. Some were from large, well-known wineries, including Beringer ("classy") and Mondavi ("ripe and bold"). Some were surprises. Our second-favorite was from Davis Bynum Winery, which we remember more for a wonderful old man in the tasting room named Manny than for its wines. Its consulting winemaker was Gary Farrell, who makes fine and very expensive wines under his own name, and this Chardonnay was a shocker. "Lots of taste after it's gone," we wrote. "Shy, in an interesting way. Long, woody finish that lasts forever, with all the taste in the back and a little bit of pine wood at the end. Like a slow-blooming flower in your mouth. The taste grows. A winemaker's wine."

It wasn't the best of our tasting, though. That was, instead, a wine that we can still taste. "Fruity, soft, approachable, creamy, and lovely," we wrote. "Elegant, with lots of fruit, but confident enough to be restrained. Wow." This was a wine that we could enjoy on many levels—so very drinkable, yet also extremely complex, with a luscious finish. It was from Rombauer Vineyards, and a steal at the time at $27.99. If you think "a steal at $27.99" is an oxymoron, try an unfamiliar, high-end Chardonnay that you discovered yourself. There's at least a good chance you'll see just what we mean.

We can't tell you which Chardonnay you'll like, but try this: Next time you drink a Chardonnay, close your eyes and smell it, and then take a big sip. In all of the various smells and tastes, can you sense plump, ripe fruit? Whether the Chardonnay costs $7.99 or $50, that is the bottom line. If your Chardonnay doesn't have a base of good fruit, try another. If you've found a Chardonnay that pleases you, great. But with all of the Chardonnays out there, don't stop experimenting. Chardonnays don't all taste alike, and you might find one you like even better—and maybe for less money, too.

One last tip: Australia is making some very good, and very affordable, Chardonnays with a kind of round, woody plumpness that we find comforting and easy to drink. We like Lindemans, Jacob's Creek, Hardys, and Alice White among well-distributed Chardonnays under $20. For higher-priced Australian Chardonnay, look for Penfolds. In addition, if you want to see how different Chardonnay-based wines can taste, try a white Burgundy, even an inexpensive Mâcon (see Chapter Five), or a Chablis (see Chapter Six).

Wine Notes

General advice: Eight wineries have been among our favorites in Chardonnay tastings at least twice, and most are widely distributed: Beringer, Byron, Bogle, Cambria, Estancia, Gallo of Sonoma, Hahn, and La Crema. The following Wine Notes show the results of our most recent under-$20 and over-$20 tastings. Don't overchill fine Chardonnay. It is best at cool room temperature. We have noted the "woodiness" of some wines below because people ask us about that. Remember that the prices are the prices we paid at the time of our tastings. We list them only to give a relative idea of cost. The vintage tasted is noted in parentheses. *Food pairings:* We find that a nicely chilled, inexpensive Chardonnay is great with any kind of spicy food, from jambalaya to Thai dishes. Better Chardonnay demands more elegant, sensuous foods, such as dishes with luscious cream sauces, and Dottie's favorite: rich, crispy-on-the-outside, succulent-on-the-inside sweetbreads.

Under $20

Bogle Vineyards (California). $9.99. VERY GOOD/DELICIOUS. Best of tasting and best value. So crisp that it seems colder than others. Like eating just-picked grapes, with nice acidity for food. Tastes expensive and classy. (1999)

Louis M. Martini Winery (California). $10.99. VERY GOOD. Quite juicy, with tons of ripe fruit and not much evidence of oak. Real mouth-feel, just a hint of nutmeg. Good with food. (1999)

R. H. Phillips Vineyard (Dunnigan Hills). $9.99. VERY GOOD. Very nice, with toast, crispness, and plump fruit. Peaches and cream, with some complexity. Still young. (1999)

Atlas Peak Vineyards (Napa Valley). $16.59. GOOD/VERY GOOD. Pleasant, though perhaps a bit heavy. Not subtle, but charming. (1999)

Callaway Coastal (Callaway Vineyard & Winery; California). $7.99.

GOOD/VERY GOOD. Fresh and alive, with good fruit left alone to taste good. Mandarin oranges and tropical fruits. Good for oak-avoiders. (1999)

Gallo of Sonoma (Sonoma County). $10.99. GOOD/VERY GOOD. Soft, with nice mouthfeel, a little bit of cream, and some lemon, but all in nice, relaxed balance. (1999)

Guenoc (Guenoc and Langtry Estate Vineyards and Winery; California). $12.59. GOOD/VERY GOOD. Creamy, fruity, with a little edge. Delightful. (1999)

Markham Vineyards (Napa Valley). $15.39. GOOD/VERY GOOD. A nice balance of crisp fruit and broad, oaky tastes. (1998)

St. Francis Winery & Vineyards (Sonoma County). $9.99. GOOD/ VERY GOOD. Crisp, with lemon and butterscotch tastes. Nice fruit, though maybe a bit too woody. (1999)

Over $20

Rombauer Vineyards (Carneros). $27.99. DELICIOUS. Best of tasting and best value. Great ripe fruit/oak balance. Creamy, rich nectars with nutmeg. Soft and approachable, yet a very serious wine. Lots of fruit, but confident enough to be restrained. Endless, voluptuous finish. (1998)

Davis Bynum Winery (McIlroy & Allen Vineyards Limited Edition; Russian River Valley). $28.99. VERY GOOD/DELICIOUS. It's good in the mouth, but even better after it's gone, like a slow-blooming flower in your throat and mouth. It lingers like a nice dream. (1997)

Robert Mondavi Winery (Napa Valley Reserve). $37.99. VERY GOOD/DELICIOUS. Smoky, heavenly nose. Ripe, bold, mouth-coating fruit and a long, gorgeous finish. (1996)

Canepa Cellars (Gauer Vineyard "Adobe III"; Alexander Valley).

$34.99. VERY GOOD. Aggressive, lemony fruit. Austere instead of plump. Honeyed, with lots of mouthfeel. It's way too young, will just get better with time. (1996)

Long Vineyards (Napa Valley). $35.99. VERY GOOD. Intense, tight fruit, with tropical flavors, nice acids, and a little cream. Great balance. (1997)

Byron Estate (Byron Vineyard; Santa Maria Valley). $35.99. VERY GOOD. Interesting and aggressive. Toasty and very American, with lots of fruit and wood. Proud to be big. (1996)

Beringer Vineyards (Napa Valley Private Reserve). $34.99. VERY GOOD. Classy, with great fruit that seems to leap right out of the glass. Beautifully made. (1997)

Pine Ridge Winery (Napa Valley, Stags Leap District). $35.99. VERY GOOD. A totally lovely drink-now wine, with generous, easy-to-like fruit and plenty of it. (1997)

Don't Be Embarrassed
About the Blue Nun
in Your Past

It's funny how we're all shy about our "first wine"—you know, the one we look back on with a combination of affection and horror. Mateus, Lancers, Blue Nun, Asti Spumante, Hearty Burgundy. But, you know, everyone has to start somewhere, even some of the world's most respected wine authorities. For Jancis Robinson, a Master of Wine, editor of the respected *Oxford Companion to Wine,* and author of many fine wine books, it was a wine called Hirondelle. This wine, in its time, was big in Britain. "It was a rosé, which was not surprising because a lot of people start out with rosés," she told us. It was the early 1970s, "and its great claim to fame was that, un-like today, the owners weren't required to tell you where the wine actually came from. It was just bought from wherever it could be supplied most cheaply. So you weren't buying into the place but into the solidity of the brand. Of course, it's contrary to everything I be-lieve in today.

"The price was 59 pence a litre. You didn't buy it in namby-pamby 750-ml size, and it probably had a screw cap. It was a sort of student-and-just-after-student, first-flat kind of wine. It was a dis-consolate, would-like-to-protest-if-they-had-the-energy, lollying-around-young-people kind of wine."

Has she had it recently? Heavens no. "The market routed it out," she says, with some relief. Her *Oxford Companion,* an exhaus-tive, 819-page look at the entire world of wine, doesn't have an entry for Hirondelle.

We first met John Fischer more than ten years ago, when he was in charge of wine at a swanky restaurant near our apartment. Over the years, we followed him to other New York restaurants. Now he is service instructor at the Culinary Institute of America. When we asked Mr. Fischer about his first wine, he got a faraway look on his face and said, "Mouton Cadet."

Andrea Immer, one of only a few women in the world to qualify as a Master Sommelier, is author of the book *Great Wine Made Simple*. Her first wine was Cella Lambrusco in screw-cap magnums. "My friend Trish in high school first turned me on to this, and it endured right through college until and even after I had my wine epiphany at my first wine-tasting class. It was just so, well, yummy. And the first few times I had it I remember thinking how fashionable I felt, just like the preening groupie-model types flanking that guy Aldo Cella on those commercials where you first learned to 'Chill a Cella!' "

Larry Stone, a celebrated Master Sommelier and wine maven of Rubicon restaurant in San Francisco, and formerly of Charlie Trotter's in Chicago, grew up in a home where wine was always present. He says his mother had a "predilection" toward sweeter wines, so they sometimes drank a wine called Moselmaid, a brand name for a blend from Germany. In college, he says, he was a bit wild and played in a band that performed in a park. The wine that fueled those performances was Gallo Rhine Garten. Gallo told us this wine was most often a blend of grapes like Chenin Blanc, French Colombard, and Sauvignon Blanc. It was medium-bodied, fresh, and on the sweet side, and it doesn't exist anymore.

Mary Ewing-Mulligan and Edward McCarthy, another wine-writing couple, have written several books, including *Wine for Dummies*. Mary told us: "My very first wine was Mateus rosé, in 1970." From Ed: "The first wine that I can remember drinking was Christian Brothers Port on Thanksgiving Day. Around eighteen or nineteen, I discovered the inexpensive, rather sweet German wines—some Mosels, like Zeller Schwarze Katz and Liebfraumilch." Liebfraumilch is the slightly sweet, simple wine with the great name that's made almost exclusively for export. The most famous one in our youth, of course, was Blue Nun.

When we wrote about first wines in the newspaper, the responses we received were laugh-out-loud funny.

• Rick Allen of Jamestown, California: "I've tried each one you mentioned and loved them at the time. I've forgotten the headaches, but remember the memories (at least the ones that included sex)."

• Pamela Parker of New York City: "Although I'm nearly horrified by the thought now, I have good memories of times spent with classics like a Boone's Farm strawberry wine and a Beringer White Zinfandel. Now that I aspire to wine snobbery, it's hard to admit I once quaffed these unsophisticated beverages. But it sure was fun at the time."

• Adam M. Carmel of Denver: "Your article reminded me of one of my favorite expressions from the '70s: 'Mateus keeps you loose.' How many times have I wished that I could go back."

• Thor Thorson of Redmond, Washington: "I was interested (alarmed?) that except for the Hirondelle, I have vivid memories of every wine you mentioned. Some are more pleasant than others. Did you ever hear the old saying, 'Speed kills, but Ripple cripples'? It was the source of my first and worst-ever hangover."

We hadn't had Lancers, Mateus, or Blue Nun in many years, so we bought some, all at around $6 or $7. The Blue Nun was kind of charming, with a lovely "nose" of apples and a pleasant, fairly neutral and slightly sweet taste. The Mateus seemed charmless, with very simple, sweet tastes. The Lancers wasn't pleasant at all, slightly sulfuric and hard to drink. Surely these were much better wines when we were younger. Or, as Burt Lancaster said in the movie *Atlantic City*: "Atlantic Ocean was somethin' then. Yes, you should have seen the Atlantic Ocean in those days."

Don't be embarrassed about any wine you drink. Even now, we'll try anything once. We're proud to have tried pineapple wine from Hawaii and sweet red wine from Moldova and homemade garlic wine. It's all part of the joy of discovering wine.

Chapter Two

Sauvignon Blanc

A Surprise in the Grass

We love detours. We both have a lousy sense of direction, so we've gotten lost all over the world. Fortunately, many of our most memorable moments have occurred on these unintentional detours. There's something about the lack of expectation, the spontaneity, that makes such experiences so much fun. Wine is the same way. When we find ourselves taking the road less traveled—either on purpose or because we somehow got lost—we usually have a good time. In writing this chapter, we took a detour all the way across the world, and we were glad we did.

Let's start at the beginning.

To us, one of the most perfect wines for summer is Sauvignon Blanc. It's crisp, refreshing, lively, and goes perfectly with summertime foods such as cold poached salmon and curried chicken salad. Not only that, but it tastes like summer to us, like sunshine, melons, citrus fruits, and fresh-mowed grass. A good Sauvignon Blanc should have an unmistakable nose: not "hints" of fresh-mown grass, not "redolent" of fresh-mown grass, but it should smell as if you're standing in the middle of a field. After it's rained. The wine might have a little tinge of green, and in the mouth it's crisp, aggressive, and almost haylike, herbal. The freshness and acidity, combined with that unique grassy quality, make this wine so very refreshing and gulpable.

The Sauvignon Blanc grape makes some well-known wines in France, like Pouilly-Fumé and Sancerre (see Chapter Seven), and is sometimes called Fumé Blanc or Blanc Fumé in California. It also makes some great dessert wines, like the famous Château d'Yquem, in which it's blended with Sémillon (see Chapter Thirty-four). Sauvignon Blanc is so versatile that it's made in any number of styles. Sometimes winemakers give it a lot of barrel aging, the oak making it rich and creamy. Sometimes they put it only in stainless steel, preserving the pure fruit and letting the grapes speak for themselves. Sometimes they put it in steel and oak.

Sauvignon Blanc has become popular as a simple, easy-to-drink, re-freshing—and inexpensive—wine. In fact, it's the second most popular va-rietal white wine in America, though it's far, far behind Chardonnay. We first conducted a blind tasting of American Sauvignon Blancs in 1998, and we were disappointed with what we found. Most California producers, ap-parently in an effort to make Sauvignon Blanc more appealing to a greater number of people, had toned down or eliminated that vibrant grassy char-acter. What was left tasted like lemon water. Why bother? Our notes about one of these wines read: "Nice and friendly, but stripped of character. Soft, could be anything. No varietal taste." When we ripped off the bag, the wine was from Field Stone, a delightful little winery whose wines we usu-ally enjoy. There was this note on the front label: "A hand-crafted varietal blend with a crisp, non-grassy herbal and spice character." Geez. When was the last time you saw a label that told you what something *didn't* taste like? In the long run, our tasting then didn't yield many Sauvignon Blancs we could recommend, but we did like the Kunde Estate "Magnolia Lane," a distinctive wine that tasted of wood, cream, and grass, and the Chateau Ste. Michelle from Washington State, then a great buy at less than $10. We also reported at the time, though, that we had thrown in some Sauvignon Blancs from New Zealand and South Africa, and found them filled with the kind of character that we missed in the American versions.

We tried again the next year. Once again, the Chateau Ste. Michelle was among our very favorites, and we also liked the Beringer, a reliable name for both low-end and high-end wines. We waited a couple of years and tried once again. We bought the first fifty American Sauvignon Blancs we saw from the most recent vintage. We also bought a few Sauvignon Blancs from New Zealand. We had become increasingly fond of the juicy, distinctive white wines from there, and we thought a back-to-back tasting might be fun. Alas, our tasting of U.S. wines again was disappointing. We found most of them simple and watery. Winemakers know that Americans like Chardonnay, so they made Sauvignon Blancs into a kind of junior Chardonnay, stripped of varietal character, although, once again, the Kunde Estate "Magnolia Lane" showed well. So we decided to bag that tasting and try again a few months later with the next vintage. Meantime, though, we went ahead and tasted the handful of New Zealand wines we bought.

Whoa! The first blind flight of these blew us away. They exploded in our mouths with juicy, clean, fresh-fruit tastes. The wines still had a great deal of grassy character, yet they were balanced and easy to drink. Moreover, they were all interestingly different from one another. Some might have never touched oak, while others clearly had a little bit of oak fermentation or aging, and others had more. Some tasted like they were 100 percent Sauvignon Blanc, while others might have had a touch of Sémillon, the grape with flatter, earthy tastes that is often paired with Sauvignon Blanc. Fascinating. We were so impressed that we decided to conduct a large blind tasting of New Zealand Sauvignon Blancs under $20.

If "New Zealand wine" is a novel idea to you, you're not alone. In *Wine Atlas of Australia & New Zealand*, James Halliday writes of New Zealand: "The wine industry of today is effectively less than 30 years old." Indeed, in 1992, by far the most common grape variety in New Zealand was Muller-Thurgau, a white grape better known for its productivity than its quality. (We love the description of Muller-Thurgau by wine writer Jancis Robinson: "decidedly mediocre but gruesomely popular.") By 2000, Muller-Thurgau had been far outstripped by both Chardonnay and Sauvignon Blanc. Exports of New Zealand wine to the United States grew accordingly—from 17,000 cases in 1992 to 278,000 cases in 1999. The Wine Institute of New Zealand says the figure grew an additional 40 percent by the end of 2001.

Sauvignon Blanc is New Zealand's best-known wine in the United States, though winemakers in New Zealand are also excited about their very flavorful Pinot Noir. The first New Zealand wine that broke into the American consciousness was Cloudy Bay Sauvignon Blanc, which was delicious, expensive, and hard to find, making it perfect for the too-much-money-chasing-too-few-wines '90s. Cloudy Bay was the first Sauvignon Blanc we had from New Zealand, and we enjoyed it a great deal, but we've since found others that we like better for less money. New Zealand wines are still something of a specialty item, which means there are many different labels out there, often with unusual names like Nga Waka, but not a mass quantity of any one of them.

As it happens, some of our favorites in our tasting were wines that are not obscure. We tried the 2000 Cloudy Bay in two separate flights, since we happened to see it twice on sale for less than $20 ($19.99 and $19.60). It was a solid "good" in both flights but was overshadowed by others. In fact, wine after wine was vibrant, juicy, and mouth-watering. These wines would make any seafood taste great. In the long run, we fell in love with one that we described in our notes as "juicy and limey, crisp and mouth-watering." But there was something more to it.

Most of the wines that rate "delicious" in our notes have various dimensions of flavor, hints of this and undertones of that. This, though, we described as "simple and uncomplicated in the best possible way: Just great fruit left alone to make a totally fetching wine." Imagine being outside in a green field on a very sunny day and popping into your mouth the juiciest, ripest, freshest piece of fruit you've ever tasted. Imagine it bursting in your mouth with flavors that stir something deep in you. That's what this wine was like. This was the Villa Maria Estate "Private Bin," which cost $13.99.

Well, this certainly set the table for our retasting of United States wines. We then bought the first fifty Sauvignon Blancs we saw from the then brand-new 2000 vintage. Whew. They were much better than the '99s. In general, we think people are overly concerned about vintages, but this appears to be one case where vintage really does matter. In California, 1999 was a cool year, and Sauvignon Blanc grapes like warm weather. Perhaps that's why we found so many of the 1999s simple and watery. The 2000s were quite different. One of our favorites, for instance, was interestingly complex. It seemed simple and slightly dusty at first, but, as it warmed, it grew more and more charming, with lovely green-pepper juiciness and lovely fruit. Dottie described it as "a satisfying mouthful, very varietal and young." Surprise: This was Canyon Road, which cost just $7.99. The best of our blind tasting, we wrote, was "crisp, clean, and grassy. Rich and layered, with mouthfilling fruit and tropical-fruit acids. Lots of lovely taste. Varietal and more, with some weight and complexity. Lots of finesse, lots of layers." We then wrote "tastes expensive," and we were wrong. This was the Geyser Peak 2000, which cost $10.99. We also liked the '99 Geyser Peak, though not as much.

As we researched these wines after our tasting, we found that both our best of tasting and our best value were made by the same company, Peak Wines International, a part of giant Fortune Brands. Coincidence? We called to find out. It turns out the same three winemakers worked on both wines, which were made at the same place. One of the winemakers, Chris Munsell, said the company has "a niche carved out in Sauvignon Blanc." It's not coincidental that the wines have strong varietal characteristics, like the grassy ones we like from New Zealand and Australia. "They've got that Down Under influence style in mind," he said, noting that Daryl Groom, the executive vice president for operations and winemaking, came from Penfolds Winery in Australia, as did one of the winemakers, Mick Schroeter.

The 2000 growing season was warmer and the grapes matured better than they did in 1999, Mr. Munsell said. The winemakers wanted varietal tastes without vegetal characteristics. They wanted the wine to "show more of the melon and citrus" qualities of the grape and they did nothing to strip it of its "fresh, fruity characteristic," he told us. The difference in the wines' prices, as you might expect, is due to the cost of the grapes they're made from, and that varies depending on factors such as the location of the vineyards.

So we have two bottom-line pieces of advice: Try a Sauvignon Blanc from New Zealand for a brand-new, exciting taste. And demand character and taste from your American Sauvignon Blanc. If it doesn't taste distinctive, try another.

Wine Notes

General advice: Buy the youngest Sauvignon Blanc you see. Many age beautifully, but we like the crisp, bouncy flavors of youth. Below are notes from a tasting of New Zealand wines and U.S. wines, all under $20. Kenwood, Kunde, and Chateau Ste. Michelle have all been repeat favorites in our tastings. In New

Zealand, Marlborough is a hotspot of good Sauvignon Blanc, so look for that region on the label. Chill well.

Food pairings: Cold salads, including seafood salads, and other picnic foods. Lighter fish.

American Wines

Geyser Peak Winery (Sonoma County). $10.99. VERY GOOD/DELICIOUS. Best of tasting. Crisp, clean, and grassy, with rich, layered, mouthfilling fruit and nice acids. Lovely tropical fruit flavors, with some weight and complexity. Real finesse. Tastes expensive. (2000)

Canyon Road Winery (California). $7.99. VERY GOOD. Best value. A shocker at the price. Give it a little time in the glass to warm up. Nicely varietal and charming, with lovely fruit. A satisfying mouthful of wine. (2000)

Kunde Estate Winery "Magnolia Lane" (Sonoma Valley). $12.99. VERY GOOD. Refreshing and fruity, with an extra dimension, some extra richness and depth. (1999)

Kenwood Vineyards (North Coast). $10.99. VERY GOOD. Fresh and lovely, like a just-picked green pepper. Juicy and unrestrained. (2000)

Groth Vineyards & Winery (Napa Valley). $15.99. VERY GOOD. Good fruit, plenty of varietal character, and nice minerals—slate, chalk, gravel—give it a serious complexity that would make this great with food. (2000)

R. H. Phillips Vineyard (Dunnigan Hills). $7.99. GOOD/VERY GOOD. Fresh and spritzy, with nice melon tastes. Charming, and seriously grassy. (1999)

Sterling Vineyards (North Coast). $12.59. GOOD/VERY GOOD. Crisp and ripe, with plenty of character. Piquant, refreshing, and perfect for a picnic. (1999 and 2000)

Fetzer Vineyards "Echo Ridge" (California). $11.99. GOOD. Clean, ripe, and lovely. Another good value from a reliable producer of value wines. (2000)

Cakebread Cellars (Napa Valley). $19.31. GOOD. Interesting and crisp, like a fresh head of lettuce, but with interesting pepperiness at the back of the mouth. (2000)

New Zealand Wines

Villa Maria Estate "Private Bin." (Marlborough/Hawkes Bay). $13.99. DELICIOUS. Best of tasting and best value. Utterly fetching, like biting into a perfect piece of fruit. Juicy, limey, mouth–watering. (2000)

Goldwater Estate "Dog Point" (Marlborough). $16.99. VERY GOOD/DELICIOUS. A winemaker's wine, complex, sophisticated, and elegant. Fresh and fruity, but with some depth, too. Some of these wines are aperitifs; this is a meal. (1999)

Grove Mill Wine Co. (Waihopai Valley Winery; Marlborough). $13.95. VERY GOOD/DELICIOUS. Nicely balanced. A classy introduction to this wine. It's true to the varietal without being overwhelming. (1999)

Babich Wines (Marlborough). $9.99. VERY GOOD. Juicy and vibrant. Lively and crisp, with lovely acids. (2000)

Vavasour Wines "Awatere Valley" (Marlborough). $19.99. VERY GOOD. Crisp, with plenty of grassiness and some interesting depth at the end. (1998)

Kim Crawford Wines (Marlborough). $13.95. GOOD/VERY GOOD. Melon with limes. Very sharp and aggressive—whoa! It reaches out and grabs you. (1999)

Selaks Wines (Marlborough). $10.99. GOOD/VERY GOOD. Bellpeppery and quite distinctive. It's so varietal some might find it off-putting, though it softens after a while. (1999)

Nobilo Vintners "Fall Harvest" (Marlborough). $8.99. GOOD/VERY GOOD. Interesting and filled with bell-pepper taste, but, interestingly, the finish is clean and filled with oranges and lemons. (2000)

Decoding the Wine List:
It's Easier Than It Looks

Ordering wine in a restaurant should be one of the pleasures of eating out. Instead, for too many people it's a chore, something to be dreaded. The wine director of one of America's most famous restaurants once told us that often when he hands the wine list to people, he feels he's tossing them a hot potato. He mimicked the recipient of the wine list virtually throwing it to someone else at the table. "No, *you* do it." "No, *you!*"

This is a tragedy. After all, you're spending plenty of money to eat out. The experience should be special, and wine helps make dinner special. Not only that, but right there on that wine list—hidden, like a piece of gold in a mine shaft—are treasures you may never see anywhere else. Wineries, importers, and shippers like to see their wines on fine restaurants' wine lists. It's good exposure for them, and it's likely the wines will be treated well, too. Restaurants want to have impressive wine lists so they can offer wines that equal their spectacular food.

So there you are at the restaurant, and you've been handed this seemingly incomprehensible list, filled with wines from all over the world. What do you do? Relax. Truth is, it's easier than you imagine. Don't think of the list as one big Tower of Babel. Think about how you decode things every day in your life. That's what you need to do with any wine list, no matter how thick. Just go through these simple seven steps. Think of them as a kind of Gaiter/Brecher Secret Wine List Decoder Ring.

(1) Take your time. A few seconds after handing you the biggest wine list in the world, the waiter will come over and ask, "Have you made your selection?" or "Do you need help?" Just look up, smile, and say, "You have such an interesting list. It'll take me a few minutes to decide." At this point, the waiter will think you know what you're doing and will leave you alone.

(2) Decide if you want red or white. If you're with a date or business colleagues, just ask: "Hey, do you like red or white?" If it's lunch, the answer will almost always be white (it's easier on the remainder of the day). The rest of the time, the answer will usually be, "Whatever you think." So if it's lunch, go with white. Otherwise, think about what kind of restaurant you're in. Look at the menu. Does it seem to specialize in the kind of lighter dishes that you like with white wine, or heavier dishes that you prefer with red wine? This single decision of color cuts the wine list in half. (If we're at an unfamiliar restaurant, we ask to see menus right away so we can make a quick determination if we're more likely to order "white" food or "red" food.)

(3) Does the restaurant specialize in a certain type of wine? If there are twenty Italian wines listed and five American wines, the owner cares more about Italian wine. Go with it.

(4) Eliminate the showcase wines. Many restaurants that have huge lists specialize in expensive French first growth wines, like Château Lafite Rothschild. Are you going to order those wines? Of course not.

(5) Now, among what's left, look for wines you already know—and cross them off, too. Hey, if you can buy the same wine from the corner wine store for half the price, it's not going to be much fun drinking it at a restaurant, is it? If this is a make-or-break business meal or if you're proposing marriage, however, you might *want* to go with what you know is a sure thing. Otherwise, look for something new. Remember that restaurants often have wines on the list you won't see anywhere else. Sometimes they're small-production wines rationed by the winery to certain chichi restaurants. They're not available in wine stores at any price. Ordering something you've never seen before and may never see again makes the whole issue of "markup" irrelevant.

(6) Decide what you're willing to spend. Maybe you had planned to spend $25, but there's just about nothing on the list at

$25. Think about $35. Whatever the price—and be flexible; c'mon, you're eating out—set a limit and mentally strike out everything else.

(7) You've decided red or white, focused on what the restaurant specializes in, eliminated the showcase wines, crossed off wines you already know, and decided what you can spend. How many wines could possibly be left? Just a handful, we'd guess. So pick two or three. At this point, say to the waiter, "I can't decide among these wines"—and, wait, the next sentence is the key. Do not say, "What would you recommend?" Sad to say, in many restaurants, the waiter really won't have a clue and will simply choose one. Instead, ask, "What can you tell me about them?" This may flummox the waiter, who will then send over someone who actually knows something about wine. Ignore what he says. Instead, watch his eyes and his body language. You'll know which wine he's most excited about.

Order it. And don't worry about it. If it's not terrific, it's still something new and different. If it is terrific, then, maybe you'll have an experience like this one, from years ago, that we still remember as if it were yesterday:

There was a small, very elegant restaurant called Hubert's in our old neighborhood in New York. We walked down a couple of steps and into the kind of hushed, intimate, carefully lighted place that said Manhattan all over it. Dottie ordered sweetbreads, one of those organ meats that thoroughly gross out John, who ordered veal. Chardonnay seemed like a good match with both dishes, and, in any case, there was something so rich about the restaurant that a rich Chardonnay seemed perfect. On the list was something we had never seen before: a Fisher Vineyards 1980 Chardonnay. We knew nothing about it, so we ordered it.

The combination with Dottie's sweetbreads was glorious. The wine was rich and almost heavy with fruit, with a round, woody plumpness that filled our mouths with taste. Its voluptuousness paired perfectly with the slightly crisp richness of the sweetbreads and the rich and creamy Champagne sauce. This all seemed so right that even John took a bite of the sweetbreads. Then he took a sip of the wine and another bite of the sweetbreads. He had never eaten sweetbreads before and has never eaten them since, but he loved them that night. Such was the power of that wine.

Twenty years later, whenever we see a Fisher wine, we think of sweetbreads, and whenever we see sweetbreads, we think of that Chardonnay and of a romantic dinner at Hubert's.

Chapter Three

Pinot Gris

"Like Drinking the Cold"

Our book agent invited us to dinner one summer night at New York's fashionable Café des Artistes with her husband, who is a famous author, and another famous author and his wife. Naturally, when the wine list came, all eyes turned to us. Gulp. What's worse, the women planned to order soft-shell crabs while the men (to the women's horror) were all ordering wiener schnitzel (it's a guy thing). We needed to find a wine that wasn't too expensive, since we weren't paying; was interesting enough to impress our dinner companions; and yet would almost surely be enjoyed by everyone at the table. The pressure was on.

Fortunately, on the short but well-chosen list, we both saw the same thing at the same time: a Pinot Gris from King Estate Winery in Oregon. Whew! How did it go? Will we ever get another book contract? Let's start at the beginning.

Hot new wine regions, and their hot new specialties, pop up all the time. In the past twenty years or so, Oregon has become a wine hotspot. What you're most likely to hear about are Oregon's Pinot Noirs, which are filled with berrylike fruit and elegance. But Oregon has another, less well-known specialty, and it's one of our very favorite summer wines: Pinot Gris.

Pinot Gris is one of those grapes that's grown everywhere, but has different names just about everywhere: for instance, Pinot Grigio in Italy, Tokay in Alsace (though it's also sometimes called Pinot Gris on the labels),

Grauburgunder in Austria, and Malvoisie in Switzerland. It's hot now in California, where the number of tons crushed went from just 36 in 1990 to 6,596 in 2000. We think Pinot Gris hits its stride in Oregon, and, fortunately, some of the biggest and best-distributed wineries in that state make some of the best ones.

A well-chilled Oregon Pinot Gris is refreshing and bracing, with some real weight to it. It has a richness that always makes Dottie think of crème brûlée or flan. The big taste makes this an excellent wine with slightly heavier summer food—say, cold roast pork—while its nice acids give it a slight lemony quality that also makes it clean and fresh. In fact, it can be so complex that it seems a mass of contradictions. After our tastings, when we look at our notes, we find that we have sometimes described the same wine as light and rich, sprightly and deep, good with food and tasting like dessert. It's a good summer wine, but it has real body—and real alcohol (sometimes above 13 percent). It is richer, fuller, and fruitier than Sauvignon Blanc, but lighter on its feet and more distinctive than Chardonnay. This is, in short, a wine that's hard to put your finger on, and that's exactly why we like it.

But it's always refreshing and a little bit different. That's why, when a colleague of ours, Amanda Bennett, moved to Portland, we gave her two words of advice: Pinot Gris. As soon as she arrived, she bought a bottle and sent us this note: "It reminded me of an experience I used to like a lot, when I was in Toronto. There was this German restaurant that used to keep some sort of not-too-sweet German wine in the refrigerator and serve it really, really cold. I remember drinking it on the patio in the summer and thinking it was just like drinking the cold. The Pinot Gris felt a lot like that—like drinking the cold."

That's also why we thought the Pinot Gris would be a good choice at dinner with our agent. It was a hot day, so we needed a blast of cold. We figured the wine wouldn't overpower the soft-shell crabs but would have enough weight for the wiener schnitzel. Fortunately, we were right. The crisp richness of the wine and the crunchy salty-sweetness and pleasant mustiness of the crab were excellent together. The same wine did wonders for the breaded, herbed veal cutlets, offering enough muscle to stand up to the men's manly meal. It wasn't just that the tastes of the wine and food were marvelous together in both cases, but that the different textures played well off each other. The first bottle was gone in no time—always the best sign of a successful wine choice. (At a business lunch once, John ordered a rare and special Chardonnay from a winery called Flowers that he'd always wanted to try but had never seen until then. It was big, bold, and tasted almost thick. John found it quite distinctive and interesting. At the end of lunch, none of his four colleagues had finished their first glass. This was not a successful wine choice.)

Oregon Pinot Gris can be a little hard to find, but more are hitting the shelves all the time. Trust us, it's worth the effort to find them, as we found in two large, blind tastings. In our first tasting, in 1998, we found that even wines that just rated "good" still showed more character and verve than most wines we drink. For instance, we liked the Yamhill Valley Vineyards even before we tasted it because it smelled so rich and creamy. In our mouths, it reminded us of lemon-meringue pie, an interesting combination of acid and cream—a surprising taste we found in all of the wines. Amazing. One memorable bottle was from a winery called WillaKenzie Estate. Check out these notes: "Cold, crisp, with soil and some chalk. BRACING in your mouth. Tastes a bit like Champagne without the bubbles. Fruit is so crisp it shocks your system. Almost a little menthol. Sort of crackles on your tongue. Round when you swallow, but jagged in your mouth. Really coats your tongue. More serious than Muscadet or Pinot Grigio. Nuttiness, too, like Champagne. Age-worthy."

One of our other favorites was from Eyrie, for years one of the consistently fine wineries in Oregon. In fact, Eyrie says on the label that it was the first producer of Pinot Gris in America. Experience shows. The nose was massive. The taste was complex, with layer after layer of flavors. Although not all of the layers were entirely pleasant, that kind of complexity in a white wine is remarkable. In that tasting, our favorite was from King Estate. That's when we first discovered that its Pinot Gris is a wine worth seeking out. "Fresh, vibrant nose," we wrote. "Explosive lemon-zest taste! Real character. Filled with fruit. Superripe grapes. Complex, with crispness yet depth. Is that wood?"

As we've said, many lighter white wines never see the inside of a barrel. They're fermented in stainless steel and then bottled to keep their freshness intact. But we were sure we tasted wood here. We called the winery, and we did taste wood in that '96: 15 percent of the crush was aged in

French oak for six months, then blended with the 85 percent of the wine put in stainless steel.

In a more recent tasting, after our first blind flight of wines, we were sure that the Sokol Blosser, one of the most reliable names in Oregon wines for years, would turn out to be our favorite. It was so very fresh, yet it had real character, with fruit flavors and a hint of minerals. But we were even more impressed in a later flight by the Pinot Gris from—once again—WillaKenzie Estate, which had a complex combination of real mouthfeel and lemon sprightliness. It was deep, with a taste of the earth that made it special. "It tastes like a meal," Dottie said.

So what makes Pinot Gris from Oregon special? Why does the same grape make so many watery, simple wines in Italy and wines of such character in Oregon? And what about age? We generally think Oregon Pinot Gris should be drunk young, but we've had some outstanding bottles with some age on them. What gives? We called WillaKenzie to find out. Laurent Montalieu, a partner and winemaker, said that by letting the grapes stay on the vine until they reach full ripeness, the wine that results is "round and fleshy," with real mouthfeel. He said the vines are "true Pinot Gris clones from Alsace," where the wines that they make are known for having long lives. As for the difference between Oregon's Pinot Gris and Italy's Pinot Grigio, Mr. Montalieu said he and others in Oregon are "pushing the maturity level and making wines that are rounder" and richer. In Italy, he said, the cool nights and high altitudes where the grapes are grown make Pinot Grigio that is fresh and crisp, and has higher acids.

So when it's hot outside, go look for a Pinot Gris from Oregon. We don't think it's a wine to sip by the pool—it's a bit too heavy and too serious—but we can't think of a better wine to recommend with many summertime dishes. More broadly, if you haven't yet discovered the wines of Oregon, you should. Every winery mentioned in the attached index is a well-known producer of fine wines, and it would be hard to go wrong with anything they make. Try an Oregon Pinot Noir, for instance, with salmon, either grilled or cold-poached.

Here's another tip: Don't forget our dinner experience. This is a great wine to give as a gift, take to a friend's house for dinner, or order for company, since most people haven't yet tried a Pinot Gris and, as far as we can tell, always love it when they do.

Wine Notes

General advice: *In the following list, we have included a recent tasting and an earlier tasting (which included different vintages) because we have found all of these producers consistent, not just with Pinot Gris but with other kinds of wine, too. Chill well. These are good young and good older, so don't worry about the vintage.*

Food pairings: *Heavier fish. Soft-shell crabs. Heavier summer salads. Cold roast pork and, yes, wiener schnitzel.*

WillaKenzie Estate (Willamette Valley). $13.99. VERY GOOD/DELICIOUS. It's all there—a hard-to-describe combination of lightness and real mouthfeel, with a taste of the soil and hints of all sorts of summer fruits. Light enough for a summer day, heavy enough for food. Quite bracing. (1996, 1997)

Sokol Blosser Winery (Willamette Valley). $15.99. VERY GOOD. Crisp, flavorful, and refreshing, with a tiny bit of burnt-sugar taste, good minerals, and real character. So yummy it sometimes seems like dessert, yet it's surprisingly light on its feet. Lovely. (1998)

The Eyrie Vineyards (Willamette Valley). $15.99. GOOD/VERY GOOD. Rich and refreshing at the same time. Deep. "You can almost taste the earth," Dottie said. Some weight, yet a lemon sprightliness. (1996, 1997)

King Estate Winery. $12.99. GOOD/VERY GOOD. The 1996 was our best of tasting in 1998, with a fresh, vibrant nose and an explosive lemon-zest taste, real character, and superripe fruit. Crispness and depth combined into a wine of real complexity. For a tasting in 1999, we bought a dusty old 1995 to see how it was aging. It was showing some age, with a bit too much of a caramel taste, but it reminded us of luscious flan. We also liked the 1997. A name to look for. (1995, 1996, 1997)

Yamhill Valley Vineyards. $12.99. GOOD. Nose is yummy, like creamy wood. It smells thick and tastes like lemon–meringue pie. Remarkably big. (1996 and 1998)

Cristom Vineyards. $15.99. GOOD. Midrange between the lighter and heavier Pinot Gris. If you happen to see Cristom's Pinot Noir, grab it. (1997)

You're an Expert on Wine, and We Can Prove It

"I don't really know anything about wine, but . . ." People say that to us all the time. They're wrong. They're experts on wine, and so are you. Maybe you don't think you are, but you are, and we can prove it. Just follow these ten easy steps.

(1) Go to your local wine shop or supermarket. It doesn't have to be a fancy place.

(2) Buy two bottles of the same kind of wine from different wineries. For instance, buy a Kendall-Jackson Chardonnay and a Glen Ellen Chardonnay or maybe an Estancia Chardonnay.

(3) Take them home. Remove the metal bottlenecks and take out the corks. Put the corks in your pocket.

(4) Put both bottles into identical bags. We find that our daughters' brown-paper lunch bags work perfectly. Twist the top of each bag tightly around the neck of the bottle, then tape it, leaving just an inch of the top of the bottle showing. There should be no visible clues to the wines' identities.

(5) Put the corks back in (you should have no idea, at this point, which cork is going into which bottle). If you're trying white wine, put the bottles in the refrigerator. In any case, don't look at the bottles again for a while.

(6) Number the bottles No. 1 and No. 2. If someone else is there, and you've done the previous steps by yourself, let them do this.

(7) Get out two glasses for each taster.

(8) Pour No. 1 into the glass on the left. Pour No. 2 into the glass on the right.

(9) Taste No. 1. Decide what you think about it. Taste No. 2. Decide what you think about it.

Know what? They're going to taste different to you. Maybe one will taste better than the other. Maybe they will taste equally good. But they will taste *different*. Don't open the bags yet. Keep drinking. You might find, as time goes by, that your opinion changes. First you liked No. 1 better. Now you like No. 2. Does this mean you're a wimp and can't make up your mind? No. It just means wine changes depending on its temperature, how long it's open, what you're drinking it with, and your mood.

Don't feel you need to be thinking about or talking about the wine constantly. In fact, it's best if you forget you're doing a tasting. Too much talking and thinking can sometimes warp the experience, make it less genuine.

At some point, tear off the bags and see which wine is which. Maybe you liked the less expensive wine more. Maybe you liked the "bad" vintage instead of the "good" vintage. And that leads you to the last step, which is the most important point of all:

(10) Trust yourself. If you paid $14 for one wine but only $7 for the one you liked better, don't say to yourself, "Gee, I guess I really don't know anything about wine." You don't have a problem; you have a bargain.

If you ever think your own taste is pedestrian because you like a "common" wine, remember this story: Our bosses once asked us to conduct a blind tasting for the *Wall Street Journal* Health Care Summit in Washington, D.C. The staff at the National Press Club, where the tasting was held, put eight different American Chardonnays in bags—we had chosen the eight, but we didn't know which was which—and poured them for several hundred people. There were many doctors in the crowd, and we've learned over the years from their letters that, as a group, doctors are quite passionate about their wine. These doctors were no exception. During the blind tasting, they talked very knowledgeably about wines they'd had and about their various preferences.

At the end, people voted for their favorite. The No. 1 wine beat the runner-up by a 2 to 1 margin. What was it? Gallo of Sonoma (Russian River Valley), which then cost $8.99. The health care folks were shocked and amused and, actually, a little embarrassed. All of which made for a very interesting and in-structive experience.

The bottom line: There are many wine experts out there. But there is no one—no one—who is more of an expert on your taste than you. A good wine is a wine that tastes good to you.

Chapter Four

Viognier

We Pronounce It "Ek-se-lent"

What do you do when you're having a traditional "red wine" meal such as steak or lamb and you don't like red wine? For that matter, what do you do in the dead of winter when you want a big, bracing wine but you just can't drink another hearty red? We have one word of advice, but because it's a hard word to pronounce, we fear many people will ignore us.

People tell us all the time about their angst over wine pronunciation. One said: "You write about so many interesting wines, from so many interesting places, but I often can't request them at a wine shop because I can't say the name." Another: "My lack of confidence in saying the names of what I am looking for keeps me from giving the names to my local helpful wine merchant. Help! I feel stupid and uneducated."

Some people avoid foreign wines altogether because they don't know how to pronounce the names. What a shame. To some extent, this is yet another of the wine industry's self-inflicted wounds. Too many people have walked into a wine store and asked for "Mur-low," only to be sniffed at and told, "You mean Mare-low"—not to mention, of course, scarier words like Puligny-Montrachet and Tokaji. But this isn't something to worry about. After all, except for linguists, few people are going to know exactly how to pronounce the names of every wine in the world, and even experts disagree on pronunciations sometimes. Heck, there's a photographer out west named John Brecher who pronounces his name "Brecker," while John pronounces it "Brecher," with a soft "ch." Dottie's more comfortable with foreign languages, and John butchers every language he goes near, but it has never kept him from ordering a wine. If a wine merchant laughs at you because you didn't pronounce the name of a wine correctly, find a wine merchant who's not a jerk.

This brings us to the big, aggressive white wine we're talking about here: Viognier. How is that pronounced? Many pronunciation guides differ, at least a little. We, and others, say vee-own-YAY, but after we printed that pronunciation once, we received a very nice note that said: "I love your column and read it religiously. But on pronunciation: Viognier is surely pronounced vee-on-yay, with the short o sound, rather than the Americanized long vowel in vee-own-yay." That might well be correct, but our point here is that, as long as a wine merchant can figure out what you're talking about, this is just one more of those wine things that you can stop worrying about. And, heck, you can always write it down and hand it to him.

In any event, Viognier is an unusual grape from the Rhône Valley of France that's so big and heavy it's sometimes blended into the region's massive *red* wines to take a bit of the edge off them. In the past decade or so, more and more American winemakers have been experimenting with Rhône varietals with unfamiliar (and, yep, difficult-to-pronounce) names like Roussanne, Mourvèdre, and Viognier. Chardonnay will always be popular, but for those who are looking for an alternative, some American winemakers, including very smart marketers like Kendall-Jackson, are putting money on Viognier. Indeed, the amount of Viognier crushed in California soared to 7,709 tons in 2000 from 2,720 tons just two years earlier. Not only that, but Viognier is available from more places now. We've had excellent ones from Australia (Oxford Landing) and Virginia (Horton); even Long Island wineries are making some.

The heft of Viognier is one thing that makes it perfect to drink even in winter. If you prefer white, this is what you should drink by the fire with hearty food, but be prepared for something really different. Viognier is a serious wine, often relatively high in alcohol. It tastes very much of minerals and earth—we think of it as tasting "dirty," although, obviously, it's not—and it reminds us of melons. This combination of crispness, dirt, and melons makes us feel as if we're in the middle of a cantaloupe field on a sunny day. Viognier has a great deal of mouthfeel—so much so, in fact, that we sometimes compare it to chicken soup because it has the same warming, almost comforting quality. Still, Viognier hasn't really caught on with the public, as far as we can tell. This is a shame, but that also means you can try something—or serve your guests something—that's still unusual and special. It also means that, because Viognier isn't being made in bulk, most of it still reflects the personalities of winemakers who are passionate about making it in small quantities.

Not long ago, we gritted our teeth and spent $59 on a California Viognier we'd never seen before, called Failla Jordan "Alban Vineyard" from Ehren Jordan Wine Cellars. It's apparently quite rare, and it was some bottle of wine. Our notes: "Exotic, with tastes of vanilla, pineapple, mango, and passion fruit. Some hints of chalk that give it grounding. Nice earth. Elegant and big. Like white velvet."

In our first tasting of Viognier, back in 1998, our favorite was from Qupé, which is one of the premier producers of Rhône-style wines in the United States. Qupé wines tend to be expensive, but if you see one, grab if for a special experience. The biggest surprise of that early Viognier tasting was the R. H. Phillips EXP, a lovely, serious, and very well-made wine. It was one of the least expensive we bought—then about $12—and a great buy. We suggested then that this would be an excellent way to take a chance on this very different wine.

For a more recent tasting, we bought every American Viognier we could find, regardless of price, for a blind tasting. Keep in mind that most stores carry only one or two, at best, and almost all are made in limited quantities. We found, once again, that this is a highly individual wine. Winemakers clearly are still having fun making these wines, and that makes it fun to drink them. They were all big, with that "dirty melon" taste—you'll have to try it to see exactly what we mean—and an almost chewy weight. Unlike most white wines, these need hearty food to show their best.

In this tasting, the EXP was once again quite good. It's a lush wine, with a hint of peaches and a nice crispness that leavens the heaviness. In our notes, we called it "chicken soup for the soul." Even though the price had risen to $13.99, it was still a great bargain. It also appears to be one of the more widely available Viogniers.

Our best of tasting this time came from a winery that was a favorite of ours for a long time, Joseph Phelps. This was the Joseph Phelps Vin du Mistral (Napa Valley), which cost $31.99. That's expensive, but this is a very serious, complex wine with real intensity that's also remarkably easy to drink. It's a wine you'd remember for a long time. The Phelps was also one of our favorites in the previous tasting.

On the whole, we were both pleased and fascinated with our blind tasting. It's clear that the wineries experimenting with this grape are giving it a great deal of attention and care. While there were obvious differences— some were bigger than others, some were fruitier, more forward in their fruit—almost all had earthy tastes and large personalities. Run out and try a Viognier. It'll be a new, fascinating taste that will make your dinner more interesting.

Wine Notes

General advice: R. H. Phillips is a great place to start exploring Viognier; it's a good buy and generally available. Pick up any Viognier you see, chill well, and serve with dinner. This big wine will be fine with some age, so don't worry about the vintage. In addition to those below, names to look for include Qupé, Gregory Graham, Calera, and Andrew Murray.
Food pairings: Hearty foods like white bean and pork casseroles and veal stews.

Joseph Phelps Vineyards Vin du Mistral (Napa Valley). $31.99. VERY GOOD. Best of tasting. Creamy melon. Big yet pleasant, with nice weight, real intensity, and some power. Serious wine. (1997)

R. H. Phillips Vineyard EXP (Dunnigan Hills). $13.99. GOOD/VERY GOOD. Best value. Chicken soup for the soul, with plenty of chewy mouthfeel, peaches, and tropical fruits. Lush, but nicely crisp, too. (1999)

Edna Valley Vineyard (Paso Robles). $21.99. VERY GOOD. Rich color. Good fruit, nice acids, and plenty of character, yet still so easy to drink. Rich with melon tastes, and a lovely, long finish. (1999)

Sobon Estate (Shenandoah Valley). $15.88. GOOD/VERY GOOD. Pepper and spice, with real stuff. Classy, with melon undertones. Easy to drink, with plenty of character but no heaviness. Nice finish. Classy. (1999)

Bonterra Vineyards (North Coast). $17.99. GOOD/VERY GOOD. Toasty and oaky, with some caramel. John found it overly heavy, but Dottie did not. (1997)

When Wine Is a Pain:
The Headache Issue

From the number of questions we get about wine headaches, it's amazing anyone drinks wine. It's startling how many people are affected, and how differently they're affected.

Valentina Korutz of Pennsylvania gets headaches from Chilean and South African wines, while Jennifer Schuman of Del Mar, California, wrote us: "Contrary to common experience/wisdom, I seem to get headaches after drinking WHITE wine while suffering no ill effects from reds, including Chianti." Timothy Cole of Stamford, Connecticut, gets headaches from American wines but not French wines, and Frances Alferman of St. Louis can drink only Shiraz free from harm. Stephen Glass of Claremont, California, wrote: "I have a friend who contracts extremely violent migraines when she consumes wine—any kind of wine—with any kind of dairy product. She can, however, consume either the wine or the dairy products with complete impunity."

So, let's talk about headaches. No, not hangovers. If you drink too much and you're like most people, you will get a headache. And we're not talking about migraines or cluster headaches, which are sometimes triggered by wine. Those are special cases, and you should be talking to a doctor about them anyway. We're talking about otherwise headache-free people who drink a glass of wine and are seized by headaches. We're not doctors, and even doctors have disagreements about why some wines cause headaches. But because we're asked about headaches and wine so often, we did some research. Here's what we found:

First, sulfites. Many people seem to think that sulfites in wine cause headaches. The scientists and physicians we talked to said that's not true. Every one of them. "Sulfites can cause allergy and asthma symptoms, but they don't cause headaches," said Frederick Freitag, associate director of the Diamond Headache Clinic in Chicago and a board member of the National Headache Foundation.

We hear all the time from people who were on vacation somewhere overseas, had a wine that didn't cause headaches, and figured the wine didn't contain sulfites because, unlike wines in America, the label didn't say "Contains sulfites." Actually, sulfites occur naturally in all wine. It's just that in the United States, the government requires winemakers to print that on the label because sulfites can trigger severe reactions, even death, in some people, especially asthmatics with this sensitivity. Almost all winemakers also add small amounts of sulfites to their wines to help preserve them and to kill wild yeasts that can ruin a wine's taste. "I grow a small number of grapes and make my own wine," said Dr. Freitag, "and if you don't do something to shut down the native yeasts and bacteria that come in with the grape skin, you're going to get wine that is absolutely horrific. Sulfites are the most benign way of doing that, but they don't cause headaches."

Some people think wines labeled "organic" don't have sulfites, but that's not true, although the wineries that make them might not add any additional sulfites. Frey Vineyard, of Mendocino, California for instance, doesn't add any sulfites, and its labels say that. Lolonis Winery, also of Mendocino, makes "wines that are low in sulfites or have a small amount added, but sulfites will never have anything to do with headaches," said Maureen Lolonis. "Without sulfites," she said, "a wine has no shelf life." On some labels these days you'll see "No added sulfites." That doesn't mean there are no sulfites, just that no extra sulfites were used.

Although experts say more study is warranted, and there is dissent, much research suggests that the headache culprits might be histamine and tyramine, other chemical substances that are naturally present in wine. Histamine dilates blood vessels and tyramine first constricts then dilates blood vessels—ouch! Dan L. Keiller, a founder of the Medical Wine Interest and Education Society in San Diego, said several studies from Europe show that "red wines, in general, contain more histamine than Champagnes or sparkling wines and those usually contain more histamine than [still] white wines." Indeed, headaches from red wine are so common that the phenomenon has its own name, "RWH syndrome"—that's "red wine headache." But, Dr. Keiller hastened to add, "Histamine content does not correlate consistently with color, bouquet, or taste characteristics of the wine."

People who most often have trouble with histamine in wine, Dr. Keiller and others told us, are those who lack an enzyme in their intestines that can help them metabolize histamine. Tyramine, meantime, can cause blood pressure to rise, and that triggers headaches in some people. These same people might get headaches from aged cheeses, smoked or cured meats, and citrus fruits.

Dr. Freitag, who has studied the health effects of wine for more than a decade and makes Riesling from the eighteen vines in his yard, said, along with other researchers, that other substances which contribute to the flavor and special characteristics of wine, such as congeners, are also suspect. Even the wood in which the wines are fermented or aged can make a difference. "Some people are sensitive to the differences in the growing regions. Some can drink a California red wine but God help them if they drink a French Bordeaux or Burgundy," Dr. Freitag said. "There are different characteristics of the soils that are picked up and translated into the chemical mix in the grape itself."

The amount of tyramine varies depending on the type of grape, Dr. Freitag said. "Riesling is one of the higher tyramine-containing wines," he said. "Chardonnays and Sauvignon Blancs are low. . . . Chiantis are higher than Rieslings, Sauternes are low and Bordeaux are low. Californians are, as a rule, pretty low. A lot of European wine country is very rocky, limestoney, and how the grapes grow and the amount of protein they produce, maybe even differences in the kinds of yeasts that are used, may make a difference."

But once again, nothing here is absolutely clear, or without controversy. When we asked for information from the Wine Institute, the California-based industry advocate, it sent a 1996 paper on wines and headaches by Mark A. Daeschel, professor of Food Science and Technology at Oregon State University. We tracked Dr. Daeschel down while he was harvesting Pinot Noir grapes for a friend. "There's really nobody out there who wants to support the type of research that needs to be done to definitely nail all of this down," he told us. "We can't go to the federal government. They'll say 'just stop drinking.' And wineries are hesitant because they don't want to raise the issue that there may be a problem. But it's a complex situation. It's a combination of things and also the physiology of the consumer. Some people's triggers go off quicker than others'."

There is some research that indicates psychological issues also are important. Several researchers noted that people responded differently to substances that cause them headaches depending on their state of mind, which might explain, in part, the-wines-on-vacation syndrome. Think about the common question: Why does Champagne give me such a headache? Maybe the answer is that the bubbles carry alcohol to the bloodstream faster. But maybe part of the answer is that people drink more Champagne than they think they do during the festive occasions at which it's often served, and they aren't eating food with it.

And that brings us back to alcohol. When we posed the question of headaches and wine to Stanford professor and heart surgeon Thomas Fogarty, the owner of a California winery by that name, he straightaway said with a chuckle, "The most common reason is overdose. The other is histamine in wine."

Elizabeth Holmgren, director of Research and Education at the Wine Institute, suggested you drink in moderation and with food, and that if you're sensitive to histamine, consult your doctor and take precautions. Some doctors and researchers say taking antihistamines, ibuprofen, or aspirin before drinking wine is effective in preventing headaches. Also, Vitamin B_6 can help metabolize histamine, some say. But, remember, some people can have harmful reactions to the use of these over-the-counter drugs with alcohol, so ask your doctor first. Drinking plenty of water when you're having wine also might help. Dehydration can cause headaches, too.

Dr. Freitag told us, "I would recommend that someone choose a white wine over a red and drink modest amounts. If you drink wine with any regularity and if you find there's a type of wine that you enjoy and that doesn't give you headaches, try to stick with it or something similar. If you're at a dinner and you get headaches from red wine, there's nothing wrong with taking a few sips of it, but your glass should never get terribly empty.

"If you're sensitive in general," he said, "most people tend to tolerate the wines from California, Washington, and Oregon more than European wines, grape type to grape type."

Quite a few of our readers have home remedies. Personally, when we go to a tasting where we will be trying many different wines, we take two aspirin before the event and drink plenty of water before, during, and after. That works for us. Bill Roy of Atlanta wrote: "The key for most people is to drink citrus or fruit juice after drinking wine, especially red wine. This prevents headaches by pulling histamines out of the body (through urine). Even a bowl of sorbet can aid this process. I've told this to hundreds of people over the years and inevitably I get calls the next day saying it really works."

And then there is this, from P. J. Burkhart of Houston: "I always suffered from major headaches drinking red wines. A friend's father who is seriously into good wine told me to choose reds that are at least three times as old as the length of time it was aged in the wooden barrels. So far this rule has worked perfectly. I now enjoy red wine with no headaches."

The bottom line: This is such an individual matter that you really should try to find out which wines hurt you and which don't, and which remedies work for you and which don't. And you really should talk to your doctor. You might find that there's an easy solution that will allow you to go back to enjoying wine without pain.

Chapter Five

White Burgundy

Just Remember Three Names

If you like Chardonnay, get to know white Burgundy. If you don't like Chardonnay, you owe it to yourself to get to know white Burgundy. We know it's not easy. There are so many different kinds of Burgundy, from the famous Montrachet to the simple Mâcon. There are few simple château names, but instead a head-spinning array of Grand Crus, Premier Crus, village names, shipper names . . . eeek! How complicated is this? Consider that it goes all the way back to the French Revolution, when the vineyards of Burgundy were chopped up. They've been chopped up even more as the years have gone on, so the situation has become more and more complex. The same vineyard can be owned by dozens of people, each making a separate wine. It's enough to make you go straight to the California Chardonnay section of the wine store, where you'll find something easy, like "Raymond, Private Reserve."

It needn't be so complicated. We have an easy solution, and it's worth the trouble because white Burgundy is a very special experience. It has inspired many exclamation points in our notes over the years. "Effortlessly wonderful! Nutmeg, fruit, and cream in perfect balance" (a 1992 Puligny-Montrachet). "One of the greats! Fruity, yet with lemon, earth, soil, and a tremendous lemon-cream finish. Despite all that, also crisp and clean and restrained, with a bit of sharpness. Tremendous complexity" (a 1983 Pouilly-Fuissé). "Great! Nose: Butter, straw, earth, herbs, rich. Taste: Huge, with a long finish. Clean, yet with a real bite to it. Vanilla. So big it's like a dessert wine. Take small sips" (a 1980 Meursault).

Thirsty yet?

White Burgundy is made from the Chardonnay grape, but the taste, while somewhat familiar, is very different from California Chardonnay. While American Chardonnay tends to be buttery, plump, round, and sometimes hard to pair with food, white Burgundy is often intense, filled with lovely minerals and the kinds of acids that give it an interesting structure and make it good with food. Like California Chardonnay, though, it also often has tastes of vanilla, nutmeg, and wood. White Burgundy isn't better than California Chardonnay, or vice versa. They're just different. And, as we noted about that Puligny-Montrachet, one thing that sets white Burgundy apart is its effortlessness. These wines have an easy charm and elegance. While that doesn't mean you'll drink it and say, "Gee, this has an easy charm and elegance," what it does mean is that you're likely to find the wines incredibly easy to drink. They don't have the edges and self-consciousness of some California Chardonnays.

It's all of that together—easy to drink yet serious, big yet clean, creamy yet lemony, buttery yet crisp—that gives Burgundy its marvelous complexity. When white Burgundy is good, there isn't a classier white wine in the world, or one with a more beautiful, more sensuous finish that seems to last forever. In a large blind tasting of white Burgundies under $30 in 1999, we found a lot to like from a wide range of areas, which we'll list to give you an idea of some of the various regions and producers of white Burgundy. Although our tasting was in 1999, these producers strive for a consistent style year after year:

> Pernand-Vergelesses Premier Cru from Domaine Rapet Père & Fils
>
> Mâcon Villages from Trénel Fils
>
> Saint-Aubin Les Charmois Premier Cru from Bernard Morey et Fils
>
> Bourgogne Hautes Côtes de Nuits from Domaine Gros Frère et Soeur
>
> Chassagne-Montrachet "Les Charrières" from Michel Colin-Deléger et Fils

Château-Fuissé Pouilly-Fuissé

Meursault from François Mikulski

Rully Premier Cru Le Meix Cadot from Vincent Dureuil-
   Janthial

Mâcon-Pierreclos from Guffens-Heynen

Saint-Véran "Les Bruyères" from Jean Goyon

Chassagne-Montrachet "en l'Ormeau" from Brenot

Savigny-Les-Beaune Premier Cru "Les Hauts Jarrons" from
   Maurice Écard et Fils

Montagny Premier Cru "La Grande Roche" from Louis Latour

Saint-Romain from Verget

Don't even think about memorizing them. Our point is just that white Burgundy is such a big, rich world. But, geez, who wants to try to remember all those names—not to mention pronounce them (Pernand-Vergelesses?). We have an easier way. Just keep these three names in mind: Puligny-Montrachet, Chassagne-Montrachet, and Meursault (Poo-lean-ye Moan-ra-shay, Sha-sahn-ya Moan-ra-shay, and Mehr-so). Stick with those three names and you'll be fine. These are not wines most of us can afford to drink every night, but there are so many times when we need a special-occasion wine: for a romantic meal for two, when you're meeting the in-laws for the first time. With the prices of American wines creeping up all the time, we doubt these Burgundies cost that much more than most people would spend on a special-occasion Chardonnay. And these have the added cachet of being French.

We figured we'd splurge for a tasting and pick up every one of these three wines we could find for under $40, but we didn't find many. We discovered that many more were clustered between $40 and $45.99, so we raised our cutoff point. While we did find, and enjoy, some that were less expensive than that, you should count on spending around $40 a bottle.

We spend most of our nights tasting six to eight wines "blind," in paper bags. You might not believe this, but sometimes this is a chore. Sometimes the wines are harsh and unpleasant, or just undistinguished. We'd be lying, though, if we told you that tasting these white Burgundies was work. As we tasted each of the three types against others of the same type, we gushed about wine after wine. In general, the Chassagne-Montrachet wines were our least favorite type, but that's relative.

These are intense wines, on the one hand filled with fruit but on the other hand with the fruit tightly wound up, intense, so there's no sense of flabbiness. They taste a bit sharp in your mouth at first, with plenty of lemon and nice mineral undertones that give them depth. Richness and austerity sound like opposites, but in this case, opposites are definitely attractive.

We love the finish of white Burgundies. Long after they're gone, they linger in your mouth, in your throat, and in your whole body, with a lush taste of vanilla, cream, nutmeg, lemon, and sensuous ripe fruit. This is heady stuff. Some of these are very big wines that seem to explode in your mouth, while others are shy and elegant, with more finesse. Your mouth coaxes the flavor from these. Consider some of our notes: "Woody, nutty, toasty, creamy—wow. Looong finish. It's all there. Elegant yet big, with apples, peaches, pears, vanilla. A very intense experience." That was the Meursault from Louis Jadot, which is one of the more widely distributed names in Burgundy. Or consider this: "A complete wine. Rich, fruity, yet with minerals, earth, and a long, sensuous finish. A lot of taste. Serious and very much a Burgundy. Very young yet ripe. Not as subtle as some others." That was the Puligny-Montrachet from Verget.

Keep in mind that because Burgundy is so fragmented, it's hard to find the same exact wine from the same producer twice. But this is a case where you really can just close your eyes, pick one, and feel good about your choice.

These wines are great with food, so they're perfect to take to a friend's house for dinner when you're supposed to bring a white (be sure to ask "red or white?" before you go). Arrive with it already chilled, then stand back and watch your wine wow your hosts. It's a famous name, it's French, it's Chardonnay, and its label is even pretty. It has all of this going for it even before it's poured. It's a grand slam.

One more tip: When most people think about aging wines, they think about big red wines, but good white Burgundies are usually much better with some age on them. Young white Burgundy, especially in good years, can be untamed—too much acidic taste, too many disparate flavors competing for the attention of your taste buds. Sometimes it's only in the finish that you can taste the real potential of the wine. It's very much like a person. In youth, sometimes people show wonderful attributes, but they haven't yet, as the saying goes, "amounted to anything." As people get older, they're able to tone down their edgier attributes while their best parts, if they're lucky, seem to come together into a real, rounder personality. Same thing with some wines.

Wine Notes

General advice: If you just keep these three names in mind, you'll be fine: Puligny-Montrachet, Chassagne-Montrachet, and Meursault. These improve with age, so don't worry about the vintage. More generally, the more geographically specific the name, the better chance you have that the wine will be excellent. So a label referring to a broad region, such as Bourgogne, is ranked lower than one referring to a specific village name. Ranked even higher are the Premier Cru vineyards; these will have the name of a vineyard and the village where it comes from (and also, helpfully, will probably say "1er Cru" or "Premier Cru" right on the label). Higher yet are the Grand Crus, which are individual vineyards, too. Grand Cru labels are shorter than the Premier Cru labels. The Grand Crus have only the vineyard name and "Grand Cru" on them (another way to know it's a Grand Cru will be the astonishing price).

Food pairings: Veal with cream sauce; flavorful fish and other seafood dishes; lobster, crabs, scallops.

Meursault

Louis Jadot Meursault. $42.50. DELICIOUS. Woody, nutty, toasty, creamy, fruity and just plain wow. It's all there. (1997)

Michel Colin-Deléger et Fils Meursault. $38.95. VERY GOOD/DELICIOUS. This will put hair on your chest. Intense and aggressive, with power like a burst of adrenaline. (1998)

Domaine Darnat Clos Richemont Meursault Premier Cru Les Cras Monopole. $42.99. VERY GOOD. Very pleasant, with nice fruit and lemon and a touch of richness. Especially good with food. (1997)

Henri Boillot Meursault. $29.99. VERY GOOD. Crisp, nicely acidic and a bit warming, with some steeliness and chalk. We had this with some age on it, and it was nice. (1995)

Louis Latour Meursault. $38.99. GOOD/VERY GOOD. Austere and steely, with plenty of lemon. Puckering and dry. Elegant and shy. Great with fish. (1997)

Chassagne-Montrachet

Domaine Marc Colin et Fils Chassagne-Montrachet Premier Cru Les Champs-Gains. $44.99. DELICIOUS. Toasty and rich, with a wonderful finish of vanilla and nutmeg that lasts forever. Big, and even bigger after you swallow it. (1998)

Puligny-Montrachet

Jean Pillot et Fils Puligny-Montrachet. $29.99. VERY GOOD. Lovely, with cream and lemon and good acids. Nice food wine, fabulous with seafood. (1998)

Domaine Gérard Chavy et Fils Puligny-Montrachet. $41.99. VERY GOOD. Crisp, clean, and dry, with loads of finesse. (1997)

Verget Puligny-Montrachet "Les Enseignères." $43.99. VERY GOOD. A complete wine, rich and fruity yet with nice minerals and a long, serious finish. Ripe. (1998)

Jean Boillot et Fils Puligny-Montrachet. $45.99. VERY GOOD. Plenty of body and proud of it. Bigger, longer taste than most. (1998)

How to Judge a Wine Store,
and When to Fire One

There are many bad wine stores out there, but there are many good ones, too, and we worry sometimes that people have been so turned off by the former that they never discover the latter. Some good wine stores are big and some are small. Many of our readers routinely tell us about the fine wines they found at Costco or Trader Joe's. We once dropped into a Harris Teeter supermarket in Atlanta with a better wine collection than most wine stores. In other words, there's no reason to suffer a bad wine shop.

Our model of a great wine merchant has always been our old friend Chip Cassidy, of Crown Wine Merchants in Coral Gables, Florida. What always drew us to Chip was his flat-out enthusiasm for the subject. He never said anything to us like, "You'll enjoy the bramblelike bouquet of this wine." Instead, he said things like: "This will blow your head off!"

When John was in Alpharetta, Georgia, he walked into a store called The Wine Store. One of the owners, Chris Hinton, handed him a brochure that said "Anything But California." It was a great deal on a half case of wine from all over the world—everywhere but California. "The whole idea is to try to get people to try things other than California wines, to get them away from that comfort zone," Mr. Hinton, a seven-time All-Pro offensive lineman who retired from the NFL after thirteen years, told us later.

When we were on vacation once, Bill Dailey of Rose City Liquors in Madison, New Jersey, called us twice because a customer was looking for a $6.99 wine we'd recommended. When he couldn't reach us, he called the *Journal* library and bought a copy of the article.

Len Rothenberg of Federal Wine & Spirits in Boston holds a wine tasting every Wednesday night—free—and everyone is invited. He includes the results of the tastings and his own picks, as well as news of coming wine dinners, in a weekly newsletter he sends out to anyone who wants it.

The Vineyard in Denver has several Wine-of-the-Month clubs that deliver wines to members' homes. For its special "Dealer's Choice" club, the store uses a "wine profile" form to tailor the wines to each member's preference.

On a wine reconnaissance trip to Washington, D.C., we walked into Schneider's of Capitol Hill. While we were there, the owners, Rick and Jon Genderson, were tasting a new wine, a Chase Zinfandel from S. E. Chase Family Cellars of St. Helena, California. This is from the Hayne Vineyard, whose grapes have produced wines made famous by other winemakers. We heard a commotion, walked over, and they offered us some. The wine was awesome. The winery made only 369 cases and Schneider's received 10. We ordered a case right on the spot.

How can you tell if you've walked into a good wine shop? We don't know about you, but we don't want to give the third degree to a merchant to try to determine if we like a store, whether it's a wine store or an auto-parts supplier. So here is how you can get a feel for a wine store without even saying a word:

1. The Chandon Test. Chandon is the sparkling wine made by the ton in California by Moët & Chandon. For years, we could find the regular Brut or Blanc de Noirs for as low as $10.99, so whenever we saw it for more than $15.99, we approached the shop warily. The price is somewhat higher now, so you'd need to decide on your own drop-dead point. But finding a single, popular wine like our Chandon—maybe Kendall-Jackson Chardonnay or something equally common—and using it as a comparison will be useful.

2. Climate. If a wine shop is really hot or really cold, walk out. It's not just that the wine is suffering, it's that the wine merchant doesn't care. Same thing for bright sunlight or harsh lighting. They're killers. (There are some very high-end shops where the wine on display is just for display—the wines you'll take home are in a cool basement somewhere—but that's rare.)

3. **"Do you like red or white?"** This is our all-time least-favorite and yet most-asked stupid question in wine shops. When you walk into a bookstore, no one attaches himself to your back and asks, "Fiction or nonfiction?" We sometimes murmur, "We like everything," and try to ditch the guy. If he doesn't back off, we leave and wait a few months before trying again.

4. **Déjà vu.** Many shops have the same, tired selection. You'll never find something new and interesting there. If everything looks familiar, you've outgrown the shop.

5. **Handmade signs.** If merchants are into their wines, they want to share them. Signs on shelves often indicate an enthusiastic, down-to-earth staff.

6. **Tastings.** Tastings in stores are a great way to further your knowledge without having to purchase a bottle of something. They're also a nice way for merchants to show you they appreciate your patronage and are invested in your expanding taste. Some stores offer free tastings all the time; others have tastings on Saturdays. Look for notices about them. (Because of various state laws, tastings may not be allowed where you live. Ask around.)

7. **Case discounts.** A 15 percent discount on a mixed case is a courtesy you should look for. Shops that offer discounts only on a case of the same wine are a bore. There is usually a sign about this.

8. **Dirt.** Approach a wine shop with the same attitude you'd approach any other merchant. If you go into a department store and the merchandise is dusty and appears neglected, or if the merchandise appears to be thrown around willy-nilly, you'd be skeptical. Simply bring that same sensibility to your wine store. Are the bottles dirty? Are there junky-looking wines around that clearly should have been poured down the sink years ago? Does it look as if no one cares? Of course, there are fine bargains to be found at some very

junky shops of all kinds, but you probably need to be an expert shopper to find them. Unless you're an expert shopper at such a wine store, beware.

You need to find a merchant you can trust, but you also need to learn to trust your own taste. If a merchant has sold you something more expensive than you'd planned, and you don't like it, be skeptical about returning.

Try to cultivate several wine merchants. Stores have different strengths and weaknesses. One might be big on Shiraz, another on old California Cabernets. Shop around. And once you're shopped in a store for a while, ask yourself these questions:

Does your wine merchant show enthusiasm like Chip Cassidy?

Does your wine merchant work hard to get you to try new things, like Chris Hinton?

Does your wine merchant hustle to find the wines you're looking for, like Bill Dailey?

Does your wine merchant offer free tastings, or write a newsletter, like Len Rothenberg?

Does your wine merchant do anything special to make exploring the wine world easy and fun, like The Vineyard?

Does your wine merchant have a constantly changing supply of new wines, at least some of which you've never seen before, like Schneider's?

And, most important, do you look forward to visiting your wine shop?

If your answer to these questions is no, fire your wine shop. There's a better one not too far away.

Chapter Six

Chablis

How to Drink a Key Lime Pie

You've picked out the perfect lobsters, the ones that seemed liveliest in the tank and most likely to scoot across the kitchen floor if they had a chance. Sure, they're expensive, but lobster dinners are special. Then you get the best sweet butter. No reason to scrimp here. You can already almost taste the plump, succulent meat drenched in the creamy, rich butter. Now, what wine are you going to have with it?

How about Chablis?

If you're shaking your head, maybe it's because poor Chablis gets "dissed," as our daughters would say, from both ends. On the one hand, people avoid it because it seems like a snooty French wine that's probably precious and expensive. Remember the "brie and Chablis crowd"? On the other hand, paradoxically, people avoid it because Chablis often dredges up memories of cheap wine. For years, it seemed as if every jug wine in America was called Chablis, even though it had nothing whatsoever to do with real Chablis. There was even a television commercial years ago in which one of those snooty voices endemic to wine ads talked about an inexpensive California white wine and called it "a better Chablis." Then, on top of all that, too many people have been offered a glass of Chablis at a cocktail party and found it too austere, too acidic, too crisp—and no wonder: Chablis was never meant to be drunk without food.

It's horrible that this has happened to one of the world's most remarkable—and, for the quality, one of the most affordable—white wines.

Chablis is a wonder of the wine world. It's made from Chardonnay grapes in the Chablis region of France, which is in the northern part of Burgundy. That geography is important. While California Chardonnay can get big and ripe and sometimes "fat" from the warmth of the sun, Chardonnay in Chablis struggles in a much cooler climate. That means the wines are leaner, more austere, with a crisp, acidic taste and sometimes even a little "sourness" that reminds us of a very ripe lemon. Yeah, we know that "sour" doesn't sound mouth-wateringly good, but think of a tart green apple. It's that very lemon-sour quality, together with ripe fruit, perfect acids, and just the right soil, that make Chablis such a crisp, delicious drink and a classic accompaniment with food.

If you've never tried Chablis, let's take a trip down to Miami Beach to explain its tastes. We love the Key lime pie at Joe's Stone Crab on Miami Beach. The Key lime is tart and rich, with a whisper of sweetness, while the whipped topping is creamy and not too sweet. The best thing about the pie is that it comes after the stone crab claws. After the briny, sweet, plump tastes of the claws, the clean, crisp taste of the Key lime pie seems even better. Now, imagine if you could actually drink a wine reminiscent of the rich tartness of that Key lime pie with the stone crab claws. It's hardly a perfect parallel, but if you can taste that in your mind, you can understand why Chablis is such a great wine to have with seafood. A good, well-chilled Chablis has a tartness, a flintiness, and a freshness that's like breaking open a very fresh head of lettuce. It's as edgy as a piece of ice in your mouth, with a luscious acidity that explodes, and a finish that's clean and bracing.

There are four kinds of Chablis. There's Petit Chablis and there's plain Chablis to start with. Then there is "Premier Cru" Chablis, which is easy to see: The label will say something like "Chablis Premier Cru" and then say something like "Vaillons" right underneath. Then there are seven "Grand Cru" Chablis. For instance, a label might say "Chablis Les Clos," then, underneath, "Grand Cru." In other words, there's no reason to memorize all this because it will say what it is clearly on the label—and in any case, you can generally tell from the price. Grand Cru should be more expensive than Premier Cru and so forth.

Chablis tends to be a good value because the market for it in the United States is limited. Our working assumption is that it's hard to go wrong just picking up any bottle of the real deal. In our first large tasting of Chablis, in 1998, we came away very impressed with the remarkable price/quality relationship of these wines. Our best of tasting then was a Chablis from Verget, and our best value was a Chablis from Hamelin. We also liked Château de Maligny, which was our house Chablis for years. It seems to be more widely available than most, and is usually a good deal.

We conducted another tasting in 2000, with a twist. While Chablis is a classic combination with all seafood, it is absolutely best with oysters. John doesn't eat oysters—he thinks they're gross—but Dottie loves them. This was a good excuse for Dottie to exercise her passion. We took our Chablis tasting to a local fish joint and ordered several different kinds of oysters. Dottie slurped oysters and tasted Chablis while John tried to interview her between mouthfuls.

Bottle No. 8: "This gets richer with the oysters," Dottie said. "The earthiness of the oyster seems to plump up the fruit and lemon, and leaves a nice, clean finish."

Bottle No. 9: "There's almost a nutmeg quality that comes through with the brininess. The wine cleans the palate. The oyster is briny and you taste the ocean. The wine barrels through that, so it's cleansing."

Bottle No. 8 again: "Hmm. This isn't so great with the oysters now. It tastes a little skunky."

Bottle No. 12: "Wow. This is the best combination because the wine seems to almost explode off the calm, serene surface of the oyster. Rich wine, rich oyster. Great combination. Just wonderful."

Bottle No. 12 was, to our surprise, Domaine de l'Orme Petit Chablis, which cost just $14.99. Petit Chablis is the most "common" Chablis, looked down upon by some, and meant to be drunk young. But the proof was in the oyster—which was, in this case, a Sisters Point from Washington State. "Some oysters are better with Chablis than others," Dottie concluded. "Some oysters are too flat, some are too sweet. The Sisters Point were best with this Chablis because they were the most flavorful."

Emboldened by this tasting, we continued the next night with soft-shell crabs at home—really plump ones that, to Media and Zoë's horror and delight, were still twitching as Dottie sautéed them. In the long run, after several flights, when we tore off the bags, we found a wide range of Chablis that we liked. We described our favorite this way: "Easy to drink. Flinty, lemony, and crisp, yet with a lovely, lingering fruit/lemon finish. Tastes like really ripe grapes, but not at all flabby and sweet. Warming." This was Faiveley Chablis, which then cost $26.95.

Chablis ages quite well, taking on a special depth and richness, but in yet another, more recent tasting we focused on newer vintages because that's what you're likely to find at your wine shop today. We came away convinced, once more, that it's hard to go wrong when you combine seafood with just about any Chablis. To be sure, some seemed thin and weak, without the kind of intensity or mouth-awakening vibrancy that we expect. Sadly, many of our favorites were Premier Cru or Grand Cru, which means they were pretty expensive. But not all of them were. We were utterly charmed by one wine about which we wrote: "Serious yet so confident that it's easy. It's deceptively easy to drink because it's so beautifully balanced. There's nutmeg and caramel in the throat." Our guess was that this was a simple Chablis because it didn't seem quite as rich and deep as the more expensive wines, but we didn't taste a single wine during the tasting that we flat-out enjoyed drinking as much. We're happy to say that this was Domaine William Fèvre Chablis, which cost about $20.

Our best of tasting was a rare Delicious! on our rating scale, a wine that we considered not just tasty but genuinely exciting. "Big, with lots of fruit and sourness. Rich and soulful," we wrote. "Huge and intense. Spicy, with lots of nutmeg and cream. Warming and intense. Lots of wood. Big wine. Nutmeg, lemon, great acids. Great food wine. Everything in proportion. Pretty well perfect. 'It takes your breath away,' says Dottie." This was Domaine Vocoret Chablis Grand Cru "Blanchot," which cost about $35.

At least once sometime soon, when you're picking just the right seafood to have for dinner and preparing a special meal, try a Chablis. Sure, you don't spend this much on a wine every day, but you don't have lobster every day, either. Special meals call for special wines, and special wines can make even ordinary meals seem special. We can't promise you a Delicious! experience, but we can tell you that, in general, the Chablis will enhance your seafood more than your usual Chardonnay.

Wine Notes

General advice: We find plain Chablis (as opposed to Petit Chablis, Premier Cru, and Grand Cru) to be an especially good buy. Some producers are consistently reliable. We have listed below the tasting results from our most recent tasting and an earlier tasting so that you can have the names of several good producers. The prices are the prices we paid at the time of the tasting; prices for current vintages are higher now in many cases. Chill these, but not too much. There are special tastes of minerals and fruits that you'll miss if the wine is too cold.

Food pairings: Seafood, especially shellfish.

Domaine Vocoret & Fils Chablis Grand Cru "Blanchot." $35.00. DELICIOUS! Best of tasting. Rich and soulful, huge yet intense. Spicy, with plenty of nutmeg and cream. Perfectly balanced. Just plain wow. (1998)

Domaine William Fèvre Chablis. $20.00. DELICIOUS. Best value. Serious wine, yet so confident that it's easy to drink and easier to like. Rich and deep but so beautifully balanced that it seems effortless. Beautiful. (1998)

Denis Pommier Premier Cru "Beauroy." $26.99. VERY GOOD/DELICIOUS. This tastes somewhat like a big, plump California wine to us, but it has a little bit of soil and some edge as well. Charming. (1998)

Denis Pommier Chablis. $18.99. VERY GOOD. Plenty of tight fruit. Juicy, intense, and hunger-inducing. It jumps around in your mouth, with a long, lime-cream finish topped with nutmeg. (1998)

Jean-Marc Brocard Chablis Premier Cru "Montée de Tonnerre." $27.99. VERY GOOD. Nice "sour" tastes on top of a rich base. More voluptuous than austere, with an utterly luscious finish. (1998)

Domaine William Fèvre Chablis Premier Cru "Montmains." $38.00. VERY GOOD. Mouth-coating and luscious, but the most amazing thing is that the taste seems to come back full after you swallow. (1998)

Louis Michel & Fils Chablis Premier Cru "Montée de Tonnerre." $34.95. GOOD/VERY GOOD. Creamy "sour" nose. Very pleasant and lemony, but without the intensity of some. (1998)

Jean-Marc Brocard Chablis Premier Cru "Montmains." $27.00. GOOD/VERY GOOD. Nutmeg, cream, toast, and burnt sugar. Luscious, with a long, lemony finish, though it seemed to lose its intensity quickly. (1998)

Previous Tasting

Faiveley Chablis. $26.95. VERY GOOD/DELICIOUS. Best of tasting. So easy to drink. Flinty, lemony, and crisp, with a lovely, lingering fruit/lemon finish. Tastes like real ripe grapes. Not at all flabby. Warming. (1997)

Domaine de l'Orme Petit Chablis. $14.99. VERY GOOD. Great with oysters. Young, zesty, and bold. Surprisingly big. (1997)

Jean Dauvissat Chablis Premier Cru "Vaillons." $24.99. VERY GOOD/DELICIOUS. Austere, chalky, and bone dry. Mysterious and complex. Great with soft-shell crabs. (1997)

Jean Dauvissat Chablis Premier Cru "Montmains." $28.99. GOOD/VERY GOOD. Crisp and a bit big, with a long, slightly creamy finish. Charming, with real taste that's shy and tight. Molasses, straw, and toast. (1997)

Domaine Hamelin Petit Chablis. $13.99. GOOD/VERY GOOD. Earthy, flinty, and so clean that it's like sorbet for your nose. Long, lemony finish. (1998)

Moreau Chablis Grand Cru "Les Clos." $41.99. GOOD/VERY GOOD. Really pleasant. Good chalk and lots of fruit. (1997)

Invite Your Friends
to a Wine Tasting;
Yes, You

Next time you're looking for something fun to do with your friends, throw a wine-tasting party. Oh, yech, you might be thinking, because many people figure this is akin to inviting friends over for a seminar on life insurance. All those people standing around stiffly, sniffing wine and nervously talking about nuances of this and pretensions of that. But wine-tasting parties aren't like that at all. They're easy, they're fun, and, without anyone quite realizing it, they can teach you a little something. Follow these simple steps for a great party that also happens to feature a wine tasting:

• Tell everyone who's coming to bring a bottle of the same kind of wine and set a price range—say, Chardonnay under $15. Couples can bring one bottle or two.

• Tell them to put the wine in a brown-paper lunch bag before they come over. If it's a white wine, have them bring it chilled.

• Have one glass for every guest and maybe a few spares. Obviously, at a formal tasting, you'd want to have a separate glass for every wine, but easy and informal are most important here. Have some containers around—just regular bowls or vases or big pitchers would be fine—so people can pour out wines they've had enough of. The spare glasses will come in handy because, inevitably, some people will forget whose glass is whose and will want a new one.

• Have plenty of heavy finger foods around and put out bottles of sparkling water and glasses, periodically encouraging your guests to eat and to drink water. This is important.

• Prepare a bottle of your own, in a bag. When people walk in, give them a glass with a little of your wine in it (just a little; remember, this is a tasting). Take theirs, open it, and put it on the table. Make sure the bags are closed tight just below the top of the bottle so no one will know which wine is which. Number the bags.

• If you want to start pouring with No. 1 and taste in order, great, but we'd just leave all of the bottles on the table and tell people to try them in any order they like.

What you'll find is that at the beginning people will be embarrassed to say anything about the wine and seem a little shy about the whole thing. What a difference a couple of tastes make, though. By the third glass, the noise level will increase. Your guests will probably be talking about everything except the wine. And soon they'll be helping themselves (that's why you left the wines on the table).

By the fourth glass, your guests will start to interrupt themselves to comment on the wines—"This is bound to be the Cubs' year"—sip—"wow, I really like No. 3." Bingo. They have noticed that the wines taste different and they know which one they like best. Soon, people really will be talking about the wines. At some point, ask if everyone has tasted all of them. If they have, you might want to take an informal poll on everybody's favorite, but it doesn't really matter. Each guest will have discovered which one he or she likes best. That means it's time to . . .

• Take the bottles out of the bags. This is always fun. There will be all sorts of reactions: "Oh, my God, I liked *that*?" "Just like me. I always choose the cheapest." "No one liked my wine. I didn't even like my wine!" You'll also find that, even without a poll, you can see which was the favorite because it will be the empty bottle.

At the end of the night, the wine tasting itself will have been incidental to the evening. In fact, all that the tasting has done is get your friends' minds off more pressing matters—like work—so they could relax. In the long run, that's what a wine-

tasting party is all about: good conversation and good friends—
not just wine. But don't tell anyone that. It'll be our secret. And
please, if your friends are driving, be very careful. Have a designated
driver or call a cab. You want everyone to be around for the next
vintage.

Chapter Seven

Loire Whites

The Ultimate Summer Wines

People sometimes ask us how we conduct our tastings. We put six to ten bottles in paper bags, number them, and taste each in a separate glass. John takes the notes while Dottie talks. We do it this way not just because Dottie has a better palate and weaker wrists, but also because she tends to say things like this, which John feverishly wrote verbatim: "This is charming and interesting. It's vibrant, intense, and limey. It's got an interesting combination of citrus fruits and soil. It's like if you fermented citrus and soil together, this is what you'd get. It's almost earthy. There are minerals in the nose and the taste, but you've got these tangerines exploding in your mouth. The result is a luscious, soulful wine. Doesn't it remind you of our carambola tree in Miami?"

Leave it to a bottle of wine to take us, in one paragraph, from a hilltop overlooking the Loire River in France to the backyard of our Old Spanish house in Miami, where we planted a "star fruit" tree and harvested just a few fresh, tangy carambolas every year. We were in the midst of a tasting of Sancerre, the great summer white from France, and, as you can tell, we were having a wonderful time. Sancerre is one of the wines from the Loire Valley that we consider the world's greatest summer whites—and they're bargains, too. You spend $8 or $10 on an everyday white wine without much thinking about it, right? Well, you can buy a better wine, with more character, for the same money—and it's from France, too.

Just as the Rhône Valley is associated with big, heavy reds, the Loire is known for lovely, often-inexpensive whites (though there are, of course, some Rhône whites and Loire reds). There are all sorts of names, like Savennières, which is quite trendy at the moment. But for our money— and not much of it, at that—we recommend Muscadet, Vouvray, and Sancerre for their combination of great value, distinctive tastes, and relatively widespread availability. To some extent, the three have little in common. Muscadet is made from the Muscadet grape, which is formally called Melon de Bourgogne. A few American wineries are beginning to make a "Melon" wine, and they're interesting but not cheap. (They're not easy to sell, either. A California winery executive told us he once made a "Melon" wine no one would buy—because they didn't want a wine made out of melons.) Vouvray is made from the Chenin Blanc grape, and Sancerre is made from the Sauvignon Blanc grape. What they do have in common, though, is that they are the kind of easy-to-like, chill-you-to-your-bones, not-very-serious wines that we all need in summer.

We often take Muscadet for granted because it's everywhere and so affordable. Drunk young and well chilled, it's perfect with light, white fish. It's also exactly the kind of wine you'd take to a summer picnic: fun, gulpable, and refreshing. Muscadet's taste is a little difficult to explain. It's quite dry and we always think of its taste as flat. We don't mean flat as a pejorative, but that it has broad tastes that are not sharply focused. There's an almost musky taste to Muscadet that gives it a sense of earthiness that's really quite attractive when combined with a core of lively, fresh fruit, nice acids, and a fairly light body. Much of the best Muscadet comes from the Sèvre-et-Maine area and says "Sur Lie" on the label, indicating that the wine stayed in contact with its sediment for a while, giving it extra body and complexity.

Muscadet isn't a wine to linger over or debate. It's just fun. Consider these notes from our favorite in our most recent tasting: "Yum. Some richness, lots of lemon-lime flat taste. Earthy. Minerals, yet with a spritz of lime. Sprightly, but with some body. Vibrant. Jumps out of the glass." This was Château de l'Hyvernière Sèvre-et-Maine Sur Lie, which cost just $9.99 at the time. (Through all the years we have been drinking Loire wines, prices haven't risen very much because they're not in great demand in the United States.)

Vouvray can be dry, semisweet, or sweet. It can also be a marvelous sparkler. We had a sparkling Vouvray—Foreau Brut—for $18.99 not long ago that was excellent: dry and alive, with the kind of clean finish, with a hint of chalky earth, that we associate with Champagne. Vouvray has an unmistakable tart, green-apple taste and a kind of round, creamy mouth-feel. Here's how we described one of them in our most recent tasting: "Fresh, clean, green-apple nose. Rich but clean. Apple tartness, nice weight, and some mouthfeel. Tastes like a peach that's been baked or poached in apple cider. Apple tartness but the sweetness of a peach. Almost like roasted fruit, but with some earth and nice acids." This was Domaine des Perruches, which cost $8.59. Do you get that much taste from your $8.59 wine? Our best of tasting was even better. "Lots of color. Smells like peaches. Slight spritz. Oranges, pineapples, some earth. A whole fruit basket. Very clean and a bit creamy, with lots of mouthfeel." This was Château de Goulaine (then just $10.50), and this is the bottle we decided to have with dinner on the night we tasted it. We find that Vouvray can be hard to pair with food because of its fruity tastes, but we wondered how it would stand up to Dottie's famous roast pork. We usually have an Alsatian white with pork, and sometimes a lighter German Riesling, but, to our surprise, this was even better. The vibrant, fruity earthiness of the wine matched perfectly with the juicy, garlic-herbed tastes of the pork. The wine seemed to have a little bite when paired with the food, giving the wine an added dimension that made it taste even better.

Sancerre is one of the most vibrant wines around, a classic Paris bistro wine because it's lively, fun, reasonably priced, and goes well with a wide variety of food. It has an aromatic limelike smell and a sharp, focused fruit taste that's fresh and pure. There's some of that grassiness you know from California Sauvignon Blanc, but there's an extra dimension. It's the marvelous soil. If you pay close attention, you can smell a little bit of chalk, or limestone, and you can taste it, too, especially in the back of your mouth. Even if you can't taste it, though, its presence gives the wine some grounding, almost as if it keeps these vibrant, juicy, mouth-popping tastes tethered to the good earth. One of the amazing things about a good Sancerre, in fact, is that you can often enjoy it on two levels: It's simply fun and easy to drink on one level, but on another level, if you want to really think about it, you can taste all sorts of complexity underneath that Sauvignon Blanc crispness. In any event, the bottom line is that its tart, slightly acidic tastes inevitably make us hungry for some summer-weight food.

As it happens, we conducted our most recent Sancerre tasting immediately after a tasting of U.S. Chardonnays under $20. The contrast was extreme. While the better Chardonnays were comforting and broad, they seemed, well, boring compared to the sharp, exciting tastes of the lighter, fresher Sancerre. The Sancerre that made Dottie think about Miami was Archambault's "Domaine de la Perrière," which was also one of our favorites in a previous tasting. Remarkably, though, we found some we liked even better, including another that then cost $12.99, which can't be much more than you pay for your everyday Sauvignon Blanc. "Juicy nose, with lime and minerals," we wrote. "Nicely acidic and so very drinkable. Clean and vibrant." This was Sautereau "Côtes de Reigny." As it happens, this is the same producer whose rosé Sancerre was the first we ever tasted. A small amount of red and rosé Sancerre is produced from the Pinot Noir grape. If you happen to see one, especially the rosé, grab it for its lovely hints of cherries and strawberries. Chilled, it's a great picnic wine, too.

Ultimately, it was difficult to choose a best of tasting. We found almost all of the wines charming, bracing, and mouth-watering. We finally decided that our favorite, the first one we'd rush out and buy again, was the one we described this way: "Fresh, almost prickly nose. This one has some richness. There are all those great fruit flavors, but an extra layer of depth and maybe even a hint of honey." This was Alphonse Mellot "La Moussière."

At some point soon, you're bound to prepare a special picnic and you're going to want to make sure that everything is perfect. When you do, go out of your way a little bit to pick up a Loire wine. You'll be so happy you did.

Wine Notes

General advice: The same producers are often our favorites in our tastings of Loire wines. In Muscadet, they include Château du Cléray from Sauvion, Domaine Luneau-Papin, and Morilleau. In Sancerre, Archambault's Domaine de la Perrière is worth looking for. In Vouvray, look for Champalou. All of these should be nicely chilled. While some will age nicely—especially sweeter Vouvray, which can improve for decades—we buy the youngest we can find because we like the fresh vibrancy they offer for summer. In Muscadet, look for the words "Sèvre-et-Maine" and "Sur Lie" on the label.

Food pairings: All of these are great with picnic foods. Muscadet is excellent with seafood. Sancerre's vibrancy gives life to dishes such as chicken salad. Vouvray is good with pork and with fruits and nuts.

Muscadet

Château de l'Hyvernière Sèvre-et-Maine Sur Lie (Reserve). $9.99. VERY GOOD/DELICIOUS. Best of tasting. Some richness on top of a broad, lemon-lime base. Earth and minerals, with a spritz of citrus. (1999)

Sauvion Sèvre-et-Maine. $5.99. GOOD/VERY GOOD. Best value. Plenty of fruit and plenty of character, with good tastes of minerals that give the wine complexity. (1999)

Château du Cléray (Sauvion) Sèvre-et-Maine Sur Lie (Reserve). $8.95. GOOD/VERY GOOD. Vibrant fruit, but still with that flat, slightly musky taste of Muscadet and a nice undertone of earth. Floral at first, slightly lemony later. (1999)

Domaine Les Hautes Noëlles Côtes de Grandlieu Sur Lie. $9.99. GOOD/VERY GOOD. Simple, but with such nice, lemony flavors that it's hard to resist. (2000)

Domaine Luneau-Papin Muscadet Sèvre-et-Maine Sur Lie "Clos des Allées" (Vieilles Vignes). $10.95. GOOD/VERY GOOD. Very approachable, musky fruit, and nice flavors, though a bit watery. (1999)

Vouvray

Château de Goulaine. $10.50. VERY GOOD/DELICIOUS. Best of tasting. Oranges, pineapples, peaches—a whole fruit basket, with an earthy underpinning and some weight. (1999)

Clos le Vigneau (Monmousseau). $9.99. VERY GOOD/DELICIOUS.

Best value. Complex and interesting, with cream, fruit, and minerals giving it very special depth. (2000)

Domaine des Perruches (Philippe de Guérois). $8.59. VERY GOOD. Fresh, clean, green-apple tastes, with some richness and mouthfeel. Nice acids, good earth, and altogether lovely. (1999)

Champalou "Cuvée des Fondraux." $13.95. GOOD/VERY GOOD. Round mouthfeel, with tastes of minerals, earth, apples, peaches, and other poached fruits. Easy to drink. (1999)

Sancerre

Alphonse Mellot "La Moussière." $16.95. VERY GOOD/DELICIOUS. Best of tasting. Fresh, almost prickly nose, with a little bit of honey and more richness than most. (2000)

Sautereau "Côtes de Reigny." $12.99. VERY GOOD/DELICIOUS. Best value. Juicy and drinkable, with vibrant lime and a hint of minerals. (2000)

Lucien Crochet "Le Chêne." $24.95. VERY GOOD/DELICIOUS. Aggressively crisp and lemony, with so much fruit it seems almost chewy. Quite a mouthful. (We also liked the less expensive, "plain" Lucien Crochet.) (1999)

Archambault "Domaine de la Perrière." $12.99. VERY GOOD. Bright, and clean, with a particularly fun, lively finish. An intense experience. (2000)

Domaine Thomas & Fils "La Crêle." $15.95. GOOD/VERY GOOD. Juicy and pleasant. Not quite as alive as some, but its relative calm would be good with food. (1999)

Taking Wine to a Friend's House:
Twelve No-Lose Suggestions

"I'm going over to a friend's house tonight and he really knows wine. What do I take?" We've been asked that many times over the years, and we have some ideas. But first, we always ask three questions:

(1) Do your friends know you're bringing wine? They should, for planning purposes. If you're bringing wine as a gift, and don't expect your hosts to open it with dinner, that's fine. But if it's a wine for dinner, they should be aware you're bringing something.

(2) Assuming your friends asked you to bring wine, are you supposed to bring red or white? Don't be shy about asking. You need to know. The wine needs to fit well with the dinner, and there are people who don't drink red wine, or white wine.

(3) How much are you willing to spend? We assume this is a nice dinner. You need to plan to spend real money. We'd figure about $30, but only you can decide what's appropriate. After all, if this is a pizza party, that's quite different.

Now for our advice. You don't want to take something your host buys by the case, but you also don't want to take something your host would scoff at. In the long run, it really is the thought that counts. If you've spent serious time searching the shelves of a good wine shop for something nice, or if you can say, "I read that the 2000 Oregon Pinots are really good, so I got one for you," that will ultimately matter more than the taste of the wine itself. If you take a white, don't buy it chilled in the store if you can help it—the bottle could have been in that refrigerator for years—but do chill it before you take it to dinner so it can be served right away.

Here are twelve wines you could bring along that are sure to impress your host. We're offering general advice, as opposed to specific bottles, so you have a good chance of finding these.

We think Champagne or a light dessert wine (anything made from the Muscat grape that's less than 11 percent alcohol) are great wines to bring, but we're assuming here that your host just wants a dry red or a white to go with dinner.

• Fine Bordeaux. Showing up with a good bottle of Bordeaux will immediately stamp you as a person of class and breeding, and this is easier than it seems. Look for a Bordeaux from Pomerol, Lalande-de-Pomerol, or Pauillac. The first two will be hits because they're primarily made from the Merlot grape. Pauillac is a storied name, home of some of the greatest red wines on Earth, such as Château Lafite Rothschild. But there are many lesser-known, and therefore more affordable, chateaux, too

• A good Shiraz from Australia. Wine lovers know Australia is making some outstanding Shiraz, but most folks haven't tasted some of the better stuff. Older vintages are better, since this red wine tends to be huge in its youth, but don't worry about it.

• New Zealand Sauvignon Blanc. This is the white wine the in-crowd is into. These wines tend to be crisp, grassy, and quite distinctive. Buy the youngest you can find.

• 1997 Italian red. We're not too interested in vintages, but everyone who knows about wine knows that 1997 was a great year for Italian reds. So if you show up with one, you're sure to be welcomed warmly. We think Barolo and Barbaresco are always special treats, but they will likely cost at least $40 and probably more. Consider instead a Chianti Classico, which will be delicious and soulful in a very special way. You can often pick up an excellent Chianti Classico for $20 to $25. When you hand it to your host and he smirks, assure him that this Chianti bears little resemblance to the simple, quaffing ones of his college days. After the wine is poured, you will be proved right.

• Savennières. This dry white wine from the Loire Valley of France, made from the Chenin Blanc grape, is highly trendy. It's juicy, vibrant, and flavorful, with enough weight to be excellent with food.

• Côte Rôtie. This is a recommendation we'd offer to our friends with a) money, and b) someone they really wanted to impress. Cote Rôtie is one of the most special red wines of the Rhône Valley of France. Made from the Syrah grape, it has a roasted, almost chewy redness that makes it unique. We also often sense herbs and even lilacs. It's great for colder weather and it's one of those wines that's too often overlooked, even by wine lovers, because it's so different. The downside: It will cost you $50 or so.

• A Malbec, from Argentina. This is a dark, intense red wine that even many wine lovers haven't tried. Catena and Weinert are both excellent producers whose wines you might see. Especially if you're having meat, this will be a winner.

• Pinot Gris from Oregon. Buy the youngest you can find, chill it well, and as soon as you show up, ask, "Can we open this right away?" It will be fresh, fruity, and different, which will immediately jump-start the evening and likely earn you the gratitude of your host. Remember that this is the same grape as Pinot Grigio from Italy, which should give you something to talk about, too, because everybody drinks Pinot Grigio.

• A white Graves, from France. This is a classy white wine that would be perfect for an elegant summertime dinner party. Look for Pessac-Leognan on the label (that's the best area). Graves, from the Bordeaux region, is made primarily from Sauvignon Blanc, which should make it somewhat familiar, and Sémillon grapes. For the price of a good Chardonnay, you can have something different that will take your host's taste buds to a new place.

• Chablis, the real thing from France, crisp and flinty. If your host is serving seafood, this wine will be a winner, and much appreciated. It's amazing how many people have never had a real Chablis and how rarely even wine lovers think to pick one up.

• A fine white Burgundy. These wines made from the Chardonnay grape are so very special that even wine lovers tend to save them for special occasions, so your visit will immediately become a special occasion, as well it should, right?

• Kosher wine. If your host keeps kosher or any of the guests do, a bottle of outstanding wine that just happens to be kosher would be most thoughtful. You can get just about anything kosher these days, from fine Champagne to top-rank Bordeaux. If your store doesn't have the kind of good stuff that makes you say, "Gee, I didn't realize this was kosher," try another store.

Chapter Eight

Gewürztraminer

A Little Pepper with Your Wine?

How does this white wine sound to you? "Prickly, fresh, and flowery, like roses. Serious wine, complex, with lots of layers to it, a lot of taste. Alive, vibrant, clean. Crisp and bracing. Floral, perfumey yet peppery finish. Filled with flowers." Or how about this? "Roses and apricots. Fresh, floral, alive, vibrant, bursting with fruit flavors, yet also plenty of white pepper. Mouth-watering, literally. Still young. So fresh and lovely. Pears and peaches and spice."

Here's the bad news: To try wines like this, you'll have to put on your pith helmet and venture into an unfamiliar part of your wine store, to the tiny section labeled "Alsace." Not only that, but you have to try to pronounce Gewürztraminer. But trust us here: It's worth the trouble.

People ask us all the time about good values, but it seems their eyes glaze over if we talk about wines from anywhere but California. If you're really interested in value, you can't limit yourself to one country, or one state. The Alsace region of France produces some of the classiest, most distinctive white wines in the world, and they're generally great bargains, too. This doesn't mean they're cheap—we rarely see them for under $12 or so—but their quality is so high, the experience of drinking them is so interesting, and what they can do for your dinner is so special that we consider them bargains at the price.

Maybe they're not popular because they're unusual in so many ways.

Alsace is on the border of France and Germany, and the wines themselves seem to have a little bit of a split personality. They're mostly white, like German wines, and they come in elongated German-style bottles, but they're identified by their grape type, like American wines. They're generally dry, but sometimes have a floral character that some might mistake for sweetness. Because they're usually white and the bottles look German, they often can be found in the German section of wine shops even though they're from France. Go figure.

The good news is that, once you finally find any bottle of Alsatian wine, it's hard to go wrong. Rieslings from Alsace, for instance, are full-bodied, bold white wines that are good even in winter. In a tasting, our favorite Alsatian Rieslings were from Domaine Schoffit, Willm, Zind-Humbrecht and Kientzler. Our favorite Alsatian wine, however, has always been Gewürztraminer. If you can't pronounce it, keep in mind that most pronunciation guides differ, too. Try ge-vertz-tra-mee-ner and you'll be fine (and if you just ask for a ge-VERTZ, the wine shop owner will surely think you're an expert). This is one unusual grape—it's distinctly peppery, with floweriness and juiciness that make it perfect with food. There's also a rare, expensive Alsatian Gewürz called Vendange Tardive that combines high alcohol, lots of sweetness, and traditional Gewürz pepper-spice into an astonishing mouthful of taste. Imagine this, a 1976 Hugel Vendange Tardive we drank in 1991 with pork chops in caper sauce: "Light, spicy nose. Wonderful and wondrous taste. Clean Gewürz character with lots of spice. Yet creamy and elegant. Gorgeous, sensuous finish. Ripe and big, yet lots of finesse. Perfectly made, perfect age, with no hint of old age."

Some U.S. wineries make Gewürztraminer, too. We once had a Field Stone, from the 1980 vintage, that knocked our socks off: "Delicious, fantastic! Roses in the nose, incredible floweriness in the nose and in the taste. Happy, fresh, young, and incredibly fun." De Loach makes a good one. Our notes on its 1998: "Pine-tar nose, interesting and prickly. Pear juice, clean, but with mouthfeel. Real fruit bowl, but nicely focused." It cost $15.99. But we've generally found American Gewürzes to be a bit sweet and clumsy, and since they tend to cost as much as the real thing, from Alsace, why bother? After all, the real thing is a natural wonder: extremely dry, with an unmistakable pepperiness and a little taste of earth. Our notes from a 1983 Léon Beyer Gewürz: "Delicious! Fruity and crisp, very varietal and fresh, yet actually with some cream. Beautiful!" Clean, dry, crisp, fruity, and alive—and still filled with definite tastes of pepper and spices. This is what Alsatian Gewürz is all about.

Alsatian wines, in general, age beautifully, which is surprising considering they're so delicious, charming, and drinkable in their youth. For Christmas 1998, we opened a 1976 dry Muscat from Alsace, made by Trimbach, and it was delicious. It was still full of that delightful orange-blossom taste that comes from the Muscat grape, but had reached an elegant middle age, with plenty of maturity and many more years ahead of it.

We've found over the years that Gewürztraminers, even from the United States, age well, too. There were years, in fact, when we spent a lot of time searching for old Gewürzes. In 1987, when we visited a winery called Rutherford Hill in Napa, it had a 1977 Gewürz for sale on its list of "library wines"—the old stuff. We asked the people behind the counter how it was, and they said they'd never tasted it. So we bought it, opened it right there at the tasting counter—it had turned a little dark—and drank it with them. Even at cellar temperature, it was delicious. The age—and, probably, the temperature—brought out its spicy, prickly, and austere tastes.

In a tasting of Alsatian Gewürztraminers in 1998, we liked the Willm, Kientzler, Lucien Albrecht, and Trimbach. For a more recent blind tasting, we bought every Alsatian Gewürztraminer we could find. As always, we bought these right off retail shelves, just as you would. Some stores carry no Alsatian wines. Others carry just a few. The two names you're most likely to see are Trimbach and Hugel, which is fine because they're consistently good and generally good buys. Indeed, in this tasting, the Trimbach was our best value. It's the wine we mentioned at the beginning of this chapter that was "bursting with fruit flavors." Our favorite, the one described above that one, was from Hurst. It cost $25.99 at the time, and is special enough to be worth every penny. Don't focus on any specific producer, though, because it's impossible to know what wines you'll find. For instance, we didn't even see Willm, our previous favorite, for our most recent tasting.

When we have pork, we usually drink Alsatian Gewürztraminer. To us, it's a classic combination. It also goes well with the kind of hearty winter meals that we usually associate with red wine. Many people we know also think it's the perfect wine with spicy Asian food, though we often prefer creamy reds. What's important is that this is a wine that offers new and different tastes. It won't be just another wine in your glass; it will be something you really notice and enjoy. These are beautifully made, unique wines that take your taste buds into whole new areas. Give them a try. More broadly, keep in mind that the white wines of Alsace are lovely and great buys because only you know how good they are.

General advice: Trimbach, Hugel, and Willm are always good names to look for. Chill well and have a glass before dinner because this wine is literally mouthwatering. Then it will taste great with dinner, too. Don't worry about the age.
Food pairings: Roast pork, ham, and smoked salmon. Some people prefer it with spicy Indian or Thai food.

Armand Hurst Cuvée Angélique Grand Cru. $25.99. DELICIOUS. Best of tasting. Crisp, bracing, and filled with flowers. Prickly, fresh, and flowery. Alive with taste. (1998)

Trimbach. $13.99. VERY GOOD/DELICIOUS. Best value. Roses, pepper, peaches, and apricots. So fresh and lovely. (1998)

Hugel. $17.99. GOOD/VERY GOOD. Pleasant, but without the intensity of some. Great picnic wine, lovely, juicy, and easy to drink. (1998)

Kientzler. $16.99. GOOD/VERY GOOD. Pleasant and peppery. Good fruity flavors. Mellower than most and easy to drink, but it doesn't leap off the tongue like some. (1995)

Marcel Deiss Saint Hippolyte. $29.99. GOOD/VERY GOOD. Golden, thick, and lovely, deeper-looking than most. Nectar. So luscious it could be dessert. (1997)

Hunold. $13.50. GOOD/VERY GOOD. Interesting and complex, with nice pepper, but slightly heavy. Better as it warmed. (1998)

Storing Wine: Relax!
(Unless the Cops Show Up)

You can make wine storage complicated if you want to. Just ask the police department of Coral Gables, Florida.

When we moved to Miami in 1984, we bought an Old Spanish house built just two months before the Great Hurricane of 1926. With its romantic arches, it was like a fortress, with thick walls that kept the house cool all year long—perfect for storing wine. We fulfilled a dream by having a wine cellar built into a spare room, with individual spaces for 990 bottles. Miami was a pretty rough place in 1984, so we decided we needed a security system. A security man named Tom knew a mark when he saw one, and he sold us a gold-plated, state-of-the-art system with all sorts of bells and whistles. When he saw the wine room, his eyes lit up. "You know," he said, "we could put a thermostat in here attached to the alarm system. If it gets too warm in here, we'd be notified, and we'd call you." It sounded like a good idea at the time.

Just a month later, at 2:00 A.M., we heard beeping down-stairs. It sounded like the security system, but if someone had broken in, we were supposed to hear a siren, not beeping. John, naked, crept down the stairs, Dottie close behind. As we walked into the front room, Dottie yelled, "Watch out! Someone's looking inside!" John scampered back behind the wall, and we both peeked around the corner. From windows all around the house, policemen stared back at us.

Coral Gables is a lovely suburb of Miami—charming, old, peaceful. It also has an efficient and generally not-very-busy po-lice force. We had no idea what was going on. John threw on some shorts and opened a window. "Your security company called," the policeman in front told us. "They said your alarm went off." The security system was still beeping. We couldn't turn it off and were afraid to open the doors for fear it would make the alarm really go off. But from the flashing lights on the control panel, John figured out what had happened: It was a warm Miami night, and the wine room had gone above 55 degrees. The wine room had flashed a message to the security company, which had called the police instead of us.

Under those circumstances, what would *you* tell the cops? We told them we were sorry, that the system was new, that there was something wrong with it—and thank you very much for coming. We were horrified. The wine, however, was unharmed.

This needn't ever happen to you because most people don't need a wine room. Obviously, if you have a large collection of fine wines, it is better to keep them someplace special, like a wine room with a temperature-sensitive alarm, or maybe even one of those wine-storage units that some companies sell. But if you're like most people, and just want to keep a few bottles around, this isn't necessary. We fear many people don't keep any wine in the house because they've been convinced it's so precious, so delicate, that it will quickly disintegrate if it's not treated like a hothouse flower. Not true. Wine is tougher than you think. And while, sure, wines kept in sublime conditions age more gracefully, you're probably not keeping your wines forever, just for a few weeks. Here's all you need to do with that case you just bought:

(1) Identify a place, perhaps the bottom of a closet, that has a fairly constant, moderate temperature (not too hot, not too cold), doesn't get much light and isn't disturbed very often.

(2) Carefully put the box of wine on its side so the bottles in the slots are horizontal, or just lay the bottles on the floor. It's important they rest on their side, instead of being stood up, so the wine stays in contact with the cork. This prevents the cork from drying out and allowing air in, which is bad for the wine. This is especially important if you plan to keep the wines for a while.

(3) Take one out when you want to open it.

That's it. Now, try it. Go out today and buy a mixed case of wine. You'll find that it's so much easier, and so much more fun, to have a few bottles of wine in the house than to run to the wine store every night (and, admit it: Sometimes you'd like to have wine with dinner but you're just too tired to pick up a bottle, right?). Most important, you will discover that it's easy to keep wine around the house, and that it won't spoil in a flash.

In time, you may see your collection grow. People often ask us how to start a collection of wine. The answer, to us, is to let it happen organically. Buy wines that you like, or think you might want to try, and then, if you enjoy them, buy another bottle or two. In time, you will find that you have a very nice collection of wines that you like—and that's the only collection worth having.

Chapter Nine

German Wines

Imagine the Taste of a Rose

Ungsteiner Honigsäckel.

Still there? Good. We'll bet some people turned the page before they even got to the sixth syllable. Imaging running into that tongue-twister at your local wine shop. It's enough to make most people grab a beer. This is a shame, because German wines such as Ungsteiner Honigsäckel are among the wine world's great gifts. They're delightful, they're low in alcohol, they're light and easy to drink, and they're even good values.

We know how you feel. Wachenheimer Königswingert? That sounds like the punch line of one of John's father's jokes. But stick with us here because we're going to tell you a very easy way to choose a good German wine—and we're *not* going to draw you diagrams of how to read a German wine label. Who wants to study how to read a label just to have a good bottle of wine?

We, too, avoided good German wines for our first few years together. We'd had Blue Nun, the then ubiquitous Liebfraumilch, and we figured all German wines were like that—sweet, inoffensive, and forgettable. Our first experience with a good German wine was so stunning that we still remember it. The wine was a 1975 Steinberger Kabinett from Rheingau. We can still taste its remarkable combination of backbone, aggressive fruit, pear-apple charm, and soil. We began to dabble earnestly in German wines and were amazed. Consider these notes from a Rüdesheimer Berg Rottland Spätlese 1971, which we bought in 1980 for $8.99: "Delicious!

Pure gold. Big nose, burnt almost, with peaches and cream. *Big,* spicy, creamy (got creamier with air in mouth). Incredibly *long,* spicy, smooth finish. Strong peaches. Fluffy! Incredible complexity of nose and taste. Coldness made it crisper!"

So when the *Journal* asked us to travel to Frankfurt to conduct a tasting for big advertisers, we jumped at the chance. We're really bad at directions and geography, but even we could see that the great Rhine river was somewhere very close to Frankfurt. We figured we'd take a couple of extra days and visit the Rheingau region. Our first surprise: Even though we couldn't figure out how to get out of the airport in our rental car and circled it three times, we were on the Rhine in just forty minutes, less time than it takes us to get from San Francisco to the Napa Valley.

The Rhine has so many hundreds of years of winemaking history that we felt very special to have a chance to see it. Of course, the Rheingau is just one of the great wine regions of Germany. Along the Rhine, there are also Rheinhessen and Rheinpfalz, or Pfalz, and, along the Mosel River and its tributaries, the famous wines of Mosel-Saar-Ruwer. To us, Rhine wines seem to have a little more pepper and backbone, while Mosel wines seem more flowery (and, by the way, it's MO-zuhl). It made sense that our first destination in Germany should be the Rheingau region, since one of its wines started our own personal journey of discovery of German wines.

As always, we made few plans and simply knocked on the door of anyplace that looked like a winery. We never identified ourselves as wine writers. Everywhere we knocked, the best English speaker of the household escorted us into a little room where we sat at a table and sampled one delicious wine after another—mostly whites, but also some reds from the Spätburgunder grape, which is the German name for Pinot Noir. It was a great trip, but sad in a way, too, because winemaker after winemaker told us that they just couldn't sell their wine in the United States. There's no market. German wine sales in the United States have been so flat for so many years that it's now outsold, more than 2 to 1, by Canadian wine.

The great grape of Germany is Riesling. Riesling is grown all over the world—a few American wineries make good Rieslings—but it reigns in Germany. Climate, soil, and generations of winemaking experience combine to make Rieslings of tremendous finesse. The best ones have tastes of all sorts of fruits—peaches, pineapples, kiwi, melons, Granny Smith apples—but such clean, crisp, fresh flavors that they seem ephemeral in our mouths and throats. They have crisp acidity and a bouquet of flowers in the nose and on the tongue. Imagine if you could taste the essence of peach nectar without any of the heaviness—or if you could actually taste what a bouquet of roses smells like. Even dry Riesling has a "sweetness" about it that's not from sugar but from the very vibrancy of the grape. And sweet German Riesling is unlike anything else.

Uh-oh. The "S word." Sweet. Americans say they don't like sweet wines, and they think of German wines as sweet, which probably has a great deal to do with the wines' unpopularity. People involved in the German wine industry, knowing this, go to great lengths to avoid the word "sweet," so if you really want to understand what they're saying, you need to work through various matrices, terms like "must weight," and the difference between ripeness and sweetness. Then, of course, there are the labels themselves, which the German government and wine industry keep making more and more exact, and therefore more and more difficult to understand.

Here's the most important thing to understand about the "S word": Yes, some German wines are lusciously sweet. But many are dry. "Trocken" on the label means just that, dry. But even the sweet wines aren't "sweet" in the kind of cloying way you might be thinking. Good German wines are so clean, so crisp, and so beautifully made that the sweetness is fundamental to their charming taste, not a film of sugar blanketing the taste. So much of the sensation of sweetness has to do with the balance of sugar and acid, and German wines have lovely acids. The result: Most of them have less obvious sweetness than your average White Zinfandel. Put that in your glass and drink it.

One of the pleasures of drinking German wines is that they seem so effortless. You taste the grape, not the winemaker. You can't sense any gears turning. There are no fingerprints on it. As Chardonnay falls out of fashion among some aficionados, who find it too heavy, too obvious, and too much an extension of the winemaker, more are turning to Riesling because of its purity. It's clean, it's crisp, and it tastes like grapes, not like wood. It tastes like nature. And German wines have a self-confidence that makes them easy to be with.

Some people consider German wines perfect companions to food, because they're so clean and fresh, with such nice acids, that they complement instead of clash, and we do sometimes drink German wines with dishes like chicken with creamy mushroom sauce or pork with sautéed apples and plums. But on the whole, we find their delicate, flowery tastes best enjoyed on their own, as an apéritif, an after-dinner wine when the girls are finally asleep, or on a sunny day with a picnic in Central Park. They're generally lower in alcohol than other wines, which also helps make them great for sipping without food.

In case you want to know, the first name on the label, like "Niersteiner," just means it's from Nierstein, and the second name is the vineyard. Because, in many cases, quite a few producers make wine from the same vineyard, it's just as important to find a producer you trust as a vineyard. In any case, "Prüm" is a lot easier to remember than Lorenzhöfer Mäuerchen. But you don't have to remember any of that. You just have to remember these two words:

Riesling Kabinett.

It's that simple. Riesling is the grape. Kabinett is the lightest and usually driest kind of fine German wine (going up the ladder in terms of ripeness, and usually sweetness, are Spätlese and Auslese, followed by the awesome and expensive great dessert wines Beerenauslese, Trockenbeerenauslese, and Eiswein). The label will have "Riesling" and "Kabinett" displayed prominently, and that's all you need to know. You will get a quality wine that's light, refreshing, and not too sweet. Ignore all the other stuff and just try a bottle. If you like it, you can learn more and try a great Auslese, perhaps.

To test that thesis, we bought dozens of Riesling Kabinetts and had a delicious tasting. One wine after another was delightful and fun. Quite a few had a little bit of a spritz that made them particularly fetching. Here are some words we used over and over again, both in this tasting and in a previous tasting:

"Charming."
"Lovely."
"Flowery."

"Bright."

"Delightful."

"Like nectar."

"Light on its feet."

"Like a bouquet of flowers."

"So clean."

"Refreshing."

"Peachy."

"Crisp."

"Pure pleasure."

Consider this, our best of tasting: "Really interesting. This really tastes German. Lots of melons. It's got all of these tropical-fruit tastes, with real mouthfeel, but it doesn't taste sweet. Lovely, clean finish that still coats your tongue. It's like a bouquet of flowers. Lovely and effervescent. Here, the sweetness comes from the fruit and it has all sorts of dimensions and layers." This was the Joh. Jos. Prüm Graacher Himmelreich 1998, from the famous Mosel-Saar-Ruwer region. It cost $19.99.

German wines age beautifully. Every year for Christmas, we open something very special. For Christmas 1998, we drank a bottle of Trittenheimer Apotheke Beerenauslese from the 1975 vintage. It had turned golden, with a nose of roasted almonds and peaches. Even at that level of sweetness, the wine was vibrant, not cloying or clumsy. It was light and frothy instead of thick, with a clean, light, orange-nectar finish. Yum!

And one more thing: When we were in the Rheingau, winemaker after winemaker was most excited about their Trocken Spätlese wines—dry wines made from very ripe grapes. To us, they were a revelation along the lines of our first Steinberger. They were dry yet flowery, with an unmistakable taste of soil and minerals that gave the wines stature and complexity. They seemed to have little body but, at the same time, a peppery flavor and bold tastes.

Go on. Try one of these outstanding wines. You'll be really glad that you got through the syllables.

Wine Notes

General advice: Look for "Riesling" and "Kabinett" on the label and you'll be fine. Many wine shops carry only a few German wines, and they're off in a corner gathering dust. Don't buy them there. These are charming, ephemeral wines, and if they've been kept poorly, they may have been harmed. Chill well, which will make the wine crisper—although, as an experiment, you might try letting a bottle warm up. You'll be surprised to suddenly taste some earth and a bit of tough backbone that are carefully hidden most of the time but actually give these wines their surprising depth.

Food pairings: Ham, roast pork, pâtés. After-dinner fruits and nuts.

Joh. Jos. Prüm Graacher Himmelreich (Mosel–Saar–Ruwer). $19.99. VERY GOOD/DELICIOUS. Best of tasting. Tropical-fruit tastes and real mouthfeel. Lovely and clean, with ripe fruit and the taste of flowers. Many layers of tastes, yet effortless. (1998)

Willi Schaefer Graacher Domprobst (Mosel–Saar–Ruwer). $15.99. VERY GOOD/DELICIOUS. Best value. Delightful and fun, a bit spritzy. A happy, uncomplicated wine with all sorts of bright fruit. Dottie called this "a makes-you-smile wine." (1999)

Pfeffingen "Pfeffo" Ungsteiner Honigsäckel (Pfalz). $16.99. VERY GOOD. Absolutely delightful. Pineapples and peach nectar, with a little bit of a spritz, but light as air. (1999)

Joh. Jos. Prüm Wehlener Sonnenuhr (Mosel–Saar–Ruwer). $26.10. VERY GOOD. Granny Smith apples, tangerines, and pineapples—and an earthiness that gives it backbone. Very fruity but not sweet. (1998)

Toni Jost Bacharacher Hahn (Mittelrhein). $21.99. VERY GOOD. A beautiful wine, with a nice balance of fruit and acid and a lovely finish. The finish seems to last forever. (1998)

J. L. Wolf Wachenheimer Königswingert (Pfalz). $18.99. VERY GOOD.

Unusual. Toasty, creamy, and rich, like dessert. It seems oaky and a bit thick, with some wood, toast, and brown sugar, a bit like crème brûlée. (1998)

Reichsgraf von Kesselstatt Josephshöfer (Mosel-Saar-Ruwer). $12.49. VERY GOOD. Stewed peaches. Dottie says this is a wine of substance, with extra layers of tastes: "There's a lot going on in there." John says it's just heavy. (1998)

Max Ferdinand Richter Wehlener Sonnenuhr (Mosel-Saar-Ruwer). $12.99. GOOD/VERY GOOD. Very flowery, with the taste of ripe, just-picked grapes. (1998)

Müller-Catoir Mussbacher Eselshaut Trocken (Pfalz). $24.99. GOOD/VERY GOOD. Quite dry, with lemons, grapefruit, and green apples. Clean and dry. Great acids. (1999)

Dr. von Bassermann-Jordan Deidesheimer Paradiesgarten (Pfalz). $17.50. GOOD/VERY GOOD. It seems a bit sweet, but it's crisp and flavorful. Serious wine. (1999)

Karlsmühle Lorenzöfer Mäuerchen (Mosel-Saar-Ruwer). $14.99. GOOD/VERY GOOD. Peachy, a good aperitif. Refreshing and delightful. (1999)

Reichsrat von Buhl "Armand" (Pfalz). $16.79. GOOD/VERY GOOD. Lots of taste and interesting character, with weight and complexity. (1999)

Do Vintages Matter? Sure.
But Should You Care?

The emphasis on "good" and "bad" vintages is one of the many things that make drinking wine so intimidating. Do vintages matter? Well, sure, because weather makes the grape-growing season different every year, but the question is whether you need to spend any time worrying about whether a bottle of wine on the shelf is from a "good vintage." The answer: No, you don't. Here are six reasons why:

• It's exceedingly rare that the difference between two recent vintages is the difference between perfection and vinegar. Instead, in general—and there are always exceptions—the differences tend to be more subtle, between years when the weather was perfect and the grapes were picked nice and ripe, and years when the weather wasn't so perfect and the grapes were less ripe. Are you such an aficionado of wine that you would find yourself enjoying a 1997 Barolo but spit out your 1998 Barolo? We think few people fit into that category.

• Some properties make good wine even in off years, while some properties make bad wine in good years.

• Even within regions, vintages differ. Who wants to keep track of the difference in vintages between the northern Rhône and the southern Rhône?

• You're not likely to have a choice anyway. Few wine stores carry multiple vintages of the same wine, so it's not like you really need to decide among vintages. In Italy, 1990 was a terrific year for Barolo. But are you likely to see a 1990 Barolo in your local wine shop tonight? What's important is the producer. Joh. Jos. Prüm, for instance, makes fine wine every year in Germany. Look for the name, not the year.

• Wines mature differently depending on the year. So the 1998 might be from a "better" year than the 1999, and might be better five years from now, but the 1999 might be a far better wine to drink tonight, more supple and easier to enjoy.

• Price matters. When a year is declared "the vintage of the century," which seems to happen a lot, prices for those wines skyrocket. Therefore, a wine from, say, 2000 might cost far more than the same wine from 1999. Is it really twice as good? Unlikely.

So why should you even notice the vintage on a bottle? Two reasons, one of which is a very good reason indeed.

First, if you're buying, say, a fine Bordeaux or a great California Cabernet Sauvignon that you hope to save for a special occasion, you'd probably want a wine from a good year if you could get it, because it will age better. Or if you were buying an older fine wine, you'd want to know the vintage to get an idea whether it's ready to drink, or over the hill, or could age longer. If you collect good stuff, you'd want to have an idea of vintages so you'd know, in general, when to open the bottles. Sometimes when we're at a restaurant, we'll see an older bottle from a good year that we haven't seen in stores in some time, and we'll grab if it we can afford it. But not many people care about those issues. The second really important reason to notice the year of the wine is simply this:

To know how old it is.

We're not being facetious. Many wines—Pinot Grigio, many Sauvignon Blancs, Beaujolais, and others—are better when they are young. You want to buy the youngest you can find. It's important to look at the vintage to make sure you're doing that. If you see one Pinot Grigio from 2000 on the shelf and another from 2001, you want the 2001. If anyone tells you that you really want the 2000 Pinot Grigio because it was a "better" year, look at them like they're crazy.

We lead very full lives and so do you. We've got all sorts of stuff in our brains—the date of the kids' orthodontist appointment, when the dog needs his next rabies shot, that teacher-parent conference in a week, when that employee's evaluation must be done. Not to mention all of the birthdays we can't let slip by. These are important things we *need* to know, things we should not forget. We don't use many brain cells committing to memory which vintages were great and which weren't, although, naturally, some of that has stuck over the years.

There are people who memorize stuff like that and use it to wow people with their knowledge. Hats off to them. Truth is, though, if you really want this information, it's so readily available that you shouldn't worry about it not being in your head when it can be as close to you as in your wallet. We have charts from wine books and we've helped ourselves to free charts that wine shops place near their cash register. They're all pretty much the same. If you don't know by heart whether 1999 or 2000 was better in Burgundy, don't worry about it. If you really want to know, just consult the chart in your wallet. Don't be embarrassed to look at it, especially if you're considering an expensive purchase. We'll consult ours in a minute if we're curious. We don't need to impress anyone, and neither do you.

Chapter Ten

Pinot Grigio

. . . and Blue Suede Shoes

If we had written this book ten years ago, we probably would have skipped a chapter on the white wines of Italy. Until recently, Italian whites, at least the ones imported into the United States, were hidden off in a corner somewhere—an Always Elvis kind of wine.

Always Elvis?

When people visit our house, they're sometimes intimidated by our wine collection. They figure our cellar is filled with rare treasures from France and irreplaceable liquid gold from California. That's when we pull out our bottle of "Always Elvis." The label, black and bright gold, shows The King, in his later years, singing into the microphone. On the back is a poetic tribute to Elvis, "Written for all the Fans Worldwide, BY THE COLONEL." What's inside is an Italian white wine called Frontenac Blanc d'Oro. We bought two bottles of this, for $3.29 each, at a Grand Union in Miami in 1980. We opened one right away. Here are our notes, in their entirety:

"Slight sparkle. Little character."

That pretty much summed up Italian whites back then, when we saw them at all in stores. Italy, after all, is known for its red wines: Chianti, Barolo, Dolcetto, and so many others. When we thought of dinner at that little Italian place on the corner, we thought of red wine, regardless of what we were eating. In just the past few years, though, white wines from Italy have exploded onto the scene in the United States. Everywhere we turn, we hear: "I'll have a glass of Pinot Grigio." Even bad wine shops offer a huge array of Italian white wines, most of them inexpensive, in an effort to satisfy Americans' insatiable thirst for cold white wines.

What are these gazillion Italian whites? It's often impossible to say. Unlike the French, whose wines come from specific, formal viticultural regions that are known for their specific styles, Italy is something of a free-for-all, despite government and industry efforts over the years. "Pinot Grigio," for instance, doesn't tell you much, since it's simply the name of the grape and could come from just about anywhere. Even when geographical regions or zones are on the labels, they're not much help. And the quality designations—from Denominazione di Origine Controllata (DOCG) to Denominazione di Origine (DOC), then down to Indicazione Geografica Tipica (IGT) and vini da tavola (table wine)—aren't hugely helpful for a number of reasons, including the fact that they include some of the country's best and worst producers.

We love all wine, of course, but we've found Italian whites over the years to be so simple, so much like lemon water, that we haven't made them a regular part of our lives. Our favorite description of Italian whites is from Tom Stevenson in *The New Sotheby's Wine Encyclopedia,* which is an excellent reference book: "Freshness, crisp acidity, and purity of varietal character personify the wines of the northeastern regions of Trentino-Alto Adige, Friuli-Venezia Giulia, and the Veneto, but beware the mass-produced wines, which are so clean and pure that they lack any fruit."

We had an eye-opening experience at a charming restaurant in Manhattan called Le Madri, which was so eager for company in the dog days of August that it offered an outrageous deal: Come in, have lunch, and—for free—drink all you want of a huge array of Italian wines served by the importers themselves. So there we were, on three successive Fridays, indulging in four-hour lunches. We may have overdone it, but we learned something important: Some Italian whites, whether Pinot Grigio or Soave, are better than others. A lot better. These had a depth and a sophistication we hadn't seen outside Italy, and we suspect that not many of these are available in wine stores in the United States. But which is which and what is what, and how in the world can you tell?

Over the years, we've found Pinot Bianco from Italy and a wine called Arneis to have more character than Pinot Grigio (try one and see what you think). While we have tasted some small-production Pinot Grigios with depth, style, and character, most have been colorless, aromaless, and charmless. Just something cold and white and wet. But because Pinot Grigio is so popular, we decided to buy several cases' worth from the most recent vintages, since they should always be drunk young. Then we tasted them blind over several nights. As always, we weren't trying to find the "best" Pinot Grigio. We just wondered if there were some good ones out there and, if so, what they tasted like and how much they cost.

Pinot Grigio is the same grape—Pinot Gris—that makes bracing wines in Oregon (see Chapter Three). Some clever California winemakers are producing Pinot Gris now and calling it Pinot Grigio. Pinot Grigio can be from just about anywhere in Italy, but the hot spots are in the Northeast—Friuli-Venezia Giulia, Veneto, and Trentino-Alto Adige.

We waited for hot days for our blind tastings, since Pinot Grigio should be light, refreshing, and perfect for summer. What we found is that there's an ocean of simple, not terribly pleasant Pinot Grigio out there. We found, as Tom Stevenson suggested in the *Wine Encyclopedia,* that most of these wines lacked fruit—and, therefore, much character. Especially considering how much these must cost as "a glass of Pinot Grigio" at the bar, this is inexcusable. On the other hand, we found some delightful ones at very reasonable prices and some more serious, more expensive styles that could give you a whole new view of what Pinot Grigio can be.

Among the less expensive bottles, a wine we'd never had before called Tiefenbrunner, at just $9.99, showed quite well, as did good old Bolla, which we saw for both $8.99 and $9.99. We think these are pretty much what most people hope to find when they buy a bottle of Pinot Grigio: lovely, easy-drinking wine with nice citrus flavors. At the same time, they weren't just throwaway whites. The Tiefenbrunner was so alive it seemed to sparkle, and the Bolla had a little bit of weight and some nice mineral tastes and good acids that would make it excellent with seafood.

Some of our favorites were expensive, including $22 for a wine called Elena Walch that we described as "a Pinot Grigio with gravitas." Now, we're not suggesting that anyone spend $22 for a Pinot Grigio to sip from a plastic cup on a rubber raft in the pool. But you might consider spending a little bit more than usual once, perhaps on a brand you've never seen before, just to see what Pinot Grigio can taste like. In fact, all three of our favorites were wines we'd never seen before, indicating once again how important it is to grab something new every time you go wine shopping.

Which brings us to our favorite. "Real wine. Weight and real character. Rich melon tastes with a little bit of chewiness. Some earth and lots of fruit. 'Every citrus in the world is in this,' Dottie says. Grapefruit, tangerines—layers of tastes. Complex, with real mouthfeel. A real meal. Think about it with halibut." We wouldn't have believed it ourselves—a Pinot Grigio with that kind of character. It was Ca' Montini "L'Aristocratico," from the Trentino region. It was $13.99 and worth every penny. At which fancy, snobbish, precious little wine store did we buy it? Stew Leonard's supermarket, proving once again that you can never tell where you'll find good wine.

After our tasting, we can say this with certainty: If your Pinot Grigio is simple and forgettable, try another. There are good ones out there that taste more like wine than water—and they don't cost more than what you're used to buying.

Oh, by the way, we once mentioned Always Elvis in the newspaper and received a note from a reader telling us that a Dallas wine merchant had a bottle of it in the window for $300. Maybe our wine cellar is filled with rare and expensive treasures after all.

Wine Notes

General advice: Buy the youngest Pinot Grigio you see. If it's from the Trentino-Alto Adige, Veneto, or Friuli-Venezia Giulia regions of northeast Italy (you'll see one or more of those words prominently displayed on the label), that's often a good sign. Chill very well.
Food pairings: Light fish, chilled or fried shrimp, oysters. Crisp, cold salads on a hot day.

Ca' Montini "L'Aristocratico" (Trentino). $13.99. VERY GOOD/DELICIOUS. Best of tasting. Serious wine of weight and character, with a whole bowl of citrus flavors. Layers of tastes and luscious fruit. (2000)

Tiefenbrunner "delle Venezie." $9.99. VERY GOOD. Best value. Crisp, refreshing, juicy and vibrant. Lively and mouth-watering. Nice weight, yet lively and exciting. "It sparkles on my tongue," Dottie said. (2000)

Elena Walch "Castel Ringberg" (Alto Adige). $22.00. VERY GOOD. Distinctive, with citrus, honey, and some taste of the earth. Makes you sit up and notice. A Pinot Grigio with gravitas, yet easy to drink at the same time. (1999)

Bolla "delle Venezie." $8.99. GOOD/VERY GOOD. Tropical flavors and nice mineral tones give it a pleasant bit of complexity. Hints of pineapples, Key lime, and all sorts of tropical fruits. All that and good mouthfeel make this particularly enjoyable. Good with seafood. (2000)

Vigneti del Sole "delle Venezie." $7.49. GOOD. Real body and taste, with luscious hints of very fresh cantaloupe. A whisper of Chardonnay tastes. (2000)

Campanile "Grave" 2000 (Friuli). $7.99. GOOD. Crisp, slightly tart, and refreshing—think of it with shrimp cocktail. A little bit of an edge, maybe even a hint of bitterness, make it interesting, although it seemed a bit sweet on the finish.

Castello Banfi "San Angelo" (Toscana). $12.99. GOOD. Some soil and slate for grounding and nice, mouth-watering acidity. Light, but nice grapefruit-melon tastes. Lovely by the pool. (2000)

Mezza Corona (Trentino). $8.99. GOOD. Refreshing and pleasant. Not complex, but filled with pleasant fruit. Simple, a nice summer wine. (2000)

Red
Wine

Chapter Eleven

Cabernet Sauvignon

The Meaning of "Glassiness"

Cabernet Sauvignon is the most consistently great red grape in the world, the grape of the impressive first growths of Bordeaux and of those famously expensive, impossible-to-find California "cult" Cabernets. This is the classic wine to have with dinner because its complex structure makes almost all foods more interesting. We have had, over the years, dozens of outstanding Cabernets, but the Heitz Cellars Martha's Vineyard 1968, one of America's most famous wines, was among the greatest. We drank it on New Year's Eve 1993. Consider these notes: "Huge nose, like tar. Look is so rich it looks like Cognac. Intense fruit on the nose with raspberries and cherries. No hint of age. Taste is incredible. HUGE, RICH, with an incredible explosion in mouth that goes from chest to ears. Really! Wow! Bold. Smells, looks, and tastes thick, but it's not. Tingle in the nose. Nose is *overwhelming*. Completely forward taste."

Unfortunately, in several tastings over the past few years, we have found that there is trouble in Cabernet land. A great deal of today's Cabernet Sauvignon from the United States is undistinguished. We think there are at least a couple of reasons. Call the first a Merlowering of standards. Winemakers know that Americans love Merlot because it is approachable, round, simple, and easy to drink. A good Cabernet, to us, has more structure, more class, and more intensity than Merlot. It has a brightness that we often refer to as "glassiness." It's hard to describe, but by glassiness we mean it has a sharpness, like a pin-focused, clear, distilled taste that fills your mouth with distinct layers of flavor at the front and leaves a lingering depth of flavor at the back. You know what a pane of glass looks like when it's clean and glistens in the sunlight? We think of Cabernet like that. It should also have ample tannins that, especially in youth, make your mouth pucker. Too many Cabernets today taste like Merlot, lacking the guts and breeding that any Cabernet should have. And a Cabernet shouldn't have to be expensive to be outstanding. Consider what happened in a tasting in late 1998—a tasting with remarkable and unintended consequences.

We had decided we'd try dozens of American Cabernet Sauvignons under $20 to see, generally, how they were. As always, our mission wasn't to find the best Cabernet for under $20. Instead, our goal was to discover, in general, whether we could expect to get our money's worth by spending $20 or less on a Cabernet right off the shelf. One stood out. It stood out so much, in fact, that we were sure there had been some sort of mistake. We keep our wines in our wine closet very carefully. We separate the wines we drink for our *Wall Street Journal* column from our own private purchases. The night before, we had had one of our own wines—a 1982 Château Grand-Puy-Lacoste from Bordeaux. It was great, everything a fine old "claret" should be. Well, we were convinced that somehow, instead of putting one of the Cabernets into a bag for the blind tasting, John had picked up another bottle of that '82. "Lovely, complex nose, very much like an aged claret," we wrote. "Tastes like a real claret, rich yet filled with crisp layers of taste. Alive in your mouth. Dust, soil, and oak."

At the end of the tasting, we ripped off the bag, fully expecting to see an old Bordeaux from our own stash. Instead, it turned out to be a Gallo Sonoma, from the 1992 vintage. Cost: $9.99.

Gallo?

All of us started somewhere with wine. We drank Mateus in college. Our first bottle together was Cold Duck. But, to some extent—metaphorically—everyone started with Gallo, and nobody's proud of it. It's like looking at pictures of yourself when you were in your twenties. "Oh my God, look at that hair!" Not only that, but for those of us who came of age in the '60s, Gallo's epic battles with the late labor organizer César Chávez, not to mention its reputation as a ruthless competitor in the marketplace, made the company as unsavory as its wine. We had recently read about how

Gallo really was making good wines, but we didn't believe it. Gallo is a big advertiser and a major player in the industry. We weren't sure how much that had influenced the coverage. Well, we admit it: we were wrong. The '92 had the advantage of being one of the oldest wines we tasted, but it came right off the shelf of an everyday wine store, and we saw it at other wine stores around New York. Gallo made 43,000 cases of it, which is quite a bit, and wine stores in New York and other states said they were still getting it by the case in early 1998.

When we wrote about this wine in late 1998, it created a sensation. We were deluged for weeks with calls, letters, and e-mails asking how to find it. Wine stores, which usually sell out of whatever we write about by the evening the column appears, sold out hours earlier. Gallo itself went on a mission to find every possible bottle, and set up a special contact for anxious wine drinkers. One sad reader told us he'd gone to his wine store to get a bottle and found a line of people asking for it. Another had just missed the last bottle of it.

What did that Gallo, ultimately, have going for it? Good fruit, pure and simple. That brings us to the second thing that has created problems with Cabernet, which will sound familiar from the Chardonnay chapter. With such great weather and so much sun in California, winemakers can essentially put Cabernet vines out in the sun, let the grapes ripen until they're really plump, get huge crops, and make serviceable wine out of them. But without the right combination of soil, care, sunshine, and coolness—not to mention cutting back the crop to concentrate the flavors—the grapes may get ripe, but in the end they lack the acids and "stuff" that make a wine balanced and interesting. The wines are essentially superficial fruit-alcohol bombs—too alcoholic to be pleasant, and filled with tastes that seem overly sweet. It's not great winemaking, but it's profitable, and it's clear that many of the wines we have tried in our tastings were produced more as cash cows than as expressions of the quality of the vineyards and the skill of the winemakers. A surprising number had stinky smells of yeast and sulfur. Others seemed to burn our throats. Quite a few had an off-putting sense of sweetness. Some weren't unpleasant, just so simple that we would have preferred to be drinking our kids' Kool-Aid. In all, especially under $20, we have found that it's harder to find good value than it should be.

That said, in our most recent tasting of Cabernets under $20, we did find some wines that had real personality, were pleasant to drink and had the layers of taste—clean, rich fruit, leather, soil, and cedar—that good Cabernet Sauvignon should have, at any price. Perhaps not surprisingly, several were familiar names: Benziger, whose Merlot was our best of tasting in an earlier tasting; Columbia Crest of Washington, whose Cabernet was one of our best in an earlier tasting (we described the wines both times as edgy and a bit risky); Rodney Strong, whose Alexander's Crown Cabernet Sauvignon was our best of tasting in an earlier high-end Cabernet tasting; and, yes, once again, a Gallo, this one a Gallo of Sonoma. Our best of tasting was a familiar name, too. It had real character, and even had enough confidence to have a little bit of "tightness"—hard, intense fruit that we had to come to—as opposed to simple, approachable fruit. This gave it some nice layers of flavors that surfaced with each sip, real complexity. "Very serious," we wrote. Can you imagine all that wine for under $10? It's true. This was Beringer Vineyards Founders' Estate.

Interestingly, our two favorites were blends of several grape types. While Americans often think that a wine that is 100 percent of a certain varietal is best, many fine wines gain complexity from the addition of other kinds of grapes. The Beringer, for instance, had small amounts of Syrah, Petite Sirah, Merlot, and Cabernet Franc. The Benziger had all of those, plus a little Malbec and Petit Verdot. (The wines can be called Cabernet Sauvignon as long as they're at least 75 percent Cabernet Sauvignon.)

So, having decided that Cabernet under $20 was a crap shoot, we wondered if we'd do better if we moved upscale. We bought the first fifty Cabernets we could find between $20 and $50. As always in our upscale tastings, we picked up wines from large producers and small producers, because many high-end wines are made in limited quantities by passionate winemakers and it wouldn't be fair to leave them out. We tasted them blind, in paper bags, over several nights, giving all of them a chance to open and change over time, and trying each with and without food.

In general, it was a far more successful tasting. Some of the wines were elegant and rich, with the kind of acids that made them excellent with food. Some were a bit edgy and controversial, which we always enjoy, because it indicates a winemaker with some personality at the controls. Midway through the tasting, we were sure we had a winner. As soon as we poured it, we said, "Whoa," because it was just about black, with dark purple edges. The nose alone was heady. We felt we'd had a glassful before we even sipped it. "Real American wine," we wrote when we did. "Guts galore. Layers of 'stuff.' An old-fashioned American wine, unrestrained and huge. Hyper-wine. Intense and concentrated." We always tell folks to take chances on wines they've never seen before. Sometimes they're small-production wines that are intensely personal efforts and offer exciting experiences. This was an example. It was Cafaro Cellars, a wine we'd rarely seen and never tasted. To us, our tasting was now like a baseball game with a 9–0 score in the fifth inning. It seemed unlikely the Cafaro could be overtaken. But then . . .

Our tastings tend to be pretty clinical. We talk about tannins and tight fruit and weak finishes and whether there's too much Cabernet Franc in the blend. But sometimes, rarely, we take a sip of a wine and turn to each other and just say, "Wow." Such was the case with this wine. It was quite dark, with flashes of rich garnet colors. There seemed to be fire in the glass. The wine smelled like big, plump grapes and rich, sweet earth. "This is so fragrant I could put it behind my ears," Dottie said. The taste was just as good, almost majestic, with the perfect balance of ripe fruit and restraint. "This is what wine should be," said John. It wasn't just good. It was genuinely exciting, earning a rare Delicious! on our rating scale. What was it? Fife Vineyards Reserve, Napa Valley. We had never tasted this wine before, either. It was $43.99, and worth every penny.

One more thing: If you can stand to put a wine like this into a drawer for a year or two, you'll be amazed what happens to it. Good Cabernets (and the wines made from it, such as many Bordeaux wines) are the classic made-to-be-cellared wines. Good Cabernet can live for decades, and even inexpensive, well-made Cabernets can get better with some age. In 1994, we opened a 1971 Cabernet from Washington State's Chateau Ste. Michelle, which makes reliable, generally inexpensive wines. If you asked any expert if this was one of the great Cabernet makers in America, the answer would be no. But age does wonderful things to good wine. Our notes: "Delicious! Despite a low fill, nose is huge, rich, and room-filling. Big, rich, massive, with an amazing nose of tobacco. Oddly, it's like a terrific old Burgundy. Rich and 'sweet' with fruit and mouth-filling. Lots of layers, from fruit to vibrancy. Raspberries."

Still, that wasn't perfection. This was:

On a Saturday morning in 1986, a wine-drinking friend of ours in Miami named Bob Radziewicz called us, breathless. "There's a little wine shop out on the Tamiami Trail that's selling '78 Diamond Creek for $14 a bottle!" he yelled into the phone. In minutes, we were headed way out to western Dade County where, in a little strip shopping mall, we found a liquor store that, incredibly, was selling one of America's most famous Cabernets for $14.19. (It had been marked up twice. Under the $14.19 label were labels for $12.19 and $13.19.) We bought several bottles and kept them for years, until August 1998. Then we opened one. Here, uncensored, are our notes:

"Cork smells great. It's so sweet with fruit that bugs have gathered around the glass! Awesome, sweet nose with lots of chocolate. Black color. Taste is simply awesome, soft yet enormous. Fruit without a single hard edge. Absolutely perfect on first sip. Only age will accomplish this perfect combination of fruit and softness and depth. Plums, cherries, wood, tobacco, chocolate with an awesome finish more in the mind than in the mouth. Perfect NOW!

"After ten minutes, gets backbone and verve under the fruit. Awesome grapes. Even the empty glass is awesome!

"After one hour, it's rich and creamy and chewy without a hint of decay. It's mouthfilling in a fluffy kind of way. Deep, dark, rich, very California. Aged, powerful, big, bold, elegant—a Sean Connery kind of wine.

"Rich, round, sensuous, and plump, with layers and layers of fruit, plums, and taste.

"It's simply perfect. Perfect."

Wine Notes

General advice: Six wineries have been repeat favorites in our Cabernet Sauvignon tastings and are good names to look for: Beringer, Columbia Crest, Gallo Sonoma, Geyser Peak, Silverado, and Rodney Strong. The following notes are from tastings of Cabernet Sauvignon under $20 and from $20 to $50. Napa

Valley is a Cabernet hot spot—note how many of our favorites among the more expensive wines were from Napa. If your Cabernet Sauvignon tastes like sugar, tastes hot, or tastes alcoholic, try another.

Food pairings: Fine Cabernet deserves fine steak, great lamb, or a majestic roast. We feel that a well-aged Cabernet is perfect with Thanksgiving dinner because its darkness goes well with the heavier parts of the meal and its softening tannins go well with the lighter parts. Less expensive Cabernet goes well with casual, comfort foods like meat loaf, grilled meats and vegetables, and pastas with tomato-based sauces.

Under $20

Beringer Vineyards (Founders' Estate). $8.49. VERY GOOD. Best of tasting and best value. Plenty of character, with rich earthiness and several layers of taste. (1997)

Benziger Family Winery (Sonoma County). $14.99. VERY GOOD. Rich, spicy, and a slight bit tart, giving it nice complexity. Interesting and classy. Can age. (1997)

Gallo of Sonoma (Sonoma County). $10.99. VERY GOOD. Rich, plummy, and a bit intense, with a taste of the earth that's quite fetching. (1996)

M. Trinchero Vineyards (Family Selection). $10.99. VERY GOOD. Earthy, with a long, peppery finish, but more elegant than that sounds. Interesting, with personality. (1997)

Columbia Crest Winery (Columbia Valley). $15.99. GOOD/VERY GOOD. Rough, raw, and charming in its own way. A wine for people willing to take a risk. (1996)

Rodney Strong Vineyards (Sonoma County). $11.99. GOOD/VERY GOOD. Light on its feet, with nice structure and a hint of cranberries. Elegant instead of poweful. Lovely. (1997)

Geyser Peak (Sonoma County). $16.99. GOOD/VERY GOOD. Toasted and roasted and a bit serious. Can age. (1997)

Cypress (J. Lohr Winery; Central Coast). $9.99. GOOD/VERY GOOD. Charming. Fruity and comforting, like a good carafe of red wine in an Italian restaurant. (1997)

$20 to $50

Fife Vineyards (Reserve; Napa Valley, Spring Mountain District). $43.99. DELICIOUS! Best of tasting. Great now, with enormous fruit and tastes of rich soil. A wine of gravitas, and even better in the future. (1995)

Cafaro Cellars (Napa Valley). $44.99. DELICIOUS. Black wine, with an intoxicating nose and real American guts. Huge, intense, and concentrated. (1997)

Groth Vineyards & Winery (Oakville, Napa Valley). $44.99. VERY GOOD/DELICIOUS. Aristocratic, with class and structure. Good with turkey and stuffing. (1997)

Burgess Cellars (Vintage Selection, Napa Valley). $46.99. VERY GOOD. "Library Release" shows the value of age. It has layers of complexity and a simple elegance that comes with time. (1990)

Chimney Rock Winery (Napa Valley). $39.99. VERY GOOD. Controversial. One of Dottie's favorites. A highly personal wine, with cream and fruit and then nice acids at the end. Slightly rustic. (1997)

Clos Pegase (Napa Valley). $34.99. VERY GOOD. Interesting, with hints of cream, tar, and rich soil. Nice with food. (1997)

Gallo Sonoma (Barrelli Creek Vineyard, Alexander Valley). $24.99. VERY GOOD. Earthy and dry, with lots of big fruit. Not complex, but soul-satisfying. (1996)

Geyser Peak Winery (Block Collection, Alexander Valley, Kuimelis Vineyard). $31.99. VERY GOOD. Give it some time to breathe, and it becomes edgy and classy and very dry. Can age. (1997)

Iron Horse Vineyards (Alexander Valley). $24.99. VERY GOOD. Plenty of fruit, but still tight-knit. Can age. (1997)

Pezzi King (Dry Creek Valley). $30.99. VERY GOOD. Classy and easy to drink. Elegant, with lovely balance. (1997)

Joseph Phelps Vineyards (Napa Valley). $38.99. VERY GOOD. Complex, with some richness. (1996)

Silverado Vineyards (Napa Valley). $39.95. VERY GOOD. A nice wine to drink now, with some cream and intensity. (1997)

Decanting: When to Do It, and How, and Why You Shouldn't

You've heard you should sometimes let a wine breathe. The truth is that simply removing the cork and letting the wine sit open doesn't do much at all, since very little air is getting to the wine to help it breathe or unfold. If you really want the wine to breathe, you need to pour a glass or two and let the bottle and the glasses sit for a while. Or decant it.

We rarely decant wines. We enjoy experiencing everything a wine can show us, from that first sip of sometimes tight fruit to that gracious last taste, when the wine, almost spent, bestows its final kiss. We don't like to hurry that process. To speed it along by pouring the wine into a decanter so it can get a blast of air would be, for us, like entering a theater during the second act of a play. How much we would have missed!

Our only exception is when the wine is throwing a lot of sediment. That's when we pour off the clear wine, separating it from its sometimes sludgy stuff. This kind of decanting has to be done carefully, because once air starts getting to a wine, the wine can change very quickly. After all, if you don't decant a wine and it's so tough and hard that you think you should decant it, you still can. But if you decant it and the wine loses some of its fruit because of its exposure to air, you can't turn back the clock.

There are three reasons some people decant a wine. First, if the wine is young, air will blow off the rough edges so you can taste the good stuff underneath that ordinarily only age would show you; or you might do it because the wine is old and needs some air so it can open up a little after years of being tightly wound in the bottle. Second, if the wine's throwing sediment, you can pour off the clear wine. Third, it's just a pretty cool thing to do. That's usually why restaurants do it. Actually, now that we think about it, there's a fourth reason: to finally use that pretty decanter someone gave you as a wedding present. We figure that about 98 percent of all decanters in America were wedding presents.

If you're going to decant, forget the candle and the rigmarole (unless you're trying to impress a date) and do this:

• Stand the wine up for a day or two so the sediment sinks to the bottom. (If it's been stored on its side for some time, you often don't need to do this, but be careful not to disturb the sediment on the side.)

• Get a flashlight with a flat bottom so it will stand up with the light flashing toward the ceiling. Turn it on and stand it up.

• Get a decanter with a fairly wide mouth.

• Open the wine carefully so you don't disturb the sediment.

• Hold the bottle in one hand and the decanter in the other.

• Lift the decanter and the bottle, so the flashlight is shining through the bottle just under the neck. Start pouring the wine into the decanter. You should be able to see the wine glistening through the bottle.

• When you see sediment begin to flow into the neck of the bottle, stop! That's it. You've done it.

One last thing: Some people throw out the wine at the bottom of the bottle that has the sediment. This is a shame, because much of the soul of the wine is there. If you're squeamish, when you've finished the rest of the bottle, pour the sediment through a coffee filter into the decanter. Then drink it. If you're not squeamish, drink the sediment if it's not too thick. To us, it's always an appropriate way to honor a fine wine's very last gasp.

Chapter Twelve

Merlot

The Ben Stein of Wine

It's hard to believe now, but not long ago America's slogan was "better dead than red"—red wine, that is. We were a white-wine drinking nation, happy with our Chardonnay and Chablis. Merlot? Never heard of it. Consider this: In John Melville's *Guide to California Wines,* written in 1960, he covered all the bases, and all the grapes. The index lists "Riesling, Emerald" and "Riesling, Gray." There's "Sparkling Malvasia" and "Mondeuse." But there's not a single mention of Merlot.

Put into perspective, that omission isn't really surprising because, back then, Merlot was known mostly as a blending grape. Winemakers used its deep, flat, red flavor to round out the sharper, harder, more tannic edges of grapes like Cabernet Sauvignon. The French use it that way in many of the great Bordeaux wines. But while Merlot has stood quite well on its own for decades in the Pomerol region of Bordeaux—it is the predominant grape in the great Château Petrus—it was virtually unknown in the United States, as a stand-alone wine, until fairly recently. According to the Wine Institute, the San Francisco-based trade organization, Louis M. Martini Winery released the first California Merlot. The winery says it was a blend of the 1968 and 1970 vintages and was released in 1972. This is how we described one of our early Merlot experiences, a Sterling Vineyards Merlot from the great California vintage of 1974: "Delicious. Elegant yet very big. Flat and silky. Years left. Lots of wood, lots of power. Huge, long finish. Small sips."

Things quickly went wild after that. In 1987, California wineries crushed 6,782 tons of Merlot; by 2000, that figure was 305,152. In California alone, the number of cases of Merlot that were made rose from 800,000 in 1990 to 13.2 million in 1999, according to the Wine Institute. People who used to drink only white wine were suddenly drinking Merlot. It was soft and approachable, not nearly as challenging as more tannic, structured, and pricier Cabernet Sauvignon. Merlot became more common at bars than bad pickup lines, more common at restaurants than Caesar salad.

We imagine one reason for this is Merlot's essential flatness. It's smooth and easy. Merlot has even-toned flavors that tend to be pleasant and friendly at an early age. You know Ben Stein, the nerd who has made a career of being a boring guy with the flat, monotone voice? He's Merlot. All across America, Merlot has become the red equivalent of "a glass of Chardonnay"—simple wine with no rough patches and not enough taste to trouble anybody. In fact, to some extent, we've come full circle, because there's now "White Merlot," which, to us, is essentially the same as White Zinfandel (it's just Merlot that's left in contact with the skins for a brief time, giving it a blush color). White Merlot is not just a profitable way for wineries to piggyback on the popularity of both Merlot and White Zinfandel, but a way to soak up some of those many tons of Merlot grapes, too.

Merlot can be a very fine wine indeed, but when a wine suddenly enjoys that kind of popularity, what happens to its quality? In our experience, bad things. Remember Pouilly-Fuissé? It's a lovely white wine from France, made with Chardonnay grapes, that became wildly popular in the 1970s. Suddenly, boatloads of it arrived in American stores, much of it underripe and overpriced. Soon the boom busted. Is the same in store for Merlot? When we began our "Tastings" column in 1998, our first column was a tasting of Merlot. Since then, we have conducted a tasting every year on the column's anniversary. What have we found? Well, what we've found, in general, is that there's a lot of really bad Merlot out there. Here are some of the terms we've used in our notes:

"Green and bitter."
"Just heat and alcohol."
"Saltwater nose."
"Grain alcohol."

"Kool-Aid."

"Not very pleasant."

Many of the wines have been perfectly acceptable and inoffensive. In fact, that may be what bothers us most about them: Many seem to aspire to nothing more than inoffensiveness. Time after time, we'll pour a glass, start talking about something else, finish the glass, and then say, "Wait a minute. How was that wine?" We'd missed it entirely. No wine should be so lacking in character. It's clear that many wineries figure they can pick some cheap grapes, rush the wine out the door, and sell it quickly to unsuspecting consumers who just have to pick up a Merlot for dinner. We can't stress this strongly enough: You can do better! There are some excellent inexpensive Merlots out there—and, for just a few dollars more, you can have a Merlot that will change your mind about what Merlot can be.

What we have found, again and again, is that many lower-priced Merlots lack fruit, charm, and taste. They're rip-offs, in a word. But we have also found that some inexpensive Merlots are fine, well-made wines, with real character and the kind of comfortable red-wine taste that got people interested in Merlot to begin with. In our most recent tastings, two Merlots from wineries that we've long admired for their value-priced wines impressed us again: Fetzer "Eagle Peak" ("fruity, but with real body") and Beringer "Founders' Estate" ("classy, rich, and a bit velvety"). We paid $9.99 for the Fetzer and $8.99 for the Beringer, and both are fairly widely available. Our best of tasting? Ask yourself if your Merlot tastes anywhere near as exciting as this: "Black as night, with a big, deep, chocolate nose. Looks expensive. Smells big and classy. Still young, almost heavy with ripe fruit, but still quite approachable." When we took the bag off that wine, we were in for a surprise.

Francis Ford Coppola, the movie director, makes wine in Napa Valley, and since he's a genius at promotion, he gets a great deal of attention. But we've never been big fans of his wines. This was an exception. We found his Niebaum-Coppola Merlot to be a great buy at $15.99, easily the equal of many of the over-$20 Merlots we've tried.

The best over-$20 Merlots have generally been wines of a different color—almost literally. They tend to be darker, blacker, and far more serious-looking than most inexpensive Merlots, which really are pale imitations of the good stuff. The tastes of more expensive Merlots are often far more complex, and simply better, than wine costing just a few dollars less. To some extent, this has to do with passion. Too many Merlots these days are being made, in effect, as factory goods—just churn them out and count the proceeds. Many higher-end Merlots are still being made by winemakers with a passion for the grape.

What we found in our most recent tasting, once again, was that really good Merlot doesn't have to be terribly expensive or from precious little boutique wineries. In fact, one of our favorites was $22.95, from the well-known Dry Creek Vineyard. Another, the most beguiling we tasted, was from the old Charles Krug Winery. Interestingly, all five of our over-$20 favorites were blends. Just as adding some Merlot to a Cabernet Sauvignon can soften it and make it more approachable, adding some Cabernet Sauvignon (or Cabernet Franc or Petit Verdot) to a Merlot can add depth and structure. One of our favorites, the Whitehall Lane, was made from 86 percent Merlot, 7 percent Cabernet Sauvignon, and 7 percent Cabernet Franc. As the winery explains: "Cabernet Sauvignon was added to the blend to give complexity and weight to the wine while Cabernet Franc was added to enhance the flavors and aromas."

Our best of tasting was made from 84 percent Merlot and 16 percent Cabernet Sauvignon. It knocked our socks off: "Extremely serious wine with lots of 'stuff.' Real soul. Complex. Edgy. Very serious, with massive, tight fruit. Ripe. Lots of structure. Clearly expensive. Flowers, tobacco, and leather. Long, majestic finish. Could age forever. Dark, burnt quality. Black cherries, dark chocolate. Full-flavored. Dark, bitter chocolate, but finishes dry." When we ripped open the bag, this was a wine we'd never seen before. It was Paloma Vineyard, from Napa Valley ($44.99). It said on the back, "Proprietors: Barbara and Jim Richards" and listed their phone number, so we called. Mr. Richards said he and his wife made 1,650 cases of that wine, and attributed its complexity and depth to the grapes and the perfect, sloped soil in which they grow.

Their wines get a great deal of personal attention. In fact, Mr. Richards said, in 2000 he and his wife picked their fifteen acres thirteen different times, each time removing only the ripest grapes. That kind of care and labor is expensive, and it shows in the bottle. The Merlot, Mr. Richards said, was available in four states outside of California: New York, North Carolina, Ohio, and Virginia—yet another example that you can never tell where you'll find any particular wine. The only thing you can do is enjoy the hunt for something new.

Here's the bottom line: For an everyday Merlot, don't settle for less than a wine that tastes affirmatively good and makes you smile. There are Merlots out there for less than $10 that will do that. For a special experience, spend more than $20 on any Merlot that you've never heard of. You just might find your own Paloma.

Oh, one last thing: We called Ben Stein to see what he drinks himself. It turns out that he prefers a high-end Chardonnay. But his wife, as it happens, loves Merlot, especially Beringer. "She has marvelous taste in everything," Mr. Stein told us, "except husbands."

Wine Notes

General advice: Four wineries have been repeat favorites in our under-$20 tastings: Bogle, Hess, Kunde, and Chateau Ste. Michelle. In addition to the names below, good names to look for in over-$20 Merlot include Beringer, Burgess, Steltzner, and Swanson. Most inexpensive Merlot is best consumed young, while some of the high-end wines will age gracefully for quite some time. If the Merlot you open seems light and its taste diffuse, try chilling it. If it seems heavy and almost chewy, leave it alone and let it breathe for a while. By the way, note that almost every one of the inexpensive Merlots below, except for two of our very favorites, simply says it's from California on the label, which means the grapes could have come from anywhere in the state, while every one of the over-$20 California wines has a more specific appellation, usually Napa Valley. That tells you the grapes came from the fine grape-growing areas, where the fruit is better—and more expensive.
Food pairings: Hamburgers with less expensive Merlot. Steak with more expensive bottles.

Under $20

Niebaum–Coppola Estate, Winery and Vineyards (Napa Valley). $15.99. VERY GOOD. Best of tasting. Black as night. Big and classy. Perhaps still a bit young. (1997)

Fetzer Vineyards "Eagle Peak" (California). $9.99. VERY GOOD. Best value. Fruity, with nice acidity and a little bit of cream. Very drinkable, and it certainly tastes as if it costs more. (1999)

Hess Select (The Hess Collection Winery; Napa Valley). $15.99. VERY GOOD. Nice edges, good fruit, and real "stuff," even a hint of mint. Interesting tastes. (1996)

Beringer Vineyards "Founders' Estate" (California). $8.99. VERY GOOD. Rich and a bit velvety. Nice fruit and real mouthfeel. (1998)

Blackstone Winery (California) $10.79. GOOD. Good hamburger wine. Quite fruity. (1998)

Camelot Vineyards & Winery (California). $8.99. GOOD. Grapey, but with better acids than most, making it more nicely balanced and better with food. (1997)

Estancia Vineyards (California). $17.99. GOOD. Some depth and earthiness. Slightly tight and green, but far more serious than most. Tastes more expensive than it is. (1998)

Forest Glen Winery (California). $8.99. GOOD. Some soil and grounding—not just fat grapes. Quite pleasant. Fruity and approachable. (1998)

Hogue Cellars (Columbia Valley, Washington). $13.49. GOOD. Good fruit. Well made, with a bit of spice, some chocolate, and real character. (1997)

Meridian Vineyards (California) $9.99. GOOD. Soft, pleasant, and smooth, just what many people are looking for in an everyday Merlot. (1998)

Over $20

Paloma Vineyard (Napa Valley). $44.99. DELICIOUS. Best of tasting. A massive wine of real soul. Complex, edgy, and ripe. Lots of structure, with flowers, tobacco, leather, blackberries, dark chocolate, and a majestic finish. (1998)

Whitehall Lane Winery (Napa Valley). $27.99. VERY GOOD/DELICIOUS. Best value. Intense and serious, with layers of tastes, maybe even some licorice. Beautifully made and memorable. (1998)

Joseph Phelps Vineyards (Napa Valley). $41.99. DELICIOUS. Very pretty, with a deep garnet color. Classy and easy to drink, with a velvety, chocolaty taste in the front and then a surprisingly dry, tight finish that gives it complexity and stature. The fruit and tannins needed for a very long life. (1997)

Charles Krug Winery "Peter Mondavi Family" Reserve (Napa Valley). $35.89. VERY GOOD/DELICIOUS. Absolutely charming. Nice and plump at first, but more complex and serious as it opens up. A wine you could fall in love with. (1996)

Dry Creek Vineyard (Sonoma County). $22.95. VERY GOOD/DELICIOUS. Loaded with tight fruit, still bound up by youth. Deep, raisiny, tannic tastes that add up to a very serious mouthful. (1996)

Flora Springs Winery "Estate" (Napa Valley). $20.99. VERY GOOD. Creamy, soft, and pleasant, with a particularly fetching finish. (1998)

Robert Keenan Winery (Napa Valley). $26.99. VERY GOOD. Really fine. Elegant and restrained. Classy, with a tight, controlled taste, good fruit, and an interesting charred taste at the end. (1996)

MacRostie Wines (Carneros). $34.99. VERY GOOD. Real character, with some toughness and all sorts of interesting spices. Not your usual Merlot. Could age for quite some time. (1996)

Robert Mondavi Winery (Napa Valley). $27.99. VERY GOOD. Round, plump, and easy to drink, with lovely blackberry fruit. This is a wine we could sip all night long. (1997)

St. Francis Winery & Vineyard (Sonoma County). $23.39. VERY GOOD. Interesting, with nice tannis but also plenty of cream. Complex and yummy. St. Francis is a repeat favorite. (1998)

The "Right" Wineglass
Is Perfectly Clear

As if Americans weren't intimidated enough by the subject of wine, now there's the whole issue of the "right" glass, designed to deliver the perfect tastes precisely to the targeted taste buds. There's the Merlot glass, the Chardonnay glass, the Bordeaux glass, the Pinot glass—and if you're not sipping from the appropriate glass, well, you might as well just suck beer out of a can.

Geez, relax. It's just a glass. When we're on vacation, we often have to drink wine out of the hotel's cheap water glasses, and you know what? The wine is always delicious, because we're on vacation. Neighborhood Italian restaurants often serve their comforting red wine in small tumblers, and it tastes great, doesn't it? Experts say the best Champagne glass is a flute, because it concentrates the taste and smells and allows the bubbles to rise gracefully, but for many of us, celebrations mean those old-fashioned Champagne bowls that were supposedly patterned after Marie Antoinette's breasts. In other words, the glass that makes the wine most special to you is the best glass. The history of the glass, the circumstances under which you're drinking the wine, and all sorts of factors matter when you're talking about the "best" wineglass. Not only that, but no glass will make a mediocre wine taste great, or a great wine taste mediocre. All that said, given a choice, it's nice to have a glass that allows a wine to show its best. Here are some general guidelines we've found to be true about wineglasses:

• Cheaper is better, especially when you have a klutz in the house like John. There are plenty of terrific wineglasses out there for less than $10 a piece. We usually pay around half that. You should enjoy your glasses, use them every day. If they're too expensive, you'll put them away somewhere and save them for a special occasion, instead of making wine an everyday special occasion.

• Clear is best. We prefer glasses with no color on them anywhere. The only hue should be the color of the wine.

• Thin glass is better than thicker glass. You want to taste wine, not glass.

• The stem should be long enough to hold it comfortably. You want to keep your hands off the bowl itself, so you don't warm the wine. Some people insist that the proper way to hold a wineglass is to grasp its "foot," the part that rests on a table, but we do what's comfortable.

• The base of the bowl should be at least a little bit wide. This gives the wine, whether red or white, some room to open up and show its stuff.

• The glass should curve in ever so slightly toward the top. So much of the enjoyment of wine is in the smell. The curve helps to focus the wine's aromas into your nose. If the glass curves in too much, it's hard to get a really good whiff.

• Don't worry much about "red" and "white" glasses. Some red wineglasses tend to be more vertical, while some white wineglasses tend to be rounder, but a good everyday glass should be appropriate to both.

• Bigger is better (up to a point, of course). Partly this is because the wine needs room to stretch and breathe, but we also like big glasses for a less tangible reason: We find them generous and comforting. They make us feel as if we're drinking something special even when we're not, and they give our table an elegance even when the plates are filled with macaroni and cheese. For everyday glasses, we'd suggest something around twenty ounces, and certainly nothing less than sixteen. There are a million "howevers," of course. If we were drinking a Riesling, which is a restrained, focused wine, for instance, a twelve-ounce glass would be fine, while it seems that no glass could be too big for a massive, rough Côtes-du-Rhône.

• And, yes, it is better to use a Champagne flute that's thin and elegant. It captures the bubbles better and makes them explode into your mouth and onto your nose and tongue. But if a traditional Champagne glass with the wide bowl makes the mood more celebratory, you can't get a better glass than that.

We once conducted a kind of "taste-off" among dozens of wineglasses that we ordered from several merchants. Our winner was the Spiegelau Vino Grand Burgundy, which was more than eight inches high and held twenty-five ounces (it cost $54.95 for a set of six at that time). After we wrote about that and some other good glasses, we received this letter from Lynnie Sullivan of North Carolina: "You listed your favorite glasses as containing between 20.5 and 25 ounces of fluid. This would seem to make your wine tastings more exciting than ours, with our mere six- to eight-ounce glasses. The use of these glasses would also save us quite a bit of change at our local restaurants, as we would order by the glass and no longer by those puny carafes. I see why you like the longer stems: for balance. Maybe 25 ounces should have been .25 liter, but, hey, party on, dudes."

So, maybe we should make this point more clearly: Don't fill up the glass. No matter how big it is, just put a little wine into it. You can swirl the wine, look at it, smell it—and that doesn't even include the best part: drinking it.

Chapter Thirteen

Zinfandel

Spirit "R" Us

We have learned many things since we began writing our newspaper column, but none more dramatically than this: There are few wines that incite more passion in Americans than Zinfandel. And why not? It is, after all, a uniquely American wine. Other fine grapes, such as Cabernet Sauvignon and Chardonnay, are associated with France, while Zinfandel is all-American (though its roots, as it were, almost surely go back through Italy).

Zinfandel reminds us of our youth. When we were headed down to the Florida Everglades in the winter of 1986 to get a good look at Halley's Comet, there was no question what wines we'd drink as we lay on the cold ground trying to see this once-in-a-lifetime ghost image. Zinfandels, of course. They would be big, bracing, warming. We were right. We wrote of our favorite on that trip, a Sherrill Cellars "Oct. 29th Zinfandel" from the 1974 vintage: "Tastes like it's on fire"—and we meant that as a compliment.

This was California Zinfandel in the 1970s; wild, unrepentant, large—a John Wayne kind of wine—and we loved it. When we say we cut our teeth on Zinfandel, we mean that almost literally. It was wine that we didn't so much drink as chew. We had one marvelous Zin experience after another, from Amador Foothill 1982 ("classic") to the Sutter Home Late Harvest 1980 ("sweet, big, long, clean finish") to this, a 1984 from A. Rafanelli: "Delicious! One of the greats. Huge and classy, like a late-harvest Zin but with the class of a Cabernet. Almost black in its taste, with awesome intensity, yet lots of layers and character. A huge, memorable, black-berry wine."

To us, a good Zinfandel isn't just a wine but an experience. It should have zest and pepper, ripe fruit and real darkness. We don't just mean that it should look dark, but it should feel dark, with a depth that touches you somewhere inside. Zinfandel really should taste like America, with spice, pepper, real zest, and an independent spirit. As a matter of fact, "spirit" is just about the perfect word for a good Zinfandel. Let Bordeaux be classy, Chianti be rustic, Barolo be majestic. Zinfandel should have spirit—American spirit.

We have so many great Zinfandel memories. In fact, it was Zinfandel that led to one of our more bizarre wine experiences. On February 15, 1980, John was visiting St. Petersburg, Florida, for a newspaper-writing seminar and, natch, he dropped into local wine shops, where he found something we'd never seen before: Woodland "California Zinfandel." It was nonvintage, but the simple label said: "To combine the best qualities of separate vineyard areas and vintages, Woodland Zinfandel was blended in August 1974. The wine is ready for immediate consumption but will repay the cellarer handsomely for allowing it to age in the bottle for a few years." The wine had no price tag and the shopkeeper had no idea how much it was because, incredibly, he had never noticed the two bottles of Woodland, had no other bottles of Woodland, and knew nothing about the winery. John bought the two bottles—they settled on a price of $3.35 each—and we opened one right away. It was so good we tried to find out who the mysterious Woodland was. John sent Woodland a letter, but it was re-turned. So he sent a letter to the Wine Institute in California. "Please," he wrote, "can you tell us *anything* about Woodland? This is driving us crazy."

On March 12, 1980, a J. V. Ingalls wrote back from the Wine Institute: "This was a label used by Montcalm Vineyards of Acampo (later merged into The Felice Winery). Both firms no longer are in business, which probably accounts for the mystery." Then the letter added: "Your dealer must not sell much wine if a bottle stayed on his shelf that long."

Obviously, we couldn't bear to open that second bottle. But by May 27, 1996, we couldn't stand it anymore. Remember: This was "blended" in 1974, lost in a wine shop until 1980, and then moved, with us, from Miami to New York, back to Miami, then back to New York. It was at least twenty-two years old. "Delicious!" we wrote. "Remarkable after all these years. Intense and raisiny, with lots of intense fruit and a real black hardness. Not at all over the hill."

Alas, since our youth, some bad things have happened to Zinfandel. The first is White Zinfandel, which has become so popular that it now outsells the real stuff about 7 to 1. Every time someone refers to our old friend as "red Zinfandel," it makes us cringe. Winemakers often tell us that we should be grateful to White Zinfandel because if it weren't for its popularity, many Zinfandel vines would have been pulled up ages ago. Because we understand market pressures, we do get their point. So, yes, we understand our debt to White Zin, and have found a few we like (see Chapter Twenty-four).

The other thing that has happened to Zinfandel is more ominous: In our tastings, year after year, we have found that the Zinfandel of our youth has become an endangered species. In a tasting in 1998 of Zinfandels under $20, we found that many weren't well made. They were simple, grapey, and lacking character. We never would have guessed that most were Zinfandel. Instead, they tasted like some sort of cheap grape, rushed out of the winery with little care or thought. Almost all of the wines we tasted, even those that cost close to $20, would have been better chilled, which is fine with Beaujolais, but not a compliment to a red wine that should have some weight, and certainly not a compliment to the noble heritage of Zinfandel. Our best of tasting back then: St. Francis Winery. Best value: Rancho Zabaco, which is owned by Gallo.

Zinfandel shouldn't have to be expensive to be good. Over the years we've had oceans of inexpensive Zinfandels from Louis M. Martini Winery that were excellent when purchased, and became even better with some age. But we figured maybe we needed to spend over $20 these days to find a really good Zin. So, still back in 1998, we conducted a new tasting of Zins that cost between $20 and $50. We were pretty disappointed again. So many seemed clumsy and poorly made, though the best upheld the proud tradition of Zinfandel. Best of tasting then: a tie between Ridge Vineyards and Gary Farrell, which are both top names in California wine. We were also very impressed with a wine we'd never seen before called Bannister, which reminded us of Jack Nicholson in *A Few Good Men*: "You want real Zin? You can't handle real Zin!" This 1995 was an awesome, intense wine.

The letters. You would've thought we insulted somebody's mother. Writer after writer told us that we were all wet, that we couldn't possibly know what we were talking about, that there are boatloads of great Zinfandels out there. Had it been just a few years earlier, we're sure we would have been called Communist dupes. So we tried again in a more recent tasting. We picked up the first fifty Zinfandels we found under $20 from well-known producers. As always, we weren't trying to find the best Zinfandel. We were only trying to determine whether you'd have a good chance of picking up a nice wine if you grabbed an inexpensive Zinfandel on the way home tonight. The answer: no. Sorry.

Over and over, we found the Zins to be cheap-tasting wines of little character. They were hot, alcoholic, and lacked depth. The alcohol content itself—often over 14 percent—wasn't the issue. The problem was that the alcohol wasn't balanced with enough fruit and other tastes, so what was left was a wine with the worst of both worlds—high alcohol and thin, wimpy tastes. There often was nothing underneath the alcohol except what appeared to be sugar. "These taste like cheap floozies," Dottie said at one point. That doesn't mean they were all failures, of course. The Cypress, from J. Lohr Winery, was a delightful, easy-to-drink wine for just $8.99. The Franciscan was a beautiful wine, with the herbs and pepper that we associate with Zinfandel. The Rodney Strong—a name we have recommended twice for its Cabernet Sauvignon—was quite controversial, which isn't a bad thing for a Zinfandel. Dottie felt it had a nice balance of cream, oak, backbone, and spice. John felt it had nice flavors, but not enough fruit, leaving the component parts too obvious.

In our last flight, we finally found a wine we could recommend without reservation. "Dark, intense, and peppery. The real thing," we wrote. "Lovely dark color, terrific, blackberry-spice nose. Taste is intense, clearly Zin. Nice tannins, but in check. Well balanced, with nice fruit. Not swimming in alcohol or sweetness. Real stuff. Some elegance, not just power— like an 'all grown-up' Zin." This was Gallo Sonoma "Barrelli Creek Vineyard," which cost $19.85. We have recommended the Gallo Barrelli Creek Cabernet Sauvignon twice, so it's clearly a name to look for.

We tried another big tasting of the higher-end stuff, too. For our tastings of less expensive wines, we focus on well-known wineries that produce relatively large quantities of widely distributed wine. But there are so many small producers that specialize in Zinfandel, and believe in it passionately, that it wouldn't be fair to leave them out. Many wine stores do carry some small-production Zinfandels. There are so many of them that you can almost always find one you have never heard of. And a small, passionate producer of Zinfandel is often likely to make a wine that you'll remember for a long time.

We found in our tasting that upper-end Zinfandel continues to be a highly personal thing with winemakers. There are still some inelegant, overly alcoholic bombs out there just waiting to go off in your mouth. And there are still some simple and superficial wines that lack the guts and intensity we expect. But the others . . . well, it's the others that keep people excited about Zinfandel. Many good ones are intentionally edgy, not meant to be a smooth and easy drink. They are challenging. That's why, more than most wines we taste, we tend to disagree in our assessments of Zins. What John finds rough, Dottie sometimes finds exciting; what Dottie finds simple, John sometimes finds elegant; what John finds hard and tight, Dottie sometimes finds beautiful but too young. (That should give a shrink plenty to work with!)

We have often said you can't go wrong with Zinfandel if you stick with the three R's: Ridge, Rosenblum, and Ravenswood. Indeed, once again, Ridge and Ravenswood showed well. In fact, we threw in a lower-priced Ravenswood—the 1998 Napa Valley at $16.99—as a ringer, just because we were curious how it would fare, and it was impressive. Rosenblum didn't fare as well in this tasting, but its Zinfandels have been so good for so long that we would still recommend looking for them.

Some of our other favorites in this tasting were new to us. Elyse, Franus, and some others showed that combination of class and guts, power and elegance, fruit and pepper that we enjoy so much. These wines will not be easy to find, but remember our advice: Look for Zinfandels that you have never seen before. In fact, our best of tasting was a small-production wine, but a repeat recommendation from our earlier expensive-Zinfandel tasting. This was the only Zin that knocked our socks off. "Classy and elegant," we wrote with the first sip. "Lovely, with lots of well-balanced fruit. Confident. Structured and classy, but with Zinfandel spirit, spicy and peppery. Cabernet class and structure with Zinfandel spirit and zest. There's no 'but' here. It's round and plump with rich berry fruit at the front, sinewy at the back, with a tobacco/leather finish that seems to linger forever." Now *that* is Zinfandel. And it turned out to be very much at the low end of our price range, at $21.99. It was Bannister, the "Jack Nicholson" wine, but this time from the 1996 vintage. It was splendid through the night.

Keep this in mind about Zinfandels: The good ones get better with age. In fact, for our tasting of over-$20 Zinfandels, we opened up two 1993 Zins from our own cellar—a Nalle and a Ravenswood "Wood Road Belloni"—just to see how the older stuff was faring. The Ravenswood was still too young, and the remarkable thing about the hear-the-angels-singing Nalle was that it was virtually unchanged since the last time we tried it four years earlier. It has many years ahead of it. How many? Consider these notes on a 1970 Ridge "Jimsomare," which we drank on September 3, 1997, with John's famous brisket: "Awesome, huge, sweet-fruit nose. Cedar, cigar—really smells like wine. Intense, raisin wine. Massive, sweet, long, hot finish. Untamed California fruit. Big, yet austere, without any clumsiness. Still young!"

Now, more than three decades old, that Ridge is probably really coming into its own.

Wine Notes

General advice: Think "R." Some of the most reliable names in Zinfandel are Ridge, Rosenblum, Ravenswood, Renwood, and Rancho Zabaco, and one of the greatest producers is Rafanelli. When you're looking for something special, choose a winery you've never seen before because small-production Zinfandels often offer the kind of individual tastes that good Zinfandel should have. If you open a good Zinfandel and it dries out your mouth and makes you pucker, give it some time to breathe. Save a glassful. You might even find that it's more delicious the next day. Food pairings: Light, inexpensive Zinfandel is fine with pizza and barbe- cued ribs. Better Zinfandels demand steak and hearty foods. Zinfandel is often good with spicy foods such as sausage.

Under $20

Gallo Sonoma "Barrelli Creek Vineyard" (Alexander Valley). $19.85. VERY GOOD/DELICIOUS. Best of tasting. The real thing, dark, intense, and peppery. Well balanced. (1996)

Cypress (J. Lohr Winery). $8.99. GOOD/VERY GOOD. Best value. Soft, creamy, and fun. More like a quaffable Merlot than a Zinfandel, but quite pleasant nonetheless. (1996)

Franciscan Oakville Estate (Napa Valley). $19.72. VERY GOOD. Nice cherry-berry fruit, with some herbs and pepper. Not enough dark character, but beautifully made. (1998)

Rodney Strong Vineyards "Knotty Vines" (Northern Sonoma). $17.95. VERY GOOD. Controversial. Dottie liked its oak, backbone, cream, and spice. John didn't think there was quite enough fruit to make it all work. (1998)

Dry Creek Vineyard "Heritage Clone" (Sonoma County). $15.99. GOOD/VERY GOOD. Very dark and pretty. Zesty, with a nice, toasty finish. Some herbs and blackberries. (1998)

Marietta Cellars (Sonoma County). $15.99. GOOD/VERY GOOD. Nice weight and plenty of spice. A bit alcoholic, but a real Zinfandel, with some guts and pepper. (1998)

Louis M. Martini Winery (Sonoma County). $14.75. GOOD/VERY GOOD. Light, fruity, and easy to drink. Charming, but without enough varietal character. (1995)

Simi Winery (Dry Creek Valley). $19.95. GOOD/VERY GOOD. Some guts and some depth. A bit hot, but a particularly spicy, peppery finish that says "Zinfandel" all over. (1997)

Over $20

Bannister Wines (Dry Creek Valley). $21.99. DELICIOUS. Best of tasting and best value. Classy, elegant, and lovely, with well-balanced fruit and oak. Just plain delicious. (1996)

Renwood Winery "Fiddletown" (Amador County). $29.99. VERY GOOD/DELICIOUS. This is the real thing: it seems black, with a huge, peppery taste. It takes your breath away. (1998)

Elyse Wines "Howell Mountain" (Napa Valley). $28.99. VERY GOOD. Beautifully made, with elegant cherry fruit at the front, yet a complex finish of fruit, leather, cedar, and tobacco long after it has gone. (1998)

Franus Wine Co. (Napa Valley). $23.99. VERY GOOD. Charming and pleasant, yet with enough backbone and toughness to make it very much a Zinfandel. (1995)

Mount Veeder Winery (Napa Valley). $33.69. VERY GOOD. Full-bodied and highly drinkable. Confident enough to be restrained—and even better the next day. (1997)

Rabbit Ridge Vineyards "OVZ Reserve" (Sonoma County). $31.99. GOOD/VERY GOOD. Big and gutsy, filled with blueberries and blackberries. John finds it a bit harsh. Could age for a long, long time. (1997)

Kaz Vineyard & Winery "Mainliner Lenoir" (Sonoma Valley). $34.99. GOOD/VERY GOOD. Black as night, with a huge, intoxicating, head-banging nose of blackberries and ripe fruit. It's like dessert—blackberry cream pie. Fat instead of intense but quite an experience. (1998)

Ridge Vineyards "Pagani Ranch" (Sonoma Valley). $29.99. GOOD/VERY GOOD. Quite pleasant, with lovely fruit, though lacking any real depth or complexity. (1997)

Ridge Vineyards "Sonoma Station" (Sonoma County). $24.98.

GOOD/VERY GOOD. Big, intense, and young. Powerful, with no rough edges. Easy to like despite its power. Some nice lemony acids, too. (1998)

Ravenswood "Big River" (Alexander Valley). $33.99. GOOD/VERY GOOD. Elegant and filled with black-cherry fruit. Still hard and tight. Plenty of earth to give it depth. (1997)

Should You Sniff the Cork,
or Salt It?

With some trepidation, you've finally made your choice from the restaurant's wine list, and the waiter has disappeared to get the bottle. Soon he returns and shows you the label. You say that's fine, so he opens the bottle and then gives you the cork. You're now holding this piece of tree bark in your hands. What in the world are you supposed to do with it?

This is a controversial subject—more controversial than we ever could have imagined when we wrote a column about it. We said there really isn't any reason to sniff the cork. After all, the wine itself is right in front of you. The smell of the cork isn't going to tell you as much as the smell of the wine. So feel free just to ignore the cork. But we sniff the cork anyway. Why? Because we like the way it smells. Some corks smell like wineries to us, with aromas of wood and wine and age all mixed together. One whiff takes us back to some of the best experiences of our lives.

Well, you can't imagine the outraged reaction. We received scores of letters from readers who simply couldn't believe we took part in such a silly and possibly counterproductive ritual. "I was instructed many years ago by the sommelier at one of the restaurants in the Waldorf-Astoria Hotel never to smell the cork because if the bottle is bad, and therefore the cork has absorbed this, that your nose will be 'cooked' and therefore any other wine will have this tainted nose," wrote Peter Hyzak of Ponte Vedra Beach, Florida. "I just look at and feel the cork. If I see that moisture has 'climbed' up the cork to the top then I will taste the wine extra carefully to make sure that it isn't 'corked.' " One reader told us that when he's handed a cork, he puts salt on it and bites into it, just to shock the waiter.

Others, though, simply couldn't believe that we said there was no good reason to smell the cork—Dr. John R. De Palma of Glendale, California, for one. "It would be a sacrilege to taste without examining the cork," he wrote. "It is by no chance that the first cranial nerve is the olfactory, a very old, very powerful sense that is underrated by the smarmy at heart. Smell is a much more important sense than the feeble tasting skills of the tongue, which can only detect four (4) different taste sensations: sweet, sour, salt, and bitter. Yes, examine the cork. As a physician, you must examine first, then diagnose. You can NOT examine a wine without examining the cork, the bottle, the wine color, the label, the state of the bottle, the temperature (subset of the touch sense) of the glass bottle, all before you do the feeblest task, to taste the wine."

Many others told us that the only reason you're handed the cork is to make sure it matches the label on the bottle, which might have been the original intent many years ago, to detect fraud, but hardly seems like a big issue these days.

We think all of this misses the essential point: It's your cork, it's your dinner, it's your experience, and it'll be your check at the end of the meal. You should do what feels comfortable to you. We had a friend in Miami whose wife liked her red wine chilled. At restaurants, our friend would order a wine, taste it, and then say to the waiter, "I'd like an ice bucket for the wine, please." When the waiter recoiled, our friend would simply say, "My wife prefers her wine chilled," and stand firm. Good for him. And it's not as crazy as it sounds anyway, since most restaurants serve their red wines too warm (and their white wines too cold).

There's too much fussy, prissy rigmarole in the serving of wine at restaurants. Too much decanting, too many ice buckets, too many waiters pouring too much wine into your glass. If you like your steak medium, order it medium. If you want sauce on the side, have the sauce on the side. And if you want to smell the cork, smell the cork. You've paid for it. It's yours.

Chapter Fourteen

Pinot Noir

The Queen of Wines

American Pinot Noir has become one of the most versatile food wines around, and it's quite amazing to us that we'd say that. Pinot Noir is the grape that makes the great red wines of Burgundy, which we love (see Chapter Seventeen). It has an elegant, velvety taste that tends to be less intense, less tannic, and more berrylike than Cabernet Sauvignon. We find it sensual and romantic. When people tell us that they don't like the heavy and sometimes aggressive tastes of red wines, we often suggest that they try a Pinot Noir–based wine. We also recommend it to people who say they find most red wines too dry. Pinot Noir is just as dry as Cabernet, but its rounder, fruitier, less-tannic tastes sometimes are more to the liking of people who find Cabernet's aggressive dryness just too much.

For years, California suffered a severe case of Pinot envy. Experts said California couldn't make a great Pinot Noir. Partly this is because Pinot Noir is a finicky grape that prefers cooler temperatures, and much of California is hot. Partly it's because Pinot Noir's delicate flavors almost demand a certain taste of the soil, and that's Burgundy's specialty, not California's, people said. And partly, we expect, this belief lingered because some people assumed that California's winemakers were too ham-fisted to bring out the charm of the Pinot Noir grape.

Our first experiences seemed to confirm the worst fears. "Not good. Over the hill. Iron-like, thin, very little fruit," we wrote in our wine notes about a 1970 Mirassou, from California. Of the next year's vintage of the same wine, we wrote: "Even worse. Hardly drinkable." It was hard to believe these wines were made from one of the world's greatest red-wine grapes. If Cabernet Sauvignon is the king of grapes—big, rich, deep, and "masculine"—then Pinot Noir is the queen. When you look it at, its color is somewhat light, but filled with a shimmering vibrancy. Put your nose in the glass and you might smell raspberries, cherries, and maybe some lilacs. When a Pinot is especially rich with fruit, we often call it "jammy" or "jamlike." At the same time, Pinot has a special depth and richness that belie its lightness. In a good Pinot, you can sometimes smell, and taste, a hint of cream. There should be a haunting, hard-to-put-your-finger-on taste of the earth, what the French call *"goût de terroir."* What do we mean by that? Think about standing in the middle of a field after rich, dark soil has been tilled, or in your garden after it has rained. The smell of that earth—clean and fertile and chock-full of minerals—is something that you can almost taste, something that you almost feel deep in your soul.

Swirled around in your mouth, a good Pinot should have a velvety, rich texture. When you swallow, it should leave memories of warm, fruity flavors. There are few more classic pairings than a simply roasted chicken and a good Burgundy. The chicken is smoky and dark on the outside, but juicy and vibrant on the inside. A good Burgundy—or a good Pinot Noir—should be like that. In the long run, all of those tastes should be in balance, none of them obvious. The flavors should be ephemeral, more in the mind than in the mouth. Even in Burgundy that is hard to do. In California, we were assured, it was just about impossible.

Wow. Has history proved those experts wrong. These days, we find Pinot Noir, of all things, more consistent than American Cabernet Sauvignon, Merlot, or Zinfandel. We never would have guessed that. Not only that, but some outstanding Pinot Noir is also being made in Oregon, which has made fruit-filled Pinot Noir its speciality.

In past tastings, our favorites have often been from Chalone—one of California's great names in Pinot Noir for a long time—and Saintsbury. Because Saintsbury's Pinot Noirs come in several price ranges and are fairly widely available, that tends to be the name we tell our friends to look for. Cambria has done well in our tastings, too, and we have liked the Napa Ridge, which is also a great buy. In our most recent tasting, we picked up the first fifty American Pinot Noirs we could find from well-known pro-

ducers for $25 or less. We had originally thought it would be difficult to
find fifty, so we'd planned to buy every one we saw, even from small producers, up to $35. After shopping a little, we were amazed how many were
available for less than that, and we lowered our cutoff. This led to a surprising twist in our blind tasting.

We found that good Pinot Noir is being produced in a variety of
styles and prices, and that they are, in general, very well made. Some of the
less expensive ones were quite good. Look for Fetzer and Estancia, for
about $16, and Beringer, for about $11. These tend to be light and fruity.
On the other end of the spectrum, we had a Coturri that tasted more like
Port than Pinot. We could feel our socks roll up and down as we tasted it.
Coturri is always a name to look for if you're a little bit of a risk taker
looking for a unique experience. Two of our favorites, including the best
of tasting, were again from Saintsbury. Another was a surprise: It was
soft, approachable, and classy, with an elegant, creamy, and fruit-filled finish that we can still taste. This was Clos du Bois, then just $16.99—a very
good buy.

One of the wines blew us away before we even tasted it. When we
poured the wine, it was so dark it was almost inky. We didn't have to smell
it—the bouquet rose to us, a massive, fruity, deep-black, rich smell that
made us feel as if we'd already tasted the wine. When we did taste this Pinot
Noir, it was glorious—intense and rich in fruit, yet concentrated. It was a
massive, "wow" wine, a rare Delicious! on our scale and one of the best
Pinot Noirs we've had.

Because we had bought a handful of wines over $25 before we low-
ered our cutoff, we decided we'd throw them into the blind tasting as
ringers. This turned out to be one of them, from a reliable small producer
named Daniel Gehrs. This was Daniel Gehrs "Lake Marie," Santa Barbara
County 1998, and it was then $30.59. We called Mr. Gehrs to talk with
him about the industry's experience with this notoriously finicky grape.
"The thing about Pinot Noir in California is that people grew it in so many
of the wrong places instead of the right places," he told us. "It's grown all
over Europe, but it only makes great wine in one place in Europe, only in
Burgundy. In the last thirty years in California, basically from the '70s, the
grape showed up in more suitable climates and sites, like the Santa Maria
Valley, Russian River Valley, and the Santa Cruz Mountains, to name a few.

And, lo and behold, we started to make Pinot Noirs that could compete with the good ones from Burgundy.

"Also, from a winemaking standpoint, Pinot Noir needs a different attitude, a different mind-set. The right thing to do with Pinot Noir is almost always the wrong thing to do with almost any other wine," he said. For instance, he said, paraphrasing a French winemaker, "You can't separate Pinot Noir from its lees too soon." The lees are the spent yeast cells and other sediment that are thrown off during the winemaking process. "It has to age with its lees because the soul of the wine is in its lees. You need the lees to unlock the soul of Pinot Noir. With most other wines, keeping them with their lees a long time just makes them stinky. Pinot Noir has to go into the barrel 'dirty,' as we say, with plenty of yeast lees in it." Also, he said, "It's fragile. It has to be treated respectfully, not given too much air during processing, whereas Cabernet wants to be aerated, splashed around, moved around. Otherwise, it stays closed and tight."

Remember what we said back in the Chardonnay section, that there's a lot of method in winemaking, and a lot of magic, too? Well, this is why we find wine—and winemakers—so endlessly fascinating.

Mr. Gehrs's Pinot Noir, like the others, is an excellent food wine. We recommend Pinot these days for salmon, for roast chicken, and for duck. But we also recommend some of the less expensive Pinots for less elegant meals, even barbecue. American winemakers clearly are trying to make these food-friendly wines—and they're succeeding.

How well does Pinot age? Some of the lighter ones in the Wine Notes will probably do fine for a couple of years, but then lose their charm and have little to replace it. Better, bigger, richer Pinots, though, get better and better as the years go by. We had a 1966 Inglenook in 1987 (with duck, one of our favorite pairings) and it couldn't have been more perfect. "More gold than red," we wrote, "without a hint of decay." And consider this: We bought a bottle of 1977 Chalone Pinot Noir way back in 1981 for the then outrageous sum of $30. We didn't open it until March 10, 1996, to drink with a roasted turkey. Our notes on this nineteen-year-old wine: "Wow! First taste is massive, huge, powerful. Intense fruit, totally forward. Classy and very varietal. After one hour, thins out, loses fruit—a little over—but still very good. A real powerhouse Pinot."

So much for the experts.

Wine Notes

General advice: *Saintsbury is always a reliable name in Pinot Noir. Oregon also makes some fine Pinot Noirs (for reliable names in Oregon wine, see Chapter Three). California Pinots from the cooler Carneros region have a lot going for them, so you might look for that name. Good Pinot Noirs age beautifully, so if you see a bottle that's a few years old, it's worth a try. Serve it at cool room temperature, and don't let it breathe before you drink it: Often, that very first taste after the bottle is opened is pure, sweet fruit. In time, the wine will get better, richer, and deeper, but that first sip is so very lovely. The wines below were our favorites in a recent tasting of Pinot Noir under $25.*

Food pairings: *A wide range. Salmon. Roast chicken and lighter meats. Duck. Shad roe. Inexpensive Pinot Noir, slightly chilled, is also good with less elegant meals, even barbecue.*

Saintsbury (Carneros). $24.99. DELICIOUS. Best of tasting. Cream and fruit, so very luscious. A complete wine, but still quite young. (1999)

Clos du Bois Winery (Sonoma County). $16.99. DELICIOUS. Best value. Cherry-berry fruit on top, velvety and easy, with layers of taste underneath, all sorts of peppers and herbs. Beguiling. (1999)

Saintsbury "Garnet" (Carneros). $15.99. VERY GOOD. Lovely, with plenty of drink-now fruit. Rich in fruit yet light in body, a nice balancing act. Great with roast chicken. (1999)

Benziger Family Winery (California). $17.91. VERY GOOD. Earth, jam, and pepper combine into a lovely, balanced wine with a nice hint of aggressiveness. (1997)

Cambria Winery & Vineyard (Julia's Vineyard, Santa Maria Valley). $24.99. VERY GOOD. Challenging, with lots of "stuff." Smooth yet deep. You don't drink it, you experience it, and it rewards you. (1997)

Beringer Vineyards (Founders' Estate). $10.25. GOOD/VERY GOOD.

Quite peppery and very different. Not easy drinking, but charming in its own, unique way. (1998)

Byron Vineyard & Winery (Santa Maria Valley) $22.31. GOOD/VERY GOOD. More tightly wound and serious than most, with some depth. (1997)

De Loach Vineyards (Russian River Valley). $17.45. GOOD/VERY GOOD. Pleasant and very easy to drink. (1999)

Edna Valley Vineyard (Paragon; Edna Valley). $19.95. GOOD/VERY GOOD. Great nose and an interesting taste of cherries, raspberries, and eucalyptus. (1998)

Erath Vineyards (Willamette Valley). $17.45. GOOD/VERY GOOD. Very pleasant and easy to drink, but without any depth. (1997)

Estancia Vineyards (Monterey County). $15.29. GOOD/VERY GOOD. Cranberry-like, quite winning. Nice, forward fruit and some complexity underneath. (1997)

Fetzer Vineyards (Barrel Select). $16.73. GOOD/VERY GOOD. Quite pleasant and some "stuff" underneath, but primarily just a very nice glass of wine. (1998)

Meridian Vineyards (Santa Barbara County). $13.50. GOOD/VERY GOOD. Earthy and peppery, with plenty of raspberry fruit. (1997)

The Perfect Wine to Drink Tonight?
Here It Is

Right now, how many bottles of wine do you have in the house?

If you're like most people, the answer is probably none, except for maybe that special bottle Uncle Harry gave you for your wedding that you're saving for some special occasion. That's a shame. Maybe you intended to pick up a bottle to have with dinner tonight, but you were running late, or you were too busy or too tired. So instead of enjoying a wine, you had soda instead. How sad.

Truth is, you can have the perfect wine on hand for any meal if you just go out today and buy twelve bottles—one case. Not only will this eliminate the hassle of picking up a bottle on your way home every night, but it will be cheaper. Why? Because you won't be in a rush and vulnerable and perhaps overspend, and because you will probably get a discount on the case. Storage? Don't worry about it. (See page 81.) Here's the perfect mixed case. We've focused on generally available wines that you have a good chance of finding in a good wine shop.

(1) Champagne. Sometimes you have a bad day. Sometimes you have a good day. In every day, there's a reason to pop open a bottle of bubbly. So you must have a bottle of Champagne, or sparkling wine, in the house. And don't rule out having it with dinner. Its crispness is great with some butter or cream sauces. An American sparkler or a Spanish Cava is great as a house bubbly. Keep it in the refrigerator, where it will be fine for at least a few weeks and always available.

(2) Cabernet Sauvignon. If you're having any kind of serious meat dish, like filet mignon or perhaps a veal chop, a California Cabernet will enhance the flavor.

(3) Chardonnay. Yes, it's great with any kind of "white meat"

dish, like chicken. But if you choose carefully, it's also a wine that will make you feel better when you come home, hot and tired, and just want something to remind you of life's pleasures. You can stick one in the fridge for a few days so it will be ready to drink when you're ready to drink it. Then let it warm up a bit. Don't rule out a good, inexpensive Australian Chardonnay.

(4) Zinfandel. This is what we drink with Dorothy's meat loaf. But it's also perfect with that pizza you've ordered, with grilled hamburgers, and with liver smothered in onions. You want something red, fun, zesty, and inexpensive.

(5) Muscadet. This is an inexpensive French white that you can find everywhere. Buy the most recent vintage you see. If you're having any kind of white fish or shellfish, Muscadet is a classic accompaniment. It's not a wine to linger over, but it's hard not to feel as if you're in a French bistro when you're drinking it.

(6) Alsatian Gewürztraminer. The wines of Alsace, in France, aren't very well known, which is good—that keeps prices down. The Gewürztraminer grape isn't well known, either. It's peppery, has real backbone, and, in the hands of Alsatian winemakers, it's crisp and delicious. There are few wines better with pork and sautéed apples or gently sautéed veal in a cream sauce. Some people also think this dry wine, well chilled, is a perfect match with Indian and Chinese food.

(7) An inexpensive Italian red. These budget Italian red wines always make us feel as though we have a red-and-white-checkered tablecloth on our dining room table, with a little candle in the middle. They're perfect if you're going to throw together a spaghetti dinner or make lasagna. Try something you've never seen before.

(8) Bordeaux. There are times when you just want something a little better than usual. When John makes his famous brisket in his sainted grandma Helen's special pot, it would be sacrilege to serve anything less than a fine red.

(9) German Riesling. Riesling is the flavorful, fruity grape that makes those delightful German white wines. Truth is, we don't keep these around to drink with anything, but to enjoy when we come home from work. Look for the words "Riesling" and "Kabinett" on the label and buy the most recent vintage you see.

(10) Rioja. What in the world would you have with Mexican or Cuban food? Or, for that matter, your turkey sandwiches the day after Thanksgiving? We like to buy an inexpensive red Rioja, from Spain, and chill it slightly.

(11) Beaujolais. The light, fruity taste of Beaujolais, slightly chilled, is always perfect. Try it with salmon or even roast chicken. Buy the most recent vintage you can find.

(12) Dessert wine. You don't think you need a dessert wine, but you do. Dinner's over, the children are finally asleep, and that Bordeaux was even better than you expected. How about just a small glass of something sweet?

Set a limit on how much you want to spend for this case—say, $100. You should actually be able to spend $115 or so, because of the case discount. That means you can spend $7 or $8 on some items, like the Muscadet and Beaujolais, and a little more on the Bordeaux. Now, $100 for a case of wine might seem extravagant, we know, but think about how much you spend on an ordinary bottle when you simply swoop it up on the way home.

And just think about how much fun it will be, next time you have dinner, to go to your "cellar" and pick out a wine that's already right there in your own home.

Chapter Fifteen

Bordeaux

More Affordable Than You Think

Compared to most of the wine world, Bordeaux is easy to understand. In most cases, there's an actual estate in this region of France that makes an actual wine that has a fairly consistent style every year. If you buy Château Gloria one year and you like it, you can be pretty well assured you can buy Château Gloria every year and like it, though some years will obviously be better than others. The most prominent grapes in Bordeaux wines are Cabernet Sauvignon, which everybody is familiar with, and Merlot, which everybody is *really* familiar with.

And yet Bordeaux is so famous, so microscopically examined, such a point of reference for wine experts (what other wine gets people into heated arguments about the relative merits of 1929 vs. 1945?) that it's easy to be intimidated by it. Whole books have been written about individual estates. Aficionados can talk until they're blue in the face about the differences among the various Bordeaux regions, such as Pauillac, St.-Estèphe, St.-Julien, and Graves—not to mention the differences among the great first growths (see the next chapter).

Relax! Bordeaux wines are lovely, elegant, and approachable. They needn't be expensive, and you don't have to be an expert to enjoy them. They're worth getting to know because they're really special. "Class" is a word often used to describe a "claret," which is what the British call red Bordeaux. The wines have an amazing complexity. They have lovely fruit and a certain crispness, with layers of red tastes and a depth you taste especially on the finish. You're likely to smell and taste tobacco, leather, and dark wood, as if you're in Churchill's personal humidor. They are not at all like most California reds—not better or worse, but different. They tend to have a slightly harder and edgier taste that in many cases makes them less charming to drink as a stand-alone glass of wine than many American wines, but a better accompaniment to food. These are wines, even the inexpensive ones, that can't be quaffed, because they seem to disappear from your mouth in stages and leave tastes behind that you would miss. You don't want to rush through these and miss any of their nuances.

There's something about red Bordeaux that makes moments memorable. Partly it's the wine itself, which tends to demand attention. Partly it's the centuries-old cachet. And partly it's because most of us don't drink Bordeaux wines very often, so when we do it's a big deal. What's more, you can experience Bordeaux's wonders without having to pay an arm and a leg. Here's how: Buy clarets from great producers in bad years; buy wines from producers you've never heard of in good years. No wine is hyped more than Bordeaux in good years, like 2000, which was yet another "vintage of the century." This sends the prices of the famous producers, such as Château Lafite Rothschild, through the roof. But, aficionados avoid great Bordeaux producers in so-so years, which brings their prices down. This phenomenon is good for the world.

When we were young, we couldn't afford fine Bordeaux, but 1980 was considered a mediocre year, so that's how we got to taste Château Mouton Rothschild, one of the great first growths. It was just $19.95, so we pounced. We declared it "Great! Fantastic. Absolutely wonderful nose, full of cinnamon, fruit, wood, more classy than powerful. Taste: Very fruity, round, rich, elegant, surprisingly ready to drink. Big yet not 'powerful.' Not really assertive or forward, but big with fruit and spice, with a long, red finish." We got a second bottle for even less—$18.99—and it was just as good. This is also how we enjoyed the 1974 Château Latour and 1973 Mouton Rothschild. On our budget, these were pure bliss.

But first growths such as those are a rare and special pleasure because, even at lower-than-usual prices, they're expensive. So what works best is this: Start with far more reasonable clarets, the châteaux most of us have never heard of. Many Bordeaux wines are made by little-known, small châteaux—there are, remarkably, more than 6,000 châteaux in Bordeaux—

that produce fine, reasonably priced table wine that's meant to be drunk fairly young. In a very good year like 2000, these wines are often better than good. They're really, really good, and reasonably priced. After all, people have been making wines in Bordeaux for more than 1,500 years for a reason: The soil, climate, and vines are special. Even the "minor" wines often have an easy sophistication and depth. These probably will cost you somewhere between $10 and $20, which is probably what you're paying for California Cabernet, and these will offer a whole new—and, often, better—experience.

Of course, they aren't as good as those from top makers, and none of this should obscure the fact that great wines from great years are life-changing experiences. But those wines are not only expensive, they also need a great deal of age to achieve their best possible taste. Especially in a good year, lesser-known châteaux have three things going for them: (1) They're available sooner, since they're not cared for as long, getting less time in barrels, for instance; (2) They're ready to drink now, instead of a decade (or two, or three) from now; and (3) They're affordable.

We should mention, by the way, that there are dry white Bordeaux wines, too, and they're quite special. They're primarily made from Sauvignon Blanc and Sémillon grapes, and they're tremendously classy. Many of the best are from the Graves region, and many of the best of those are from Pessac-Léognan *(Pess-sac Lay-own-yawn),* which will be prominently displayed on the label. Look for Blanc de Lynch-Bages, Château Carbonnieux, Château Latour-Martillac, and Clos Floridene, whose 1996 earned a rare Delicious! from us in a tasting.

Of course, when most people, including us, think of Bordeaux, they think of red wines. Let's start with the truly affordable stuff, the labels that few of us have ever seen. The question we asked, in several tastings over the past few years, is whether you can pick up a no-name Bordeaux with some confidence. The answer: absolutely. In blind tastings, we were regularly pleased with the quality of these wines. To be sure, some lacked enough fruit, giving them a green, viney taste, while others were so sharp that they seemed almost bitter. Moreover, these wines are so different from one another, and from such different areas, that it's impossible to offer a single description. Some were lovely, soft, drink-now wines, while others were aggressive, challenging wines that may be better with a few years of age. On the whole, though, the wines were well made and enjoyable, again and again. In our most recent tasting, Dottie fell in love with one we called "pleasant in its grapey plumpness. Lovely. Drink this week! Gulpable and friendly." It was Château Le Drot. The label just said it was "Bordeaux" and was from the 1998 vintage. Here's the kicker: The regular price was $7.55, but we bought it on sale for $6.04. Six dollars and four cents.

We also liked Château Sainte Marie, which we called "comfort wine." With comfort food such as beef stew, this would be marvelous. Our best of tasting was excellent yet still quite young. It had edges and complexity, nice fruit, and plenty of class. It was Château Duplessy. The price at the time of the tasting: $9.49. We can imagine laying down a few bottles of this and having a very expensive-tasting bottle of wine in a couple of years.

You might kiss a couple of frogs in the Bordeaux section before you find your own $10 or $15 prince, but give them a chance. Then, after you've tried some lower-end Bordeaux, if you enjoy them, you might think about moving up the ladder a bit. It's important to have your own house Bordeaux, a midrange claret that you know and trust. After all, sometimes you want to splurge a little. You're having company over for your world-famous beef tenderloin. Or you've been invited for dinner and have volunteered to bring the wine. Or maybe you just, finally, have a night alone together. At special times like these, you want to spend more than usual, but you don't want to mortgage the house. This is the time for a good midrange Bordeaux, which will probably cost somewhere between $30 and $50. Which would we recommend? We'll tell you about our six favorites, the ones that we have found consistent, year after year. All are pretty much available, not ridiculously expensive, and consistently good. If you get to know just one of them, it will make your life easier.

There have been so many advantages to getting to know this handful of wines well. It gives us a sense of history—it's fun to have had the 1970 and then the 1997. We know it's a wine we'll like, and we know our friends will enjoy it. We know the vintage doesn't matter that much because the wine is pretty consistent year to year. We wouldn't claim that these are the best midrange Bordeaux out there. They just happen to be some that we've always liked. What's important is that you find a Bordeaux of your own. It should be something that you see regularly and that you simply enjoy.

These are not inexpensive, but they do taste as though they cost more than your everyday wine. They have tightly focused, intense, dry fruit tastes that are very different from the plump, "sweeter" tastes of many California Cabernets. There is an elegance and a class about them that will make meals seem more special. Since the wines you'll buy today are likely to be on the young side, they will stretch and change the longer they're open, making the meal more interesting. They can often be like many bottles in one.

A nice Bordeaux also is always a good bottle of wine to take to a friend's house for dinner, whether you're bringing it to drink that night or as a present to open later. Any of these would be winners.

Château Lafon-Rochet. This has the class and breeding of a much more expensive wine. It's nicely dry and very easy to drink. We find this wine consistently offers the complexity we want in a fine Bordeaux, but with a more reasonable price than most.

Château Pontet-Canet. Such style and grace. This is a good wine for people who say they like their wines "smooth."

Château Gruaud-Larose. We love this wine, and we always have. In fact, we've had more vintages of it than any other Bordeaux—nineteen, going back to 1966. Maybe the reason we were drawn to it many years ago was because it's something like the California Cabernet Sauvignons we grew up with—big, rich, deep, and woody. It's a wine of real guts, often with some hints of tobacco, chocolate, and earth. With a well-marbled steak—well, stand back. We remember when Gruaud-Larose was a steal. It can't be described that way anymore, but it's still a lot of wine for the money.

Château Gloria. Probably our second-favorite midrange Bordeaux over the years. It's charming, seductive, and a bit fruity, and almost always a good buy. It's relaxed yet classy, and so very easy to drink.

Château Phélan Ségur. This is a more recent favorite of ours. We've come to like it, frankly, because it's inexpensive compared to most good Bordeaux. We once found the 1997 for just $19.95, which was almost criminal. Consider these notes: "Classy, with lots of ripe fruit, fairly forward, but lots of structure and real depth. Really special and elegant."

Château de Fieuzal. This is from the Pessac-Léognan area that produces such fine red and white wines. Fortunately for us bargain hunters, it's such an obscure name to most Americans that its wines are frequently overlooked, which means they can often be good buys for those who know them. It's very approachable, yet actually gains complexity and a bit of pleasant "tar" backbone as it opens up.

With the price of good California wines creeping up all the time, you should try to find something else you can rely on. And if you're looking for a good holiday present for a wine lover, or someone just beginning to explore wine, two or three midrange Bordeaux wines would make a pretty darn good gift.

Wine Notes

General advice: Try an inexpensive Bordeaux that you've never seen before. Then move up to a more expensive Bordeaux and find out what all the hoopla is about. Less expensive Bordeaux is generally meant to be drunk young, so focus on recent vintages. The more expensive, better stuff ages beautifully for a long time. Drink these slowly after opening them and see how they change with some air. The following Wine Notes include our favorites in a tasting of red Bordeaux under $15. Prices are higher now, but there are still many great Bordeaux bargains.
Food matches: Steak and any elegant meat dish, such as rack of lamb. Inexpensive Bordeaux can also make lasagna seem elegant.

Château Duplessy Premières Côtes de Bordeaux. $9.49. VERY GOOD. Best of tasting. Edgy, interesting, and still young. Very dry. Classy. (1997)

Château Le Drot Bordeaux. $7.55. VERY GOOD. Best value. So pleasant and easy to gulp, with plenty of approachable, friendly fruit. (1998)

Château Sainte Marie Bordeaux Supérieur. $9.99. VERY GOOD. A complete wine, so very easy to like. Comfort wine, with raspberries and earth. (1998)

Château de la Grande Chapelle Bordeaux Supérieur. $9.99.

GOOD/VERY GOOD. Plenty of fruit and depth. Grapey, but with some nice tar to give it grounding. Could age a little. (1998)

Château Haut-Guiraud Côtes de Bourg. $9.99. GOOD/VERY GOOD. Ripe fruit, with some chocolate. Nice, focused tastes. (1996)

Château Picau-Perna Saint-Émilion. $12.99. GOOD/VERY GOOD. Plenty of structure and class, but drink it now. (1999)

Château Segonzac "Vieilles Vignes" Premières Côtes de Blaye. $12.99. GOOD/VERY GOOD. Quite plump, but with some backbone and a nice, dry finish. (1998)

Why Pairing Wine and Food
Is Like Choosing a Tie

"What wine goes with this dish?" That's one of our favorite questions, because we love hearing about what people cook. Greg Sisengrath of Dallas, for instance, wrote us to ask what went well with crawfish besides beer. That left us daydreaming about crawfish and New Orleans for several minutes in the middle of a workday. What could be better? (We suggested a well-chilled, lower-end Chardonnay.)

Answering these questions is always a bit of a gamble. Sure, there are some classic pairings, like Muscadet with seafood, but so much depends on the preparation of the food, the wine preferences of the people at dinner, and even how a particular bottle of wine tastes that night. Consider this: Dr. M. Dean Jacoby of Dallas once wrote us to suggest that we try a smoked turkey from a company called Greenberg with a Riesling, which sounded like a fabulous combination to us. We tried that, along with some other wines Dr. Jacoby recommended. To our surprise, we preferred a creamy Pinot Noir to the Riesling. When we mentioned this in the newspaper, that, in turn, brought a note from Gil Smith of Helotes, Texas, who wrote that he smokes turkeys himself and "we always go for the Riesling, usually a Spätlese.

"So why the different results?" he continued. "I checked the Web for information on the source of your turkey, the Greenberg company in Tyler, Texas, and found, in a *Texas Monthly* article from 1997, that they use a hickory fire for smoking their birds. Hickory produces a very distinctive flavor in any meat that is smoked over it, and needs a fairly robust wine to stand up to it. On the other hand, I use nothing but South Texas live oak in the smoking process, and the result is a smoked meat with a more neutral flavor. That allows a gentle white wine like the German Riesling (especially a Mosel) to blend wonderfully with the bird."

It's easy to see why even experts rarely agree on the "perfect"

match. When we were looking for a perfect pairing with Grandma
Dot's famous roast leg of lamb, we looked at some good Internet sites
for advice. They suggested Merlot, Chianti, red Burgundy, Pinot
Noir, Syrah, Dolcetto, Beaujolais, Côtes-du-Rhône, Bordeaux,
Barolo, Barbaresco, Shiraz, Petite Sirah, and Zinfandel. Whew. We
decided to conduct our own test, and found that a good Cabernet
Sauvignon or a softer Bordeaux, such as a Margaux, was great with
the lamb.

Throughout this book, we've tried to recommend a couple of
good food matches with each wine. But we're not much for rules,
especially with something as subjective and sensuous as food and
wine. Being children of the '60s, we're of a mind that if it tastes
good, eat it; if you like it, drink it. Who are we to tell you that
Chardonnay doesn't go that well with peanut butter and jelly sandwiches? We've tried, though, to come up with some general
themes you might think about when you're trying to pair food
and wine, stuff that has worked well for us. In general, think of a
wine-food pairing along the lines of choosing a tie to wear with a
particular shirt. If John is wearing a dark blue shirt, he probably
doesn't wear a dark blue tie. If he's wearing stripes, he doesn't want
polka dots. How does that translate to wine? Here are some
thoughts:

• **The wine and the food shouldn't be too much alike, but
should instead be different enough to bring out the best in each
other.** You know how sometimes people say, "It's no wonder those
two hate each other—they're so much alike"? It's the same thing
with food and wine. In other words, if you're having a big, plump,
white fish, you wouldn't want a big, plump, white wine such as a
buttery Chardonnay, because they're too much alike to bring out
anything different in each other. It would be better to have a wine
with some crispness and acidity, like Muscadet or Chablis. In general,
it has been our experience that acidic wines go well with cream and
butter sauces. The wine's acid and fruit cut right through the sauces,
which helps the palate sort out the layers of flavors.

Acidic wines also can complement pretty heavy dishes because they can be refreshing and bracing. Think of the sausages, the breaded meats, and pickled vegetables of Germany and of that country's delightful, crisp, and floral white wines. Some meals, like a dish of herbed meats, roasted peppers, and garlic potatoes, could stand up to a huge, dry red as well as a huge, crisp white. Then there's that classic combo, oysters and Chablis, where the creamy and briny shellfish and the elegant, flinty white play off each other.

• **On the other hand, avoid obvious clashes.** You wouldn't have a big red Rhône with a simple filet of sole. You don't want to overpower and obliterate a dish—or a wine. A big red Rhône would, however, enliven and enhance the taste of comfort foods.

• **Think about the character of the food and wine, not their color.** For instance, one of the all-time classic French combinations is a simple roast chicken with a red Burgundy, even though chicken seems like a "white" dish. Why? Consider the taste of the smoke, the crisp skin, the juicy meat. An elegant red wine, with some soul and earth and fruit, brings out the best in all of that, more than many white wines would. A sharper, more tannic red wine, such as a Cabernet, could overwhelm the subtle flavors. But the Cabernet would go well with red-meat dishes or something with a lively tomato-based sauce, like osso buco.

• **Consider the personality of the food and the wine.** Some foods are delicate; some are robust. If you're having a rough-hewn dinner, such as spare ribs, you'd want a robust wine to match it, like a big, young Zinfandel. The fruit of the Zinfandel would enhance the ribs' smoky and spicy taste. A chilled Beaujolais would work well, too, with not only the taste of the wine but its temperature contributing to the experience. A delicate dish, like shad roe, would do well with a young, fruity Pinot Noir, the soulful mustiness of the roe balancing nicely with the spirited fruit of the Pinot.

- **Change the temperature.** If the wine and food you're having don't seem to go well together, but you're stuck with them anyway, maybe you're drinking a white too cold, or a red too warm. Take the white out of the ice bucket; put the red into an ice bucket. Wines are different at different temperatures. By manipulating the temperatures you might transform a so-so food-and-wine pairing into something memorable.

There are a million exceptions to all of this, of course. For instance, many people don't like red wine. Does that mean they should just drink water with "red wine" meals like beef stew? Of course not. But maybe they should think about a heavier white wine, such as Viognier. Ultimately, any classic food-wine match has to be a classic match for you, not for the experts. They're not coming to dinner tonight.

We discovered a delicious exception ourselves at the famous— and famously expensive—Alain Ducasse restaurant in New York City. A rich friend gave us a $600 gift certificate for dinner—can you imagine?—so we knew we could splurge. We generally have "tasting menus" at fine restaurants, and the tasting menu that night was based on asparagus. The first course was simply steamed asparagus drizzled with a white truffle sauce, and it was sublime: plump, sweet, and not at all chewy. Asparagus is one of those dishes that's difficult to pair with any wine, so we told the sommelier to choose one, and we told him to be bold.

He came back with a somewhat dark white wine in a carafe. He didn't tell us what it was, because he wanted to surprise us. It turned out to be a Sauvignon Blanc from Switzerland. It was grassy and fresh, but also had a weight to it that gave the wine real seriousness. Now, if you'd asked us if Sauvignon Blanc would go with asparagus, we would have told you that they were too much alike, that they wouldn't add anything to each other. We would have been wrong, at least in terms of this remarkable Sauvignon Blanc. It was one of the great food-wine combinations we've had. The wine was crisp and lusciously rich at the same time, with undertones of minerals and a grassiness that lifted the asparagus, coaxing the sweetness out of the pliant spears, which dripped with the most heavenly of sauces. The overall effect was to transform the asparagus into a sensuous, sweet fruit.

After all, sometimes a solid blue tie with a solid blue shirt looks good, too. Just ask Regis Philbin.

Chapter Sixteen

The First Growths

Yep, They're Special

Even if you're not rich, even if you never plan to spend $200 on a bottle of wine, you must be at least a little curious about the first growths of Bordeaux. Fashions and fads come and go, but Châteaux Lafite Rothschild, Latour, Mouton Rothschild, Haut-Brion, and Margaux endure. Year after year, decade after decade, these clarets are the standard by which red wine is judged. They incite almost sexual passion among wine lovers. Think we're kidding? Consider this, from one of our old books, a 1928 edition of *The Wines of France,* by H. Warner Allen:

> A great Claret is the queen of all natural wines, and in the present writer's opinion the highest perfection of all wines that have ever been made. It is delicate and harmonious beyond all others; the manifold sensations that it produces are of the most exquisite subtlety, and their intensity is so perfectly balanced and their quality so admirably harmonized that there is no clash or predominance, but bouquet, aroma, velvet, body are all blended into an ideal whole. For the thorough appreciation of a Château Margaux or Latour, the wine-lover must be possessed with the acutest sense of *nuances,* of those subtle shades of taste and fragrance, which are delights that belong exclusively to great wines. For this reason Claret makes great demands on the

powers of appreciation of the drinker. Its beauties are never obvious, but all the more fascinating for their elusiveness.

Whew! Over the centuries, men have paid much more than $200 for
experiences like *that*. But all kidding aside, there really does come a time in
your wine journey when your thoughts will turn to these great wines of
Bordeaux. Maybe you're celebrating something, or giving a gift to a close
friend, or you've simply gotten to the point in your wine appreciation
where you want to taste what the very best is really like. At some point, if
you love wine, you should treat yourself to a first growth, just to see what
they're about. These are very serious, challenging wines that, at their best,
can take your palate someplace it has never been before.

First, a little background. In 1855, Napoleon III ordered up a list of
the best wines of Bordeaux for the Paris Exposition of that year. They were
ranked according to their quality and price—especially their price. Ever
since then, the Classification of 1855, in which wines were ranked by
"growth," has been enormously important as a benchmark of quality. Lafite,
Latour, Margaux, and Haut-Brion were *premiers crus*, or first growths
(Mouton was added in 1973), and others were ranked lower. Wines like
Pichon-Lalande, for instance, were second growths, which isn't shabby.

The first growths are primarily made from Cabernet Sauvignon, with
some Merlot and Cabernet Franc (and, in most, a little Petit Verdot) in the
mix. Generally, the more Cabernet Sauvignon in a wine, the "tougher" and
more age-worthy it is. Its tight fruit tastes and tannins do that. The more
Merlot, the softer the wine. So it's not surprising that Latour, which is
known as the biggest of the first growths, has less Merlot than Margaux,
which is often the softest. Still, "soft" is a relative term for these wines, especially in good years. For the first few years after a good vintage (they're
not even released for three years after the vintage), these wines are extremely difficult to drink, tannic, and hard. That means it's sometimes difficult to get their true measure in youth. Consider this:

People often ask us if we ever disagree about wines. We do, of course,
but generally we come around to some sort of compromise. Dottie has the
better palate and taste memory and John has the better memory for vineyards and vintages, so between us we generally come to some sort of un-
derstanding. If we can't, well, there's always the sofa bed to sleep on. Our

usual amicable musings hit a snag with our tasting of the first growths from 1995, an excellent vintage. While we usually taste wines blind and against one another, in this case we knew what we were drinking, and we drank just one bottle a night, every night for five nights. We knew these would be challenging wines, wines that would change with each sip, and we knew we'd have to concentrate to figure out what was really going on in each bottle. As we expected, especially at that point in their development—they were infants—these wines were more an intellectual exercise than a truly pleasurable experience. The fruit, to varying degrees, was tightly wound and largely unyielding. Each of these wines had layers of wood, tobacco, and vanilla, and some had undertones of mint. But the layers, at that point, were like the layers of phyllo dough, so thin and compact they were hard to distinguish without a great deal of care and thought. We've been studying wine for almost thirty years, and for us, deconstructing young children like these is part of the fun of drinking them. We imagine first-grade teachers must have the same kind of fun as they look at each child and try to guess how he or she will grow up.

It was impossible to say which was "best" among those 1995 wines. They were all extraordinary in their own way. In fact, we disagreed about these wines so thoroughly that we kept separate notes, which appear below.

We had better luck with our tastings of the 1996, 1997, and 1998 first growths—or at least we could agree on them. Nowhere is there more emphasis on vintages than in Bordeaux. Huge sections of books are devoted to discussing every vintage going back a century or more. A remarkable number of vintages are declared "the vintage of the century." The easiest way to tell what kind of "buzz" a vintage gets is to look at the prices. We paid $1,430 for the five wines from 1995, $1,245 for 1996, $665 for the 1997 and $975 in 1998. Guess which year was considered the best of the four. Prices for the 2000 vintage, hailed as an excellent year, were outrageous even before the wines were released. Four thousand dollars for a single case of Château Lafite Rothschild? Gee.

We were disappointed with the first three wines from the 1996 vintage. Uh-oh. Finally, on the fourth night, we began to experience the kind of "Wow, can you believe this?" wine that a first growth should be. It was the Mouton, and it was gorgeous—soft and velvety, almost like a cloud of elegant tastes. This is the kind of once-in-a-lifetime experience you should expect for this kind of money. In fact, the Mouton was the best buy of the lot. Finally, though, the best of tasting was the Lafite, which rated a rare Delicious! on our scale. Everything worked together: it was intense and challenging, with a remarkable amount of tight fruit, a chewy, rich mouth-feel, and that telltale cedar on the nose that Lafite is famous for.

When the 1997s arrived, their prices were quite low, and that could mean only one thing: a year of light wines that weren't being terribly well received. These were the kind of wines that are called "charming," which is often the fine-wine equivalent of "she has a great personality." They were, indeed, on the whole, underwhelming, but there was an exception that was, in its own way, a bargain. One of the good things about an "off" year is that all the wines get painted with the same brush. Since 1997 had a bad rap, all five of the first growths we tasted cost about the same. In fact, the 1997s were so widely ignored that some stores that bought a lot of them had a hard time getting rid of them. But the Latour was clearly superior. "Intense, with a core of ripe, tight fruit," we wrote in our notes. "Some wood notes, deep and rich. Chocolaty richness. Ageable. Raspberries, blueberries, and altogether lovely fruit." Now this, to us, was a first growth, the kind of wine that we'll remember. The 1997s were drink-now wines, with the exception of the Latour. That's not necessarily a bad thing, of course, considering that most of us are drink-now kinds of people.

The 1998s were relative bargains, too—and we do mean relative—because they kind of sneaked into town quietly amid all of the hype of the 2000 vintage. We weren't crazy about the Haut-Brion, Margaux, or Latour, but the Mouton Rothschild was effortlessly elegant and charming. And then there was the Lafite. This was it. This was the kind of experience you're paying for when you shell out so much money for a first growth.

We will never forget that first sip. It was huge and deep, with an un-usual roasted quality. The wine tasted black and purple, like it was coating our tongue and staining our insides. It was chewy, with intense, concen-trated fruit and hints of cream and plums. At some point, John said, "It's as simple as great fruit," and we both laughed because there was nothing sim-ple about this wine. But so many wines today are thin, lacking the kind of great, intense fruit that this Lafite offered. It was dense, "like drinking pills of wine," Dottie said, that then exploded in our mouths with flavor. The wine was seamless despite its youth, and offered a kind of effortless wisdom that emerges when excellent fruit is coaxed to perfection by a masterful hand.

Dottie ultimately called this "a profound wine," and that's just what it was: majestic, intense, and deep. We felt it was cerebral rather than sexy. What we mean by that is that a great Burgundy, with its velvety texture and sensuous tastes, makes us want to retire to the bedroom. This made us want to talk about the wine all night. You can understand why, in general, we prefer great Burgundy, but we stayed up quite a while talking about this Lafite, and that's special, too. We were awed by it.

The Lafite cost $235 and it is very much, to us, what great wine is all about—one of the best wines we've ever had. Now *that* is a real first-growth experience.

Wine Notes

General advice: Because people buy first growths from past vintages as well as current vintages, we have included our notes going back to the 1995 vintage. The prices are those we paid when the wines were released. In great years, the prices of Bordeaux wines can rise dramatically as time passes, but that is not always the case. In fact, in early 2002 almost all of the wines below could be bought for just about the same price we paid for them at their release—and, in some cases, less. It is true that a well-aged first growth from a good year is a very, very special experience, but too many people buy a great first growth and put it away for a special occasion, then never open it. Don't fall into that trap. If you buy a bottle, find an occasion to drink it. If you drink it young, plan to sip it for several hours so you can experience it changing before your eyes (or, we guess, your nose and tongue). If you buy a first growth, shop around. Prices are extremely flexible.
Food pairings: Great steak, chateaubriand, osso buco, and other hearty roasted meat dishes, turkey, rack of lamb.

1998

Château Lafite Rothschild. $235. DELICIOUS! Best of tasting. One of the greats. Intense and concentrated fruit with cedar and chocolate undertones. A profound wine, and a profound experience.

Château Mouton Rothschild. $170. VERY GOOD/DELICIOUS. Best value. Vibrant and lively, with real edges and a long, cherry-earth-cedar finish. Utterly winning.

Château Haut-Brion. $235. VERY GOOD. Looks like velvet. Quite tight and tannic at this point, with spices and a bit of bite, but sweet fruit is already obvious.

Château Margaux. $170. VERY GOOD. A fruit bomb on the nose, with a hint of green vines. After a while, it becomes lovely—ephemeral, mysterious, and delicious, with a remarkable bouquet. Then it seems to go away.

Château Latour. $165. VERY GOOD. A bit green and alcoholic. Still very wound up, and lacks the underpinning, the complexity we'd expect.

1997

Château Latour. $129.95. VERY GOOD/DELICIOUS. Best of tasting and best value. Intense, with a core of ripe but tight fruit. This will get better with some years.

Château Haut-Brion. $129.95. VERY GOOD. Nice and interesting, with some grapey fruit, some leather, minerals, and oak. Soft, approachable, and classy.

Château Margaux. $135. VERY GOOD. Easy to drink, with class and breeding and pleasant fruit. Give it a few minutes in the glass before you try it.

Château Mouton Rothschild. $135. GOOD/VERY GOOD. Awesome purple-black color, but the taste is a bit green and not very giving, with no obvious sense of fruit.

Château Lafite Rothschild. $135. GOOD. Extremely dry, slightly green, and a bit bitter. It has breeding, but not enough fruit.

1996

Château Lafite Rothschild. $265.00. DELICIOUS! Best of tasting. This has it all: deep color, massive nose, tight, challenging fruit, great mouthfeel, chewiness, and a marvelous finish.

Château Mouton Rothschild. $190.00. DELICIOUS. Best value. Elegant and shy and simply beautiful, with a sensual velvetiness that is totally fetching.

Château Margaux. $325.00. VERY GOOD. Full-bodied and a bit plump, but with some nice, hard edges. Finishes a bit salty and green.

Château Latour. $265.00. VERY GOOD. Some deep, "sweet" fruit, but not nearly the heft and intensity we would expect. Surprisingly drinkable for a young Latour.

Château Haut-Brion. $199.95. VERY GOOD. Dark, blackberry fruit, with some hints of plums and figs. But in a short time it seems to thin out—not a good sign for the future.

1995: John's Ranking

Château Margaux. $325. Best of tasting. Remarkably wonderful when first opened—round, classy, and crisp. It turned green after an hour, indicating there's more depth there than was apparent at first. At its best, velvety, soft, and pretty well perfect. When people talk about great claret, this is what they're talking about.

Château Haut-Brion. $245. Purple, young, and grapey, like a barrel sample. An awesome core of ripe fruit that's still so tight it's almost like a fruit pill, or hard candy. It's clear there is layer upon layer of fruit, wood, vanilla, and tobacco here. It's a risky wine, edgy in its intensity. My guess is that, twenty years from now, this will turn out to be the best of the five.

Château Latour. $360. Surprisingly approachable. Packed with explosive, black fruit. The nose is so huge and creamy it can knock you off your chair. It's still tough, but filled with the kind of fruit and earth that give it tremendous character.

Château Lafite Rothschild. $250. Cedar nose, like a cigar humidor. Green and a bit harsh; very dry. Muscular and sinewy, but with a core of blackberry/cassis fruit. It tastes too much like its components, like you can feel the wheels turning. Just a little too obvious.

Château Mouton Rothschild. $250. Rich-looking, with a warm, smoky nose. It's chewy and meaty, with notes of cherry, wood, and cream. In general, it's the most generous of the wines, with plumper fruit, but also seems a bit less classy than the others. Obviously a fine bottle, but without the intensity and character of the others.

1995: Dorothy's Rankings

Château Lafite Rothschild. $250. Best of tasting. An incredibly intense experience. A winning, complete, and harmonious balance of fruit, wood, and soil. It's all there, and it's elegant and heady. This wine engages the intellect, sends you reeling with expectations. If it were a demure woman, it might be said to flash just enough throat to make you catch your breath and then sit back, resigned to the wait and certain of the reward that lies ahead when it chooses to reveal itself more fully.

Château Margaux. $325. This was, as expected, beautiful and approachable. If any of these could be said to be enjoyable in a couple of years, this would be the one. Although it played a little peek-a-boo through the night and was for a few minutes asleep in the glass, it was mostly soft and sweet and revealing. I wondered whether it had enough stuff to hang in there for several years or if its easy virtues would too soon dissipate.

Château Latour. $360. After a few minutes of a strong mineral and prune nose, this became creamy and awesome. The sweetness went down bone dry and fanned out through the chest with a glorious glow. Then, without warning, it would get a little tough, then lovely again. But the fruit makes me think this may be spectacular in several years.

Château Haut-Brion. $245. Show me the fruit! Show me the fruit! All right, so it's beautiful to look at and smells wonderful and my better half really likes it. But it was so tight that I almost had to take it on faith that it had fruit. Sure, there were hints, stingy flashes of sweetness. But getting to it was almost like cracking a jawbreaker. And yet . . . who knows in twenty years?

Château Mouton Rothschild. $250. This looked and smelled wonderful, but the fruit, while more apparent, seemed weak, lacking intensity. The least impressive of the lot.

To Chill or Not to Chill:
Serving Wine at the
Right Temperature

Pinot Noir, a red wine, sometimes should be served slightly chilled. Chardonnay, a white wine, sometimes should be served at room temperature. Shocked? We would have been, until an experience in 1981 challenged our beliefs about wine and temperatures, and changed our wine lives.

We were at an excellent but claustrophobic wine store in Manhattan called Crossroads and a young salesman there told us we just *had* to buy a California Chardonnay called Bacigalupi, from the 1979 vintage. "Drink it at room temperature!" he gushed. "It's incredible!" We were doubtful, but we took it home, let it sit for a couple of weeks, and then, skeptically, opened it at room temperature. Our notes: "Delicious! Looks like Champagne, not golden like a Chardonnay. Buttery, woody nose. Big, citrusy taste up front, very peppery, but a big, smooth-as-butter finish. Thick and incredibly long-lasting. Amazing combination of tastes and qualities. ROOM TEMPERATURE. Absolutely luscious, big and fruity and plump. Huge finish."

Since then, we have found that big, rich California Chardonnays are usually better at room temperature. These wines are meant to be bold. They're *American,* and their big flavors and verve are part of their charm. Chilling constricts those tastes, shuts them down tight. Heat pumps them up, makes them effusive. Think aromatherapy. Think what happens when a woman applies perfume to pulse points—the throat, the wrists, behind the knees. Those places warm the perfume, releasing the fragrance that then envelops her in a cloud of sensuous scent.

On the other hand, some lighter reds are better when they are lightly chilled because the tastes are so wild and diffuse that some cool air focuses the flavors. Think here of a lovely tree whose symmetry is marred by errant limbs. Pruning those suckers enhances the tree's structure, allowing the tree to flourish. Wine that is too cold is like a denuded tree, the nightmarish handiwork of a tree surgeon on speed. Its lovely branches, and the flights of fancy they might inspire, are gone. Beaujolais, and especially Beaujolais Nouveau, is the classic must-chill red wine. But we've recently tasted several lighter Zinfandels and Pinot Noirs in which the tastes are so fresh, fruity, and diffuse that you can almost feel the wine bouncing around in your mouth. These wines would be more focused, and just plain more drinkable, if they were a bit colder.

How can you tell? Trust yourself. If you taste a wine and you're not getting a lot of flavor out of it, it might be too cold. Let it warm up and see what happens. But if you taste a wine, either red or white, and its flavors seem to be all over the map, try chilling it a bit. In fact, sometimes you'll taste a red wine and you'll think to yourself, "This tastes hot," even though you know it's not. But don't think of hot as just a temperature, but as a taste. If you're tasting "hot," chill the bottle.

More generally, think of cold as pulling tastes together and warmth as letting tastes burst out. There's a big difference between "chilled" and "cold." If you can't even hold the bowl of a wineglass for more than a few seconds because the cold hurts your hand, that's too cold. If a wine tastes like ice going down your throat, it's too cold. A chilled wine should be refreshing, not numbing.

Even so, don't worry about overchilling wine in the refrigerator. There's no reason you can't put a bottle of, say, Sauvignon Blanc in the refrigerator today to drink sometime this week. If you take it out and it's too cold, you can always just leave it on the table and let it warm up. That's not a bad idea anyway, since it will show you how the wine tastes at various temperatures. That Sauvignon Blanc, for instance, might not be better warmer, but it definitely will be different.

Don't worry about underchilling wine, either, because that's easy enough to fix, too. Don't put the wine in the freezer. It's too easy to forget it's there. There's nothing quite so awful as suddenly leaping up and saying, "Oh my God! The wine!" and then finding it frozen, the cork pushed out by the icy juice (as you can tell, we've

done this more than once. "I won't forget it," John always prom-
ises—before he does). And don't just drop the wine into a bucket of
ice—that'll take forever to chill. Instead, fill a bucket with ice, add
cold water, then the bottle. This will chill your bottle in fifteen minutes. With the ice bucket around, you can pop the bottle into and
out of the cold water, experimenting with the different tastes and
temperatures. For a pretty table accent for an outdoor picnic, we'll
sometimes use a large clear-glass vase as an ice bucket and put flower
blossoms in the water.

One other thing: Restaurants almost always serve white wines
too cold. They pour you a glass of wine you can barely taste because
it's almost frozen, and then they drop the bottle into an ice bucket
to make it even colder. This is usually a tragedy, especially considering how much extra you pay for wine in a restaurant. We suspect
restaurants do this because some diners insist on all of the trappings
associated with wine drinking—you know, the whole show. But just
try this: After the waiter has poured you the first glass and you've
told him you like it, just say, "But you know what? It's cold enough.
Can you just leave it on the table, please?" This has two advantages.
The first is that the wine will warm up and taste better. The other is
that, when you're ready for another glass, if you're in a place that's
not too precious, you can pour it yourself, making your wine the
simple drink-with-a-meal beverage it was always meant to be.

Here's a simple, and very rough, guide to serving temperatures:

• Big white wines, such as California Chardonnays: Room temperature. "Room temperature" really means "cellar temperature,"
which is something around 55 degrees—cooler than most people
keep their homes. You might want to chill even a fine Bordeaux in
the refrigerator for a few minutes to up to two and a half hours (depending on how warm it was to begin with) to get it down to cellar temperature.

• Crisp whites, such as Pinot Grigio, Muscadet, Sauvignon Blanc,
Chenin Blanc, as well as Champagne: Well chilled. Well chilled

means cold. Leave it in the refrigerator for at least three hours, or in an ice bucket with water for at least fifteen minutes.

• Good white Burgundies: Lightly chilled. Lightly chilled means up to three hours in the refrigerator. Try to keep lightly chilled wines out of ice water, because they can quickly get too cold, but leaving them sitting on a little ice to keep them cool is fine. Why are California Chardonnays better at room temperature but good white Burgundies, which are also made from the Chardonnay grape, better cooler? To us, that's one of those marvelous mysteries of wine.

• Big red wines, such as Rhône, Cabernet Sauvignon, and heavy Zinfandel: Room temperature (again, meaning "cellar temperature"). We often find that well-aged red wines are better at slightly warmer temperatures than younger reds.

• Lighter red wines, such as Beaujolais, lighter Zinfandels, lighter Pinot Noirs, and some lighter Riojas: Lightly chilled. While this isn't always true, many light red wines *look* light, even in the bottle. It's not foolproof, but that's one way to try to tell if it's a lighter red wine before you open it. If that doesn't work, give it a quick taste and, if necessary, drop it into ice water.

Chapter Seventeen

Red Burgundy

The World's Most Romantic Wine

It happened to Joanne Lipman on January 31, 2000.

Joanne is a deputy managing editor of the *Journal,* founder of the *Weekend Journal,* and a person of style. Modest, she would tell you that she really doesn't know much about wine; but she and her husband, Tom Distler, have joined us for tastings, and they have pretty darn good palates. When John saw her on the morning of February 1, her eyes were big as saucers. "I had the greatest wine of my life last night," she said, a look of awe on her face. She had been at a gala dinner the night before and they'd served a special red Burgundy: Beaune Grèves Vigne de l'Enfant Jésus 1989. This was a fine wine from a very good year, served in magnum, which means it was probably in even better shape than a regular bottle, since magnums generally age more gracefully. We asked Joanne, while she was still floating from the experience, to tell us what was so special about it. "It was simply the most amazing wine I've ever tasted," she said, "one of those transforming experiences that you guys write about all the time. What made it especially spectacular was that it came toward the end of a five-course dinner at Daniel, the fine New York restaurant, with a different rare wine served with each course. So we were tasting it not in isolation (and not compared with cheap wine), but in the midst of all these remarkable wines. And yet it stood head and shoulders above the rest. It didn't taste like any wine I've ever tasted. It was way richer, with more body than any liquid has a right to have, yet without being the least bit heavy.

"Because it was a tasting dinner, I wasn't drinking a full glass of any of the previous wines—but when this came, despite the fact that I was so full I could burst, I drank it all and asked for more."

We love wine. We're willing to try anything, and we find something to like about almost everything. We think it's a mistake to decide you like only white wine, or dry wine, or French wine. There's a whole wide world of wine out there that's constantly in flux. All that's why, when someone asks us about our favorite wine, we always say, "We like everything." But if you really pinned us to the wall, if you absolutely insisted that we tell you what we think is the greatest wine in the world, we would tell you that it's red Burgundy, from the Burgundy region of France. As Joanne discovered, there is no wine in the world that can transform your life like a good Burgundy.

At a winery, we once met a Wall Street money manager, a very serious, down-to-earth guy, who was talking about return on capital and such. When he asked us casually what we thought was the greatest wine in the world, we said, Well, when it's right, we'd have to say red Burgundy. He immediately seemed caught in a spell. He said he felt the same way. Then he told us the story of a particular Burgundy he'd once had. He described the wine in almost sexual terms, then looked around the room, lowered his voice, and said: "After my first sip, I got down on my knees and prayed. I swear to God. I actually got down on my knees." We knew just how he felt.

We know it's daunting, but you will enrich your life if you taste a fine Burgundy. Some people are willing to spend $500 on an old Château Latour who have never spent $50 on a Burgundy, and we can understand why. When you buy a fine Bordeaux, you pretty much know what you're getting—one château, one winemaker, a consistent vision. Burgundy isn't like that. There are hundreds of growers, most of whom sell their grapes or wine to big *négociants,* who blend and ship the wines under their own labels. The wine itself isn't called something simple, like Château Giscours or Kendall-Jackson Chardonnay, but is instead called by its place name, like Santenay. Many people can own plots in the same vineyard. Vintages make a big difference. Few wine merchants know much about Burgundy. The Pinot Noir grape, which is the great grape of Burgundy, is notoriously fickle, so each bottle is a little bit of a gamble. One of the ways to identify a Burgundy is a hint of what is politely called "barnyard odor," which certainly doesn't sound very romantic. And on top of all of that, everybody knows Burgundy prices are ridiculous. *Geez!* How could this wine possibly be worth the trouble?

Well, it is. Red Burgundy is the wine we always recommend for Valentine's Day because we consider it the most romantic wine in the world, although explaining why is hard, like trying to explain why a sunset is romantic. It's sensual, with a soul-satisfying hint of earthiness. It's both challenging and charming, perhaps like our loved ones themselves, and the same bottle can be alternately supple and tight. While we find Bordeaux to be proper, well structured, and intellectually delicious, we tend to talk about Burgundy with words like passionate, hedonistic, and beguiling. It's "feminine" and sensual, with a creamy roundness wrapped around a hard core of ripe, forward fruit. A good Bordeaux or Cabernet Sauvignon can shout; Burgundy whispers. Good Burgundy always reminds Dorothy of a kiss, of red velvet, and, as she puts it, "of all sorts of warm, gooey stuff, like chocolate fondue." It doesn't have to cost a fortune, either.

How good can it be?

Chambertin (P. de Marcilly) 1976, drunk in 1984: *Great! Incredibly gorgeous nose, big and red and fruity and rich. Nose is very sensuous; a little earth. Taste is big, aggressive. Round, but with a backbone. Fruity. Really wonderful and rich. A bit of chocolate. Long, blackberry finish.*

Latricières-Chambertin (Faiveley) 1964, drunk in 1988 with lamb and homemade mint pesto: *Delicious! At first, it's brown and gold, flat, closed, yet fruity and chocolaty. Fifteen minutes later, it's hot. Then it's round and rich and beautiful. Chewy. Chocolaty. Sweet with fruit. Huge.*

Chambolle-Musigny (Chevillot) 1961, drunk in 1988: *Delicious! Golden and old-looking. First taste is wonderful, old and sweet and rich. Very much an old Burgundy, with velvet and gold and flat fruit. Color is Cognac, with more gold than red, less red than you'd ever guess. Old but not over the hill. As it opens up, it gets bigger and sweeter, powerful in its Burgundian flat sweetness. Classic old Pinot.*

Volnay-Santenots "Les Pelures" (Ballot-Millot) 1976, drunk in 1981: *Delicious, a real classic. Typical fine Burgundy, more horizontal than glassy. So filled with fruit that it's like sparkles, with pockets of fruit exploding in mouth. Little wood. Just very elegant and velvety and beautifully made.*

That comment in the last notes—"more horizontal than glassy"—requires some explanation (hey, we never thought anyone would see these notes but us). You know how we described Cabernet Sauvignon as "glassy"? It seems to have edges to it, all sorts of angles. We think of Burgundy as less edgy than Cabernet and Bordeaux wines. Not that Burgundy wines don't have layers and a structure of their own, but we think of them as having tastes that seem to be broad across our tongues, and therefore a more approachable mouthful, while we think of Cabernet-based wines as having tastes that seem to be more focused, tighter, on our tongues.

There are many different kinds of Burgundies, from generic Bourgogne to rare, awesomely expensive wines such as Romanée-Conti. If you really try to understand all of Burgundy, it'll make your head hurt. There's a whole book, for instance, just on Romanée-Conti. In a large tasting of many kinds of red Burgundy in 1999, we found good ones from all over. Just to give you an idea of the range, and some of the names, our favorites were:

Nuits-St.-Georges Premier Cru Les Pruliers from Chicotot Georges

Santenay from Domaine Bachelet

Gevrey-Chambertin from Antonin Guyon

Beaune-Bressandes Premier Cru from Albert Morot

Gevrey-Chambertin from Bouchard Père & Fils

Santenay Clos de Tavannes Premier Cru from F. & D. Clair

Pommard-Epenots Premier Cru from Domaine Caillot

Gevrey-Chambertin from Labouré-Roi

Chambolle-Musigny from Antonin Guyon

Chambolle-Musigny from Louis Jadot

Vosne-Romanée from Domaine François Lamarche

Chambolle-Musigny from Louis Jadot

But who wants to remember all of that? We asked ourselves: If we were going to tell a friend to pick up a red Burgundy on the way home, what advice would we give to narrow the search to reasonable proportions? Getting a good bottle requires a little bit of luck. How could we lower the odds? We decided to identify two or three kinds of Burgundy to look for. First, we considered what kinds of Burgundy we have found consistently enjoyable over the years. Then we looked at various wine stores, both in person in New York and on-line all over the country, to see what kinds of red Burgundies they carried for $45 or less. We chose that figure because it's hard to find a good Burgundy for under $25, and there appeared to be an explosion of available wines between $40 and $45. Many wine stores are weak in their Burgundy collection, and we wanted to recommend types of wine that might actually be on the shelves. Having set parameters, we bought dozens of red Burgundies and conducted blind tastings. We ultimately came down to this recommendation:

If you keep these three names in mind—Gevrey-Chambertin, Chambolle-Musigny, and Savigny-lès-Beaune—you should be able to find at least one bottle in many good wine stores for under $45, and it will be worth every penny. That doesn't mean these are the very best wines of Burgundy, but identifying the "best" doesn't do much good if you can't find it or can't afford it. You'll likely see Gevrey-Chambertin most often. It's also the most expensive of the three because it's one of the great names of Burgundy. Imagine nice, drinkable fruit bound up tightly, like the inside of a baseball. That's the remarkable taste of Gevrey-Chambertin. You know what Merlot is like—pleasant, approachable, plump fruit that presents all its tastes right inside your mouth. Gevrey-Chambertin is the opposite. It has just as much fruit, if not more, but it's challenging and complex, changing with each minute and each swallow. It tends to be powerful, sometimes with a little bite and a hint of lemons. With food, this can be a very memorable experience. These wines also age magnificently. There are all sorts of levels—premier cru and such—but your choices will likely be limited anyway, by availability or price, so don't get too worried about this.

The wines we tried from Chambolle-Musigny were far more approachable, sometimes with a nose of chocolate. We referred to some of them as "fetching." But underneath the pleasant fruit was a tight core of taste, with excellent acids for food. These are wines of real finesse.

The Savigny-lès-Beaune? Well, consider these notes from a Louis Jadot "Les Lavières": "Giving, with lots of fruit. Tastes purple. Classy but not challenging. Resonates in your throat with deep echoes of fruit, wood, and violets. Soul-satisfying." The Savigny wines we tried were charming, sometimes with tastes of raspberries, cherries, and cranberries. Here's the best thing: Because Savigny isn't well known, it tends to be a good deal. Our two favorites were then both under $30.

By keeping these three names in mind, you can go home to your Valentine with a good bottle of Burgundy.

Wine Notes

General advice: *Keep these names in your wallet for special occasions, especially special romantic occasions: Savigny, Gevrey-Chambertin, and Chambolle-Musigny (pronounced sav-veen-ye, jev-ray shahm-bear-tan, shahm-bol moos-seen-yee). There are many great red Burgundies, but this will be a good start. The big négociants Joseph Drouhin, Louis Jadot, and Bouchard Père & Fils are good names to look for. These are the wines to order for Valentine's Day. Chambolle-Musigny from Antonin Guyon was a favorite in an earlier tasting, too, so that also is a name to remember.*

Food pairings: *A classic accompaniment to roast chicken. Lamb. Any elegant, lighter meat dish, such as roast veal.*

Savigny-lès-Beaune "Les Lavières" (Louis Jadot). $29.99. DELICIOUS. Deep, dark, spicy, and giving, with real structure. (1997)

Savigny-lès-Beaune (Catherine et Claude Marichal). $26.59. VERY GOOD. Rich and earthy, with nice depth. (1996)

Gevrey-Chambertin (Coron Père & Fils). $42.99. VERY GOOD/DELICIOUS. Raspberry fruit, tightly bound. Warming, and great with food. (1996)

Gevrey-Chambertin Premier Cru "Clos Prieur." (Domaine Pierre Gelin). $34.99. VERY GOOD/DELICIOUS. Charming and challenging at the same time, with a good core of fruit. (1998)

Gevrey Chambertin "Vielles Vignes" (Domaine Heresztyn). $33.99. VERY GOOD. Rich but tart, more like the skins of fruit than fruit—wow. Right now it's like green apples, with nice acids and tightly wound fruit. (1998)

Chambolle-Musigny (Antonin Guyon). $29.95. VERY GOOD/DELICIOUS. Easier to drink and more approachable than many, but still with an interesting tight core of fruit. (1997)

Chambolle-Musigny (Domaine Magnien). $32.95. VERY GOOD. Lovely chocolate nose. Elegant and a bit fruity. Some interesting bite at the end. (1996)

Chambolle-Musigny (Jean-Jacques Confuron). $39.95. VERY GOOD. Tight, elegant, and classy. Rich berry fruit, but quite tightly wound at this point. Some pepper at the end. (1997)

Chambolle-Musigny Premier Cru "Les Plantes" (Domaine Bertagna). $39.95. GOOD/VERY GOOD. Very fruity and totally charming. No real depth, but no edges, either. Just friendly and pleasant and easy to like. (1996)

Chambolle-Musigny Premier Cru "Les Chatelots" (Hervé Sigaut). $45.00. GOOD/VERY GOOD. Soulful, rich, and interesting, with serious raspberry fruit, some depth, and grounding. Slightly rough and earthy. (1996)

Chambolle-Musigny (Labouré-Roi) $35.99. GOOD/VERY GOOD. Real fruit—it tastes purple. A bit rustic, with a long, lovely finish. (1995)

Wine and Business:
How to Impress the Boss

Wine strikes fear in the heart of many otherwise fearless people, and rarely more so than in business settings. No matter how much you know about wine, these situations, already fraught with all sorts of spoken and unspoken significance, are ready made for wine faux pas. A friend of ours is now the head of a large, well-known firm, and he's worth a fortune. But when we asked about this, he immediately recounted this story:

When he got his first job, the head of his department invited him home to celebrate over dinner with the senior members of the team. The boss was a very serious wine collector and he pulled out a very old and very serious bottle of red wine. He explained at length the significance and pedigree of the bottle, then proclaimed that only such a special occasion could move him to open it. He slowly pulled the cork and, with a flourish, poured the wine for our friend, then in his mid-twenties. Our friend, who was used to drinking Yago Sangria, tasted the wine and thought, Ugh, it's one of those heavy, French wines. But he grinned and pronounced it delicious. Joyous, the department head carefully poured a glass for each colleague around the table. Then the boss sat and took a sip—and spit the wine on the floor. "It's turned to vinegar!" he declared. Our friend was mortified. To this day, twenty-five years later, he has never been the one to taste the wine at a lunch or a dinner.

Patrick J. McDonnell, of Lake Forest, Illinois, recalled the time, about twenty years ago, when he was a new manager at a big accounting firm, accompanying a young partner to dinner with important clients. At a fancy steak restaurant, the captain handed the massive wine list to the partner, who was clearly uncomfortable. "As the captain, waiter, and sommelier hovered over his shoulder," wrote Mr. McDonnell, "he became anxious, and, after what seemed like forever, in as casual voice as he could muster, the young partner said,

'I think we'll try the Lancers,' " the simple Portuguese rosé wine that was in vogue in the '70s.

"After a very formal 'very good, sir,' the sommelier went off to find the treasured nectar. I think the vintage selected was 'September.' When he returned, he carefully poured a small measure into the crystal goblet for tasting and approval. I could hardly watch as the partner swished it about in the glass, tasted it carefully, and announced it to be 'a bit dry, but suitable.' "

What do you do when you're the one asked to choose the wine at a business lunch or dinner? Here's some advice.

(1) Prepare. A little preparation goes a long way. Christian H. Winslow, a marketing manager in Chicago, has the restaurant fax him the wine list the day before. Michael Wetterauer, senior vice president of a specialty-food company in Corona, California, isn't shy about calling someone's secretary and asking what the boss likes. He noted that the call itself shows concern and good manners. Some restaurants even have their wine lists on the Internet. All of this helps, no matter how much you know.

(2) Price matters. If you order the cheapest wine on the list and you're paying, people will notice. If you order the most expensive wine on the list and someone else is paying, they're most certainly going to notice. "I was on a business trip in Nassau, Bahamas, and took an important client out to lunch," Sheila Goodman, an advertising representative from Coconut Grove, Florida, told us. "When the wine list came I asked him to please order a wine that he would like. The wine came and was unbelievably delicious. When the bill came, it was also unbelievably high. The bottle of wine was $300!!! From that day on, I have always ordered the wine myself."

(3) Manage the sommelier. When the sommelier is leaning over your shoulder, only you and the sommelier can see what you're pointing at on the list. That leads to some clever advice from K. Ramanandan, an executive in Elgin, Illinois: "Discreetly glide the index finger right to left"—that is, from the price to the name of the

wine. "John, this looks good. Do you have a similar Cab?" Or, Mr. Ramanandan suggested, try this: "'John, do you have a Chardonnay close to Far Niente?' Generally, that wine costs about $70 at fine restaurants. Usually, the sommelier will get the hint."

Not surprisingly, most sommeliers we contacted suggested asking the sommelier for advice. After all, said David O'Day of Del Frisco's Double Eagle Steakhouse in Dallas and New York, sommeliers are not only trained in wine, but also trained how to "read" a table. But we know most people aren't going to do this, especially in a macho setting like a business lunch. So, if the person on the spot really wants to choose the wine alone, Mr. O'Day stands back. "When they want to act like they know what they're doing and you know they don't have a clue, you treat them like they have a clue," he said. "You tell them theirs is an excellent choice, play it up, and make them feel good about it."

At the Manhattan Ocean Club, Peter King said diners can avail themselves of an experienced wine staff that's trained to give advice "in a way that saves their manhood." But, he adds, "If you're not knowledgeable and you're scared and you want to be macho, that's a bad combination."

(4) Think of a trick. Sometimes, it's enough to just seem as if you know what you're doing. When faced with an unfamiliar wine list, Brian P. Daley, an insurance broker in Chicago, said, "I revert to 'the 70 percent rule.' I simply choose a wine that is 70 percent of the highest-priced selection offered. The tasting odysseys that this guideline has taken my guests and me on have been exciting, rewarding, and rarely disappointing."

And here's a trick Jerry Kolins, a doctor in La Jolla, California, discovered by accident. At a national meeting of medical experts, he was asked to choose the wine with dinner. When the wine was poured for his approval, he was too busy to taste it, so he simply smelled it and pronounced it excellent. "Diagnosing the quality of the wine based on the aroma was interpreted by many to indicate a highly evolved enologic appreciation that no longer requires the actual tasting of the wine," he wrote us. "Of course, I do not have such knowledge."

(5) Do not send it back (unless it really is vinegar). You'd be amazed how many businesspeople do this at serious lunches and dinners, whether the bottle is really bad or not. It seems to be a macho, whose-corkscrew-is-bigger kind of thing. We have heard from many diners who had to suffer through this and just hated it. Mr. Winslow still remembers "when I was hosting a dinner and, because I was younger, one of my business guests assumed that he would choose the wine for the evening. It turned into a spectacle as he ostentatiously had the sommelier turn back three bottles of wine."

(6) If you order it, don't talk about it. Your kids are amazing, but no one really wants to hear about them over a business meal. It's the same way with wine. No one is going to tell you this, but people who aren't obsessed with wine don't want to hear you talk about it. They just want to have something nice to drink with dinner. If there's anything to be said about the wine, let the wine say it. If you don't order it, do say something nice about it. Just a simple "That's a very nice wine" will mean a great deal to the person who ordered it.

What this all adds up to is this: Don't be a jerk. No one is going to judge you based on your knowledge, or lack of knowledge, of wine. What they will notice is how you handle the task. If you know about wine, are you ostentatious about it? If you don't know about wine, do you know how to ask for help gracefully? When you think about it, that's not very different from anything else in the business world, is it?

Chapter Eighteen

Beaujolais

Much More Than Nouveau

Even if you don't know much about Beaujolais, you've surely heard of Beaujolais Nouveau because of all the hype that surrounds it. "Nouveau est Arrivé!" scream the signs posted everywhere on the third Thursday of November. That's the day that year's Nouveau, made from grapes picked just weeks before, arrives from France. We love that day. Yeah, we admit it: This is a commercial event, like National Secretaries' Day, and, yep, Nouveau may be less a wine than an upscale fruit juice. It doesn't matter. Nouveau is the very first wine that will touch our lips from the current vintage in France, and that's something to celebrate.

We used to say that Nouveau was the very first wine from the new vintage, but that drove winemakers from other countries crazy, since many of them have different seasons and therefore earlier harvests. In New Zealand, for instance, harvest takes place between February and April, months earlier than in France or the United States. Wine areas all over the world celebrate their new vintages in various ways. We attended a harvest festival at Paumanok Vineyards in Long Island one early October afternoon where, while Media and Zoë took a hayride, Charles and Ursula Massoud served us their just-pressed Riesling that was still fermenting. They poured it from big glass jugs that had a hole in their tops; vents, so the containers wouldn't explode. The wine was cloudy with yeast, still very much a rough agricultural product, and tasted and smelled more like grapefruit juice than wine. It couldn't have been more lovely. Two weeks later, John was in

Germany, where, after a blowout German meal, the restaurant's owner brought out a special treat from his own vineyard in Rheinhessen: still-fermenting Riesling! It's called *Federweiss* (feather white) and it's the star of the harvest festivals in places like the Mosel region, where it's classically served with onion cake and cheese. Well, guess what? The new wine in Germany looked and tasted just like the brand-new Riesling we'd had on the North Fork of Long Island, truly making John feel as if he was part of some global celebration.

All of this explains why we, who are not big party people, throw a party every year on the third Thursday of November. Nouveau is a great excuse for a party, and this gives us a chance to see all of our best friends, whom we never see often enough during the rest of the year. Just hours before the party, John runs around to wine stores and picks up as many different Nouveaux as he can find. Then we serve all of them to our guests, who swear every year they won't be able to tell the difference between one and another—and every year they can. Indeed, some wine snobs scoff at Nouveau as a kind of grown-up Kool-Aid that pretty much all tastes the same, but we don't think that's true. At its worst, Beaujolais, the regular kind, can be thin, metallic, harsh, and so salty it tastes a little like anchovies. Really, anchovies. Don't get us wrong: we love anchovies. Just not in our wine. At its best, the regular kind of Beaujolais is fruity, vivacious, and about as much fun as any wine out there—and all of that is accentuated with Nouveau, which is basically just picked, pressed, fermented, bottled, and shipped. We loved the Nouveau of 1995, hated the '96 and found '97, '98, and '99 OK but unmemorable. We thought the Nouveau of 2000 was the best since 1995, and 2001 was charming. One consistently fine Nouveau is made by Georges Duboeuf, who did much to popularize Beaujolais and whose wines are now pretty much ubiquitous. Still, our favorite Nouveau year after year is Pierre et Paul Durdilly "Les Grands Coasses," so we'd urge you to look for that name when Nouveau next arrives.

But there is a big problem here and this is it:

There is so much excitement with Beaujolais Nouveau that too many people think that's all there is to Beaujolais, which is a real shame. By tradition, Nouveau should be drunk before January 1 (and you should never buy it after the first of the year). Beaujolais—the real thing, which gets more care and some time to calm down before it's released—is around all the time, not just in November. The "real" stuff arrives about a year after the vintage and it's one of the world's greatest wine bargains, one of the best-made, most delightful and self-confident wines on the shelves. It's the classic year-round wine, great with all kinds of foods. It's perfect in spring with lamb or shad roe, good with barbecue in the summer, and often accompanies turkey at Thanksgiving. It goes well with Mexican food, with grilled salmon, and with hamburgers. We often recommend Beaujolais for people who say they like red wines, but feel that most are too tannic, austere, or serious. It can be served at many temperatures, and it's always available and usually costs under $10, sometimes far under $10. What more could you want?

Beaujolais is produced from the Gamay grape in the Beaujolais region of France. (You'll sometimes see a wine from California called Gamay Beaujolais because it's made from the Gamay grape, but it has nothing to do with Beaujolais.) Regular Beaujolais is fruity, delightful, and meant to be drunk young. Good Beaujolais has a jazzy, blue-purple color, a fruity, lively smell, a grapey, berrylike taste, and, often, a finish we describe as very slightly salty. There's no salt, of course, but that lingering taste is, for us, one of the hallmarks of Beaujolais, and that's fine as long as there isn't too much of it. Just as the great first growths are used as points of reference—"It's big, like a Latour"—Beaujolais, for us, is the point of reference on the other end of the scale: "It's fruity, like a Beaujolais."

If you wanted to make Beaujolais complicated, you could. There is plain Beaujolais. Then there is Beaujolais-Villages, which has to come from specific areas and is often more consistent than plain Beaujolais. Then there are ten areas within Beaujolais that are allowed their own "appellations": Fleurie, Morgon, Moulin-à-Vent, Brouilly, Côte de Brouilly, Chénas, Chiroubles, Juliénas, Régnié, and St.-Amour. Each has its own character. For instance, Fleurie is flowery, while Moulin-à-Vent is the heaviest. In a good vintage, some Beaujolais, such as Morgon and Moulin-à-Vent, can keep well for a couple of years or even longer. But one of Beaujolais's many charms is that you don't have to know any of that. Just look for the most recent vintage of Beaujolais-Villages. Take it home. An hour or two before you plan to drink it, put it in the refrigerator, if you have the time. Open. And gulp.

We believe it's hard to go wrong with Beaujolais, and we have tested our theory with four large tastings starting in 1998. The one thing that became absolutely clear in the tastings was this: Beaujolais is a great buy. Most are well made and exuberantly drinkable. These are wines meant to be gulped at the bistro, not sniffed and debated. In tasting after tasting, the Georges Duboeuf Beaujolais-Villages, which costs around $8, showed well. Our very best of tasting one year was the Fleurie from Georges Duboeuf. While Beaujolais-Villages is soft, winning, and simple, and Moulin-à-Vent is somewhat heavy, Fleurie is the perfect middle ground for us. " 'Sweet,' with classy fruit," we wrote. " 'Feminine' and just lovely. A combination of charm and power, right in between. There's a lot of stuff going on in that glass, and none of it's negative." This is a serious Beaujolais—serious about being fun, a party-animal kind of wine. Find the most recent vintage of this, chill it slightly, and drink up.

In our most recent tasting, we picked up the newest vintage from various Beaujolais villages and from various producers. We were just wild about the Georges Duboeuf Brouilly. It was as though we'd stepped into a berry patch in the middle of summer, with all sorts of flavors bursting in our mouths, yet just enough structure to make it clear that this was real wine. The price for that lovely experience: $10.28.

Drinking wine should be fun, and there isn't a wine that's more fun than Beaujolais.

Wine Notes

General advice: Beaujolais from specific villages such as Fleurie are a special experience, but keep it easy at first just by looking for Beaujolais-Villages. Buy the most recent vintage you can find—except never buy Beaujolais Nouveau after the end of the year in which it was produced, because it is meant to be drunk immediately upon release. Beaujolais can be drunk chilled, at cool room temperature, or at regular room temperature. You might experiment to see how you prefer it. The food you are eating with it might make a difference in the temperature you like, too. For instance, we always like it chilled with barbecue, but at cool room temperature with poached salmon. The wines of Georges Duboeuf seem to be everywhere, and they're reliable. Also look for Pierre et Paul Durdilly and Olivier Ravier. The wines below, all from the 1999 vintage, were our favorites in a tasting in 2000. These wines are widely available in more recent vintages. The prices have been updated to reflect the prices for more recent vintages.

Food pairings: *Great with turkey sandwiches the day after Thanksgiving (especially Nouveau, because it's brand new then). Salmon, barbecue, hamburgers, Mexican food, ham, cold lamb, shad roe.*

Georges Duboeuf Brouilly. **$10.99.** DELICIOUS. Best of tasting. Creamy, rich, and yet filled with lively fruit, a virtual garden of blackberries, blueberries, and raspberries.

Domaine du Granit Bleu Beaujolais-Villages (Georges Duboeuf). $6.99. VERY GOOD. Best value. This is it, the real thing, easy to drink, fruity, and fun. It tastes like just-picked fruit. Unpretentious and friendly.

Château des Tours Brouilly. **$12.99.** VERY GOOD/DELICIOUS. A complete wine, with surprising structure yet that great Beaujolais fruit.

Clos de la Roilette Fleurie. **$15.99.** VERY GOOD/DELICIOUS. So much fruit, so much "stuff," that it's probably better with food.

Louis Jadot Beaujolais-Villages. **$7.99.** VERY GOOD. Raspberry-jam wine, but not a simple fruit concoction. You can feel it in your chest after you swallow.

Georges Duboeuf Juliénas. **$9.99.** GOOD/VERY GOOD. Ripe fruit, and nicely medium-bodied.

When Do I Open That Bottle?
A Guide to Aging

"I have a bottle of Château Whatever 1985 that I got for graduation. When do I open it?" We are asked this all the time. Truth is, the answer to that question is easy, and we provide it below. The much broader question—how can you tell when any wine is ready to drink?—is very difficult, and yet answering it is one of the great pleasures of wine drinking.

The great first growths of Bordeaux, such as Château Lafite Rothschild, can age for many years. Beaujolais and fresh whites such as Pinot Grigio from Italy are best drunk young. That's easy. Between those two extremes, however, is a whole world of wine. It is impossible to say, for sure, how any wine will age. Even two bottles of the exact same wine will age differently, based on a number of factors including, of course, how they're stored.

We tend to keep our wines for too long, to tell you the truth, because we grow attached to them as the years go on. That often leads to nice surprises. When we were looking for the perfect Champagne for our millennium celebration, we decided it was finally time to open our jeroboam of 1976 Bollinger Grande Année Champagne—three liters, the equivalent of four regular-size bottles. Our bottle was purchased at a Miami wine store on November 24, 1984, for $100, by a friend of ours, who sold it for $125 in 1985 to Dottie, who gave it to John as a present for our sixth anniversary. Because of its heroic size, it always just sat on the floor, too big to fit into the little cubbies of our wine closet. We didn't think of it as our millennium-celebration wine. In fact, we didn't even mean to keep it so long. It just sort of happened. You know what we mean.

It was a pretty good vintage for Champagne, but how would it be after all these years?

Even experts don't agree on how long certain wines should age because it's so often a matter of taste. There has always been great debate among wine experts, for instance, on whether Champagne should really age at all. The British have traditionally liked their Champagne with some years on it, while others sniff at the whole idea, saying good bubbly has nowhere to go but down after it's released. Whether any wine is still good is a function of so many factors: the integrity of the cork, the storage conditions, the size of the bottle, and, to some extent, just plain luck. We've tasted some wines that "should" have been just perfect that were clearly over the hill, and some that "should" have been too old that were delicious. The mystery of each bottle is part of the wonder of wine discovery.

Most experts didn't hold out much hope for our bottle. Even Bollinger was nervous. "Ah, it's a gamble," Guy Bizot, great-nephew of Lily Bollinger, who greatly boosted the winery's production and quality after World War II, told us through a spokesman. "Do they want to gamble on New Year's Eve? You'll still taste the great wine in it, but it could be beginning to go over the hill. I'm praying that in the jeroboam it will fare better."

Praying? Uh-oh.

We opened it on that special night with great anticipation, and some trepidation. The corked popped, which was a good sign right off. The bubbles were precious and languid. They rose slowly, elegantly, as though the liquid itself was so thick it was hard for them to float to the top. The nose was nutty, slightly caramelized, the color like golden nectar. Then the taste: flavorful and rich and deep, like an elegant old white Burgundy, but with a mouth-filling effervescence that went beyond those two little strands of bubbles. Then something special: Even after we swallowed, we could feel the ghost of the shy little bubbles, less a taste than a memory.

It was, in all, the greatest Champagne we've ever had.

So, if you're wondering if your wine is ready to drink, you'll never know until you open it. But here are some tips:

• Next time you're at your local wine shop, see if it's giving away a vintage chart. They're sometimes near the cash register, and they usually give you some idea when various wines should be drunk. All are pretty much the same.

• Remember that "heavier" wines often age better than "lighter" wines, and this is just as true of whites as reds. Just as a big, heavy Rhône is likely to age more gracefully and longer than a light Rioja, a heavier Chardonnay, one with plenty of oak, will often age better than a light Sauvignon Blanc. Wines with nice acidity often age well. German Rieslings, for instance, get more and more beautiful with age. Dessert wines tend to age well for a very long time, too.

• Trust yourself. If you buy a bottle of Zinfandel and you really like it, but it seems a bit harsh and young, think about buying more and leaving it in the bottom of your closet for a year or two. See what happens. Don't let price be your guide. Some of our greatest experiences were with wines that were inexpensive to begin with, but tasted quite expensive by the time we drank them, aged to a beautiful maturity.

• Take some risks. It's rare for a wine to go bad unless it's really abused. There are few things more thrilling than a perfectly aged wine, and it's worth taking some chances to get there. You might think, for instance, that Gewürztraminer is the kind of wine you'd want to drink young and fresh, and it is; but, in fact, we find that a Gewürz with some age on it is a remarkable experience (see Chapter Eight). In any event, usually if a wine is a little too old, it still has elegance and charm that just weren't possible in its youth.

Finally, about that old bottle you got for graduation, or from Uncle Harry, or for your wedding. Forget all the advice and the vintage charts and the books. We know this wine intimately, and we know *exactly* when it will be absolutely at the peak of its perfection:

Next Saturday night. That's right. Next Saturday night. Prepare a special meal, put the kids to bed, open it up, and drink it. Instead of waiting for a special occasion to open this wine, let the wine itself be the special occasion. Here are ten steps for preparing for the special night:

(1) Stand the wine up (away from light and heat, of course) for four days before you plan to open it. This will allow any sediment to sink to the bottom.

(2) If the wine is white, put it in the refrigerator just two hours before you plan to drink it. If it's red, put it in the refrigerator for thirty minutes or so. You might find them too warm and therefore might want to put them back in the fridge, but we often find that older, more-delicate wines show more of their charm when they're warmer.

(3) Because it's old, the cork may break easily. The best opener for a cork like that is the one with two prongs, but it requires some skill. You have a few days to practice using one. Otherwise, be prepared for the possibility that the cork will fall apart with a regular corkscrew. If that happens, have a carafe and a coffee filter handy.

(4) Otherwise, do not decant. We're assuming these are old and fragile wines. Air could quickly dispel what's left of them.

(5) Have a backup wine ready for your special meal, in case your old wine really has gone bad.

(6) Serve dinner. Then open the wine and immediately take a sip. If it's truly bad—we mean vinegar—you'll know it right away. But please, please, please: Even if the wine doesn't taste good to you right away, don't rush to the sink to pour it out. Give it a chance, give it some time, stay with it. If it's not completely, irretrievably gone, our guess is that it will be wonderful, in its own way, and reward you off and on during the night. Start eating, and slowly sip the wine.

(7) We've found that talking about the person who gave you the wine, or the circumstances under which you received it, makes the wine resonate in a very sweet and personal way.

(8) Enjoy the wine for what it is, not what it might be or might once have been.

(9) Save one last glass in the bottle.

(10) At the very end of the meal, after the dishes are done, pour the remainder of the wine into your glasses (pour it through a coffee filter if there's a great deal of sediment). Then drink up, and enjoy those very last moments of a lovely night.

We told you that wine was special, didn't we?

Chapter Nineteen

Rhône Reds

Comfort Wine with Comfort Food

When we think of certain dishes, we immediately think of certain wines. We think of Bordeaux with steak, Chianti with spaghetti. What do we drink with "comfort food"—beef stew, meat loaf and mashed potatoes, chili? We drink red wines from the Rhône Valley of France, which actually have much in common with meat loaf. They're comforting, too, in an almost inexplicable way. How do you explain meat loaf's appeal? If you were describing it to a Martian, how could you possibly make it seem appetizing? Most Rhône reds are like that. Any description of the wine will inevitably include words like "rough" and "raw." Yet there's something about a Rhône—like a meat loaf—that is so thoroughly basic and soulful that it's hard not to like. They're big, aggressive, and—well, it's impossible not to use the word "hearty." They're a Dan Blocker kind of wine, what he and Pa Cartwright might have drunk with a big steak at the Ponderosa Ranch on the old *Bonanza* television series.

The Rhône is a long river, and the valley produces an ocean of wine—some white, mostly red—so vast that even some vintage charts include one section for Northern Rhône and another for Southern Rhône. The northern part includes some of France's most distinctive wines, such as Hermitage and Côte Rôtie. The primary grape there is Syrah, a big, deep, dark, rich red that also makes those awesome Shiraz wines of Australia (and, of course, the Syrah wines of California. See Chapters Twenty-three and Twenty-seven). If you ever have the opportunity to taste an Hermitage, especially one with some age on it, it's quite an experience. The wine not only looks black, but tastes black, too, with a depth of flavor that's like staring into space on a dark night. At the same time, though, this remarkable wine manages not to be heavy, which makes it surprisingly drinkable. The downside: Hermitage is quite expensive.

Southern Rhône is home to the famous Châteauneuf-du-Pape and all sorts of wines simply called Côtes-du-Rhône. These are made from a wide selection of grape varieties, including Grenache, Syrah, and, sometimes, even some white varieties to even out the roughness of the reds. Rhône is also the source of many wines you've probably seen from time to time, but never paid much attention to, such as Vacqueyras, Gigondas, Saint-Joseph, and Crozes-Hermitage. These are generally not identified by a specific château or winemaker, but usually by the name of a big producer, who buys grapes from many vineyards (and, in some cases, makes his own wines from his own vineyards). There's Jaboulet, for instance, and Guigal, who ship many different Rhônes in fairly large quantities. Wines like these tend to be outstanding bargains since most people have never heard of them and therefore demand is weak.

Many of these wines do not aspire to class. As we drink them, we often wonder why American winemakers don't make better "rough" wines. Sure, there are American reds that are rough, but that's because they're cheap and just plain lousy. Most American winemakers who make good, inexpensive reds are trying to make something smooth, easily drinkable, and inoffensive, and we appreciate that. Inexpensive Rhônes, on the other hand, are genuinely peasant wines—proud to be a bit rough, yet, in their own way, surprisingly drinkable because they're so comfortable being just what they are: a beverage to drink with big, brown food or during a cold rainstorm. (In fact, we so closely associate Rhône reds with gray days that as soon as the sun is blocked before rain, we always look at each other and say, "Let's get a Rhône.") The nose of many Rhône reds is often a bit biting, with slight hints of green pepper and a little bit of vines. The wines often have a strong, fruity taste at the front of the mouth that grows into a sharp, earthy mouthful. The finish is often pretty hot and a bit leathery. These wines would be perfect under the stars with that kettle o' beans Pa Cartwright was cookin' up over the campfire.

Many people are already familiar with Châteauneuf-du-Pape, a wine

that seems to have enjoyed a brief flirtation with wide American popularity a while back because of its wonderful name, with pop, quite literally, at
the end. As the name indicates, the village where the wine is produced got
its name because it was the summer castle of the pope in the fourteenth
century. To us, this is a wine that has always tasted almost roasted, and
when we once spent a couple of nights in an old castle converted to a hotel
in Châteauneuf-du-Pape, it was immediately apparent why. We'll always
remember the white, rocky, hard-to-even-walk-on soil in which the grapes
were forced to grow. That's what gives the wine its character. Difficult conditions often make intense wines, and the stony soil holds in the heat of the
day. The result: big, spicy wines of real character and some serious alcohol
content (around 14 percent, compared with about 12 percent for most
table wines). Whenever we taste these big, "hot" wines, we think of the
big, white rocks, reflecting the intense sun.

It's hard to put your finger on Châteauneuf-du-Pape, and there's a
reason for that. Winemakers there are allowed to use thirteen different
grapes in their mix, and they can use as much or as little of them as they
want. So any wine might have a little more Grenache (the grape most
closely associated with Châteauneuf-du-Pape), a little more Syrah, or a little more Cinsault, and the proportions will make a difference in how the
wine tastes. That's why you might often see notes like this on the back of
a bottle: "This wine produced by André Brunel on the stony soil of
Châteauneuf-du-Pape is a blend of 65% old Grenache, 20% Mourvèdre,
15% Syrah and other varieties." Or "The vineyards are planted with all thirteen varietals of the region. Grenache, Mourvèdre, Syrah, and Cinsault
predominate." (We have generally found over the years that it's a good sign
when a label gives you a great deal of information about the wine.) Because
of the variation in the blend of grapes, some of these wines will be easy
drinking now, while others will be great drinking a few years down the
road.

We conducted a large tasting of every Châteauneuf-du-Pape we
could find under $30. The least expensive was $15.99. We were charmed,
as we knew we would be. There's something so refreshingly confident
about these bold wines. There's a noticeably spicy quality about them, and
a surprising herbal undertone to many. All of this gives the wines depth and
complexity, and that means they tend to need food, and ideally should be

savored throughout a robust meal of roast meats and herbed root vegetables, to give them time to stretch out a little.

It was a fascinating tasting for a number of reasons. The wines changed with time and air, so we found that we had to go back and retaste far more often than we usually do. That's a good sign of a complex wine. While some of the wines were soft and easy to drink and others were big and hard, what most had in common were earth and spices. One of our favorite drink-now wines, we're happy to report, was the Barton & Guestier (then $19.99). B&G is a big shipper whose wines are often available in wine stores and supermarkets.

A few of the wines seemed to balance perfectly the drink-now loveliness and the powerful intensity. "Roasted yet easy to drink," we wrote in our notes about one wine. "Lovely, with real character. Full-flavored, ripe, cherrylike. Deep, purple, and soulful. 'Grapey' in the best sense of the word. A slight bit of spice, but not too much." This was Domaine des Sénéchaux, which cost $19.99, a bargain for so much wine. Then there was this: "Charming and 'sweet,' with some depth. The intense fruit of some and the charm of others. Easy to drink, yet with lots of fruit. Has everything. Smooth and slightly creamy. Big but not challenging." This was Domaine Charvin. It was our best of tasting.

If you're willing to venture into new territory, and take a bit of a risk, there are even better bargains out there. Côtes-du-Rhône is a pretty generic name for many wines from all over the Rhône Valley. In a large tasting, we found that many inexpensive Côtes-du-Rhône wines were simple and forgettable, but quite a few were great buys. Our best of tasting: Saint Cosme "Les Deux Albion" 2000 Côtes-du-Rhône, from Barruol. It looked dark when we poured it and even tasted dark. We often describe good Rhône wines as meaty, and this certainly was. It also had hints of spices, violets, blackberries, and blueberries.

Better still, look for Gigondas, Vacqueyras, Crozes-Hermitage, and Saint-Joseph. They offer excellent value. In fact, in a large tasting of Rhône wines under $20, our very favorite was a Crozes-Hermitage. "Interesting and classy," we wrote in our notes. "Nice acids that make it bright, yet there's this soulful, fruity earthiness underneath. Spices, tobacco, and some chocolate. Juicy, mouthwatering, yet roasted and dry. Rich and earthy." This was one of those wines that, once again, proves that you need to be bold, picking up things you've never seen before. It was Tardieu Laurent 1996, which cost $19.99. We had never seen this wine before, and the extra age clearly added to its appeal, but, as always, it was sitting right there on the shelf of a wine store—and not a precious New York City wine store either, but in a store in a strip mall in New Jersey. This is the one we'd want to have with a big dinner tonight—or as the sky darkened with rain this afternoon.

Wine Notes

General advice: Red wines from the Rhône Valley can be excellent bargains. They tend to be aggressive and raw, which means they're not great for sipping. It would usually be a mistake to order "a glass of Rhône" at a bar. They are best with food. Many are better with some age, so don't worry about the vintage, though you may find that some younger Rhône wines need to get some air to calm down a bit. Simple Côtes-du-Rhône is often a good buy, as are names such as Gigondas, Vacqueyras, Saint-Joseph, and Crozes-Hermitage. Châteauneuf-du-Pape is good to look for because it's often good and generally available. Serve at cool room temperature with a hearty meal. Be careful: They tend to be high in alcohol (up to 14.5 percent). The following wines were our favorites in a Châteauneuf-du-Pape tasting, and then in a tasting of wines from Côtes-du-Rhône, Saint-Joseph, Crozes-Hermitage, and Gigondas.

Food pairings: Beef stew, meat loaf, liver, white bean and ham casserole, and other peasant food. Roasted meats. Herbed vegetables.

Chateâuneuf-du-Pape

Domaine Charvin. $26.99. VERY GOOD/DELICIOUS. Best of tasting. The intense fruit of some and the charm of others. Smooth yet soulful. Quite big but not challenging. This has everything. Good now. (1997)

Domaine des Sénéchaux. $19.99. VERY GOOD/DELICIOUS. Best value. Full-flavored and ripe. Toasted cherries and a bit of spice, but not too much. "Grapey" in the best sense of the word. Real character, with nice depth. (1998)

Château La Nerthe. $29.99. VERY GOOD. Fascinating. Almost as if it were steeped in herbs when first opened, but as it gets some air it becomes lush and giving. (1997)

Les Cailloux (Brunel). $23.99. VERY GOOD. It's a bit green at first, with plenty of herbs and real intensity. After some air, it opens into a lovely, full-throated, intense, cherry-berry wine. (1997)

Domaine Lucien Barrot et Fils. $26.99. VERY GOOD. Some cream and spice on the nose. Intense berry taste with more ripe fruit than others, more body. A fuller wine than many, with nice balance and some toastiness. (1998)

Barton & Guestier. $19.99. GOOD/VERY GOOD. Simpler than most. Easy drinking, and ready right now. (1998)

Domaine Pontifical. $29.99. GOOD/VERY GOOD. Nicely balanced, with nice fruit and some interesting hints of herbs and eucalyptus. (1998)

Domaine Roger Perrin. $21.99. GOOD/VERY GOOD. Sweet cherries and a little bit of an edge. Very drinkable and a little creamy, with nice hints of earth. Young. (1998)

Other Rhône Wines

Saint Cosme "Les Deux Albion" Côtes–du–Rhône (Louis et Cherry Barruol). $16.99. VERY GOOD. Best of tasting. Dark, rich, and meaty. Violets, herbs, blackberries, blueberries, and maybe a hint of cream. It even tastes dark. (2000)

E. Guigal Côtes–du–Rhône. $10.99. GOOD/VERY GOOD. Best value. Rounder and smoother than others, with good fruit and a nice hint of earth. (1999)

Louis Bernard Côtes–du–Rhône. $9.99. VERY GOOD. Robust, fruity, and spicy. Rich, roasted flavors, with some depth. (1998)

Domaine des Amouriers Vacqueyras (Jocelyn Chudzikiewicz). $18.99. VERY GOOD. Spicy, with an interesting combination of "berryness" and richness. Grapey at the front, with some bite at the end. (1999)

Clos du Bois de Menge Gigondas. $18.99. VERY GOOD. Curiously fetching. Light in body, but filled with pepper and spices. Easy yet complex in its own way. Very comfortable. (1998)

Eric Rocher "Terroir de Champal" Saint-Joseph. $17.99. GOOD/VERY GOOD. Pleasant and easy to drink, with nice spices and some chewiness. Big yet classy. (1998)

Tardieu Laurent Crozes-Hermitage. $19.99. VERY GOOD. Bright yet soulful. Dry, roasted tastes of rich earth, spices, chocolate, and tobacco, all rolled into an easy-to-drink whole. (1996)

E. Guigal Crozes-Hermitage. $16.99. GOOD/VERY GOOD. Pleasant, grapey and easy to drink. Simpler than we'd expect, but very easy to like. (1999)

Cherry Picking:
Wine Tastes Better
When It's a Steal

Wine lovers, no matter how successful or rich, love to "cherry pick." This means finding a rare or expensive wine at a bargain price. When wine lovers get together, they spend half their time talking about the great bottles they've had and the other half talking about the great bargains they found. Somehow, a wine tastes better when you got it on the cheap. We once spent an evening crying with laughter as Bill Plante, the elegant long-time CBS News White House correspondent and wine lover, told us about rushing down the aisles of a giant Costco store early in the morning because it was selling Tignanello, one of Italy's most famous red wines, for just $30.

When we think of cherry picking, we think of some great Burgundies we found for $1.99 each, a 1970 Château d'Yquem we found for just $30, and this:

One of the famous wines of the '70s was something called Ice Wine from Chateau Ste. Michelle in Washington State, now one of the state's biggest wineries and still one of the best. Ice wine—real ice wine, because there are fakes out there—is rare. Winemakers, often in Canada and Germany ("ice wine" is derived from the German word "*Eiswein*"), leave a few grapes on a few vines after all the others have been harvested. Then they wait for frost. When the grapes freeze, only a tiny amount of concentrated, sweet juice remains. From this, they make precious amounts of very expensive, and exquisite, wine. The fact that Ste. Michelle had made an ice wine from its Riesling was remarkable. It was so rare it was sold in half bottles, and ordinary mortals, like us, couldn't hope ever to taste it.

We were living in Miami at the time, and we went to a Cuban restaurant called 27 & 27 every weekend, sitting at the counter, nursing our *café con leche* and reading the newspaper. In the middle of the counter, where the waitresses worked, was an island, where they cut that delicious Cuban bread and kept desserts in a refrigerated case. On top of that there were always a couple dozen bottles of wine, mostly Spanish and mostly just for show. One morning, John saw something new. He couldn't believe it. It was the Chateau Ste. Michelle Ice Wine 1978. For $3.50.

Cherry picking is a very delicate art. When you make a great discovery, it's very important not to appear excited. You might raise the curiosity of the shopkeeper, who might then jack up the price. John whispered to Dottie what he'd seen, his lips barely moving. She, too, was agog—quietly. After a couple of minutes, we called over the waitress. "Um," said John, "that looks like an interesting wine. Is this price [his voice was so tight he could barely talk] correct?" The waitress didn't have a clue. So she held up the bottle and, in Spanish, yelled something across to the man at the other end of the restaurant. Soon, everyone who worked there crowded around our bottle, and us. They didn't much care about the price. They wondered who was interested in wine at nine in the morning. Three dollars and fifty cents was indeed the correct price. We bought two, all they had.

We drank the first for Christmas in 1986: "Delicious! Sweet apricot nose, golden rich color. Burnt orange. Intense nectar taste. Huge, long finish. Sweet, rich, and luscious." We still have the second bottle. And even if we never drink it, it has been worth far more than $3.50.

Then, of course, there's Lu's. If you ever want to see a silly grin come across our faces, just say, "So, tell me about Lu's."

We were at a Shell's City liquor shop in Miami, in 1985, when we spied a Champagne we'd never seen. It had a horrible little label, bright red and white, that just said "Lu's." No vintage. But it said it was from Épernay, one of France's great Champagne towns, and it looked real, and was just $9.99, so we bought it. Oh, man. It was delicious: nutty, creamy, with a real sense of fullness and richness that could only come from age. We went back and bought a case. Lu's quickly became our house wine. We kept a bottle in the refrigerator all the time. On any whim, we'd give one to friends, who would then rush out and buy a case of Lu's. When one Shell's City store would run out of Lu's, we'd find another that still had some, and buy a couple more cases.

Finally, sadly, it became harder and harder to find Lu's, and then it disappeared. We even sent a letter to Lu's—just "Épernay, France"—but it was returned, undeliverable. And that was the end of that, until several years later.

One day we were spending a few hours looking through a wine store, trying to find something new and interesting. There on the shelf was a very expensive Maxim's Champagne, with a lovely, artistic label. "We've never seen this before," we said. "Is it new?" The shopkeeper explained that Maxim's had tried once before to break into the South Florida market. "They brought their 1964 in here a few years ago," he explained, "but it was so expensive nobody would buy it. So they slapped some sort of awful label on it and basically gave it away. It was some stupid name. I can't remember it." He yelled across to one of his associates: "Hey, remember that '64 Maxim's? What did they call it?"

The associate yelled back, "I think it was Lu's. Yeah, that's it. They called it Lu's."

Chapter Twenty

Barolo

Perfect for Winter—or a Castaway

We conducted an on-line chat once just as Tom Hanks's movie *Cast Away* hit the screens, so maybe it was inevitable that someone would ask us what one bottle of wine we'd want to have if we were stranded on a desert island. We looked at each other for a moment, shrugged as if the answer were the most obvious thing in the world, and said to each other at the same time: "Barolo."

This may seem like an odd choice. We think red Burgundy, when it's just right, is the most romantic wine in the world; Sauternes can be the most majestic; and Champagne would certainly seem appropriate to a day on the beach. What's more, Barolo, the great red wine from the Piedmont region of Italy, is so massive that it might seem too challenging under such already challenging circumstances. And it would clearly overpower a modest meal of raw fish and coconut.

The reason we answered the way we did, though, is that Barolo, to us, is a particularly life-affirming and enriching experience. Made from Nebbiolo grapes, which are named for the fog that rolls in over the vineyards, it's an extraordinary red wine, truly magical. A good Barolo has plenty of fruit, but it's so tightly wound that it seems almost concentrated, sinewy. It has a taste of the earth, a soul and a power that make it special, along with a notable bricklike color, a muscular taste, and a very dry finish. There's something about Barolo that touches us deep in our souls. It's as though its tastes and smells register in our hearts, not in our mouths.

Incredibly, that becomes even more pronounced as the wine ages. Most wines, as they get older, get rounder, softer, and more approachable. Barolo gets tighter as it withdraws into the essence of itself. The sense of the earth becomes even more pronounced. What you get is pure fruit, with the wisdom of the grape.

In Miami, there's a terrific restaurant named La Bussola that allowed us to keep our own wines in its cellar along with its own excellent collection. On January 2, 1987, over dinner there, we opened our own 1971 Barolo from Casa Vinicola Dosio to share with the restaurant's owner. Our notes on this sixteen-year-old wine: "Totally closed up and overwhelming. After ten minutes, hints of fruit. First real taste only after twenty minutes. A little bitterness. Hard and austere. That's clearly how it was made. Muscular. Unyielding. Yet a hint of 'sweet' fruit. Concentrated. After one hour, delicious. Tough, with a long, hot finish. Lots of fruit and wood. Raisiny. The essence of Italian fruit."

Even on the nose, Barolo is notable for its earthiness. You can almost taste those Italian hills, and we think that's one reason why Barolo makes us want to rush out and eat earthy foods with it—richly herbed meats or pasta. Consider this:

Preparing to embark on our first blind tasting of Barolo, John uncorked the first flight of wines and then, as always, put each bottle in a paper bag so we wouldn't know what they were. Soon, the aroma of Barolo filled the kitchen, and so John thought, Hmmm, I should make some risotto. Since he was making risotto, he figured, Heck, I might as well make some veal scaloppini. Then our little Zoë, seeing this, decided she would make the salad, and she proceeded to create a masterpiece, with a selection of cheeses on the side. And then John and Zoë thought that, well, since they had done all that, they might as well make it special for Dorothy and Media, so they served it by candlelight.

This is the effect Barolo has on us, and on many other people, too. Barolo isn't just a wine. In each bottle is also a place and a lifestyle that includes lusty food and an appreciation of nature's gifts. Sometime during winter, you really need to rush out and buy a Barolo. It's expensive, but so very special that it's worth it, especially with one of your most special meals.

There aren't that many big Barolo producers, so this is one wine that you can get to know fairly easily. The top names—Ceretto, Gaja, Aldo

Conterno, and some others—can be expensive. For our most recent blind tasting, we collected all the Barolos we could find under $50. Few stores offer many, and it's rare to see the same one twice, since no producer makes very much, but we ultimately found plenty for a tasting. These aren't wines that we could taste in huge flights anyway. They're relatively high in alcohol (about 13.5 percent to 14 percent), and the power of their concentrated earth and fruit tastes demands that you take small sips and that you pay attention to them from the first sip to the last. They have such interesting and complex tastes beneath that brawny exterior. In our tasting, marvelously contradictory notes kept flowing, like "rich yet austere" and "sweet fruit and dry finish." We also commented regularly about raisins, dryness, nice acidity, and long, dusty finishes.

We were sure this would be the best of tasting when we had it: "Charming and challenging. Lots of fruit but also lots of earth tightly wound into an indescribable whole. A wine you can't ignore. On the one hand, easy because of the fruit, but when you swallow you know it's serious. Good acids for food. Could live forever." This was the Parusso "Piccole Vigne." Parusso is a reliable name in Barolo and Dolcetto (see Chapter Twenty-two). But another reliable name eclipsed it. "Sweet fruit yet tightly wound," we wrote, "without the dark, brooding quality of many. Cherry fruit, but so dry it seems like dust on the finish—maybe the driest wine we've ever tasted. Remarkable balance of fruit, tannin, and acid. It's like a meal." This was Marcarini "La Serra," which cost $41.49.

After our tasting was over, we thought we'd conduct one last experiment. The next night, we opened an old Barolo—from the 1971 vintage—from our own collection. It was from Poderi e Cantine di Marengo. And here is the amazing thing: If we had opened it as part of our blind tasting, we doubt we would have known it was more than two decades older than the other wines. It was incredible: very intense, filled with hard-candy fruit. After John took his first sip, he slapped himself in the face. This, like all good Barolos, is a wine for all of the senses, truly one of the greatest experiences in wine drinking.

With its rich, intense fruit, Barolo always makes us hungry, and when we are, our thoughts often turn to rich roasted meats, grilled vegetables, polenta, crusty bread, herbs, olives, and a superb olive oil. Barolo is a legendary wine because of its power, its long life, and its uniqueness, and because of the effect it has on some people—like us. It's one of those wines that simply makes life special, whether on a desert island or the island of Manhattan.

A postscript: The other great red wine of Piedmont is Barbaresco. In our minds, a great Barbaresco can be even more wonderful than a Barolo because it has an extra complexity that engages the intellect as well as the soul. What we've found, though, is that it's just about impossible to find an affordable Barbaresco in the United States that walks that line between power and finesse. It's worth trying to find a great Barbaresco, but your search may be a difficult one.

Wine Notes

General advice: Barolo is intense and big, especially in its youth, so you need to serve it with lusty food—and be careful, because it tends to be high in alcohol. There are some great producers—Ceretto, Gaja, Aldo Conterno, for instance—but they tend to be expensive. Buy old Barolo if you can, since it ages beautifully. If you buy young Barolo, be sure to pour a couple of glasses, take a sip, and then let the wine breathe for maybe an hour or so before you plan to drink it. "Riserva" on the label means it was aged in barrels for a long time, making it an even more intense experience. If you can bear to leave a little in the bottom of the bottle, try it the next night.

Food pairings: Meats—roasted, herbed, and sauced—and other hearty winter foods. Game.

Marcarini "La Serra." **$41.49.** DELICIOUS. Best of tasting. "Sweet" cherry fruit, tightly wound and dry at the same time. Lovely acids. Remarkable balance, and so complex it's like a meal. (1996)

Luigi Einaudi. **$29.99.** VERY GOOD. Best value. Really good fruit, with nice, lemony acids and just the right amount of dryness. Grapey, earthy, and beautifully balanced. Not as serious as some, but it's all there. (1995)

Parusso "Piccole Vigne." **$44.99.** DELICIOUS. Charming and challenging at the same time. Filled with fruit, but also filled with earth, tightly wound into a delicious whole. A wine you can't ignore, with approachable fruit at the front and an explosion of tastes at the end. Could live forever. (1996)

M. Marengo "Brunate." **$49.99.** VERY GOOD/DELICIOUS. Plums and earth. Tight and powerful, and almost like it has been steeped in rosemary and other herbs. It was even better the next day, creamy and luscious. Wow. (1996)

Marziano Abbona "Vigneto Terlo Ravera." **$39.99.** VERY GOOD/DE-LICIOUS. Rich, with fruit, with plenty of backbone and character. Easy to drink yet almost regal. (1996)

Damilano. **$32.99.** VERY GOOD/DELICIOUS. Lots of lovely, raisiny fruit. Tight structure and a loooong finish with some nice acidity. Dry enough to make us pucker. Not as giving as some. (1995)

Camerano "Cannubi San Lorenzo." **$29.99.** VERY GOOD. Raisiny and, after a while, deceptively easy to drink, so pleasant and easy yet so serious at the same time. (1995)

Gianfranco Bovio "Vigna Gattera." **$44.99.** GOOD/VERY GOOD. Lots of earthy fruit and a nice dark-cherry taste, though lacking the complexity of some. (1995)

Pira. **$39.99.** VERY GOOD. Still quite hard, but quite drinkable nonetheless. A hint of bitterness makes it interesting. (1996)

Paolo Scavino. **$39.99.** GOOD/VERY GOOD. Young and tight, but with a nice core of ripe fruit. (1994)

Prunotto. **$43.99.** GOOD/VERY GOOD. Sweet tar, earth, and plenty of acids combine into a fascinating mouthful. (1996)

The "Other" States of Wine:
The Vineyard Next Door

Looking back over our wine labels, even we are surprised how many wines we've had from states you might not associate with winemaking. We have had wine from Florida and Hawaii, from Idaho and Rhode Island, from New Mexico, Arizona, and Georgia. Virginia is getting a great deal of attention for its wines at the moment. Missouri has quite a few wineries. We were once members of Wine of the Month clubs for wineries in both Illinois and Indiana. We could go on and on, but the point is this: Wine—sometimes very good wine—is made all over the United States. There's probably a winery not far from you. What we've found is that anyone who tries to start a winery in an "other" state is likely to be someone of real personality, passion, and conviction, and those qualities often add up to wine with soul.

One of the up-and-coming wine regions of the United States is Long Island, New York. We have been visiting there since 1990, so we've seen the industry grow from a small number of pioneers to a much larger number of people with money and marketing muscle. These wineries hold an annual public tasting for charity in Manhattan, and we attend every year. Among scores of wines at the 2001 tasting, we were most impressed by one: a 1997 Merlot from Ternhaven Cellars. Many people argue that Merlot will be Long Island's great grape, but we don't buy it. We find the Cabernet Franc from Long Island to be consistently better. But this wine was certainly an exception: classy, with the structure of a fine Bordeaux and lush fruit that left a long, scrumptious finish. Ternhaven is a good example of the small wineries that dot the whole American landscape. It's housed in a tiny tasting room in little Greenport, New York, and its owner, winemaker, and tasting room manager is Harold Watts, who opened the winery while working at his "real" job as an economics professor at Columbia University.

To dramatically make our point that good wine is being made

everywhere, during the 2000 presidential race we conducted our first "Presidential Taste-Off" between the wines of Texas, George W. Bush's home state, and Tennessee, Vice President Al Gore's home state. We conducted our tasting in Washington, D.C., just down the road from the White House. We invited several wine lovers and a special guest: Representative George Radanovich, a Republican from California's Central Valley, the only commercial winemaker in Congress. Radanovich Vineyards & Winery is a 4,000-case winery that specializes in Sauvignon Blanc, Cabernet Sauvignon, Chardonnay, Merlot, and Zinfandel.

We asked the state wine associations to choose twelve of their best wines and send them to us for a blind, head-to-head tasting. To be honest, all of us approached this tasting with some apprehension. Although we were somewhat aware of the Texas wine industry— John wrote about it in 1983 for *Newsweek* and we've had the state's wines off and on for years—none of us had ever tasted a wine from Tennessee, although a few of us were acquainted with the state's other, more popular spirits.

Here's the good news: As we ate, drank, and talked about the wines, our respect for the winemakers grew. "This is surprisingly difficult," said Rep. Radanovich, and he was right. Of the five best whites, three were from Tennessee, though the best white was a Chardonnay from Llano Estacado Winery, one of the granddaddies of Texas winemaking. All four of the red finalists were from Texas, including our favorite, a Merlot from Fall Creek Vineyards of Tow, Texas. The overall winner was Texas, which gave us 100 percent accuracy in predicting the outcome of presidential elections.

But the larger point was proved: Both Texas and Tennessee wines showed well, proving again that good wines are being made everywhere. Unfortunately, the wines of one state are often unavailable in others, even states right next door, but at least you can buy the wines from the winery just down the street. You really should give them a try.

Chianti

Life and Depth in Tuscany

Chianti. Makes you smile to yourself, doesn't it? Chianti is Tuscany, big Italian meals, straw-covered bottles with dripping candles, happy times at the cozy little restaurant around the corner. But when was the last time you bought a bottle of Chianti to take home? It has probably been a while, which is a shame considering how much Americans like to cook Italian food. Maybe this is because, for years, Chianti suffered the same fate as Chablis, the marvelous white wine from France. Just about every cheap red jug wine in America seemed to be called Chianti if it wasn't called Burgundy. The name became generic for "cheap red wine." Poor real Chianti, which is made in a zone of Italy called Chianti.

Maybe it's because many people think of Chianti, even the real thing, as only a simple quaffing wine, and, of course, much of it is just that. But Chianti, in many ways, is not the wine we grew up with. The Chianti area itself has made huge strides in quality in the past couple of decades, and now, as we discovered in a large tasting, it is making classy, elegant wines that are still real bargains.

The great grape of Chianti is Sangiovese, whose name gives an idea how ancient it is: "sanguis Jovis," the blood of Jupiter. Sangiovese has a core of cherry-raspberry fruit that gives the wine a mouth-popping vibrancy. It tends to be tannic, dry, and slightly acidic. Some Chiantis have an attractive rustic quality about them, while the best also have a Bordeaux-like structure, which means you can almost taste the layers and edges. There is often a toasted-roasted quality and some nice spices, and, as Dottie said during one of our tastings, "some of them taste like they should be cinnamon-colored." An interesting combination of fruity liveliness and underlying depth is one of the things that makes Chianti so fetching to us.

When we drink Chianti, we almost always say at some point, "This tastes like red bricks." We've actually never eaten a red brick, but if you can imagine what a red brick smells, feels, and could possibly taste like, you can begin to imagine part of the taste of a good Chianti. All that said, Chianti covers a wide range of wines. The Sangiovese grape itself is variable, and different winemakers and different regions make different Chiantis, some with a little bit of this grape and some with a little bit of that. Chianti was traditionally made with at least some white-wine grapes, and many Chiantis still are. There are different regions within Chianti and even different laws governing what grapes can be used where, and how much of each. "Riserva" means the wine has been aged longer. In all, with Chianti's history going back to the twelfth or thirteenth century, whole books have been written trying to sort out the various rules and regulations that have come and gone over the years.

When we think of Chianti, we always think of an experience we had in Tuscany. We were staying at the elegant Villa Le Barone in Panzano in Chianti. Driving up and down hills, trying to get our bearings, we had passed a small, rustic restaurant that looked charming. Bruno, the concierge at the villa, made reservations for us, and we soon found ourselves in what was basically a farmhouse, with family-style seating, rough-hewn food, and rougher-hewn waiters who looked like farmers. The restaurant was part of a winery, and its various vintages of Chianti were listed in pencil on the menu. We couldn't believe it: They had both 1975, a very good year, and 1971, an even better year.

With the waiter who spoke no English looking over our shoulders, we pointed to the 1971. You would've thought we'd made some sort of indecent proposal! Dark eyes flashing and lips a bit tight, he shook his head violently and pointed to the 1975. Taking his rather forceful hint, we ordered the '75. Heck, we were almost afraid not to. It was delicious: vibrant, fruity, alive, and perfect with our roast pigeon. We enjoyed it so much that we wanted our waiter to try it. He poured himself a glass—the wine was served in plain water glasses—and he clearly was pleased with how beautiful it still tasted in 1986.

But we kept thinking about that '71. It was right there. If the '75 was that good, what must the '71 taste like? We called the waiter back over and, despite his objections—frankly, he could have blown a gasket; nothing was going to stand between us and that wine—we ordered it. It was magnificent, surely the most special Chianti we'd ever had: deep, big, rich, chewy, with a vibrating core of fruit. It was very different from the other wine, far more serious, with excellent structure. Again, we called the waiter over and offered him a glass. He shook his head. We kept trying. He kept shaking his head. We never did get him to taste the '71. Maybe he just didn't like that style of Chianti. It was an important lesson for us about how very different one Chianti can be from another.

But if Chiantis can be so different that even our own waiter liked one and not another from the same winery, what should you do? We'd offer this advice to make it simpler: Look for "Chianti Classico" on the label—that's the most famous region—or, even simpler, look for a neck seal with a black rooster on it, which is the sign of Chianti Classico. Plan to spend more than you'd expect, maybe $15 to $25. That might seem like a lot, but at a time when many people are used to spending almost that much on undistinguished, unmemorable wines, this is a small price to pay for wines that have the class of Bordeaux, the earthiness of Tuscany, and the kind of ripe fruit that many Americans love. Not only that, but they're great with food.

We bought several cases of Chiantis in all price ranges and tasted them blind. It was clear they were all related—kind of like an extended family in which everybody has the same eyes. No matter what other tastes were present in the wines, their core—the Sangiovese grape—was always evident. In this tasting, only one of the wines under $10 rated more than "Good" on our scale, the easy-to-drink Aziano from Ruffino ($8.95), which we rated "Good/Very Good." In past tastings, and in our real life, we have found inexpensive offerings from Viticcio to be reliable. Another great deal from Tuscany is Santa Cristina from Antinori, which is not a Chianti but is made from Sangiovese and a little Merlot. These wines tend to be simple and fun to drink. As Dottie said about the Viticcio during an earlier tasting: "It doesn't shoot for complexity. It's just a big mouthful of fruit—and it makes you smile." What could possibly be wrong with that?

For a few dollars more, we found wine after wine that was excellent, with special layers of flavors. Every one turned out to be a Chianti Classico, and some are fairly widely available, including the Ruffino Riserva Ducale, with the familiar gold label. It was also one of our favorites in an earlier tasting, in 1998, and continues to be an outstanding buy.

Remarkably, three of the wines rated "Delicious" on our scale. How would you choose among these three?

(1) "Classy, fruity and complete. Soulful yet also elegant. Clearly expensive, with cut-glass tastes. Lots of vibrant Sangiovese fruit but also lots of structure."

(2) "Serious wine. Dark as night. Structured. Fabulous, long, elegant finish. Round. Not a gulping Chianti. There's some deceptive softness there, and then suddenly some fire in the glass. A wow wine."

(3) "Very serious yet very easy to drink. Classy. Really good fruit with a vibrating core of Sangiovese, but a dark chocolate cover, like a chocolate-covered cherry. Long, structured finish. Yum."

No. 1 was Santedame 1998, which is made by Ruffino. It was $22.49, and we ultimately decided it was the second runner-up. We went back and forth on the other two, and never did decide, though price ultimately came into play. No. 2 was Fonterutoli 1998, which was $22.39. This was also one of our favorites in our 1998 tasting. The other best-of-tasting was clearly the best value: Isole e Olena 1998, which was $17.95. It puts most wines at the same price to shame.

It's impossible to know what Chianti you will find at your local store. Some stores carry only the lower-end stuff because it sells faster, while some stores specialize in good, more expensive Italian wine. Next time you cook Italian, just get a good Chianti. You really will be surprised.

Wine Notes

General advice: Look for "Chianti Classico" on the label, or just a black rooster on the neck ring. (That's the sign of the Chianti Classico association. Not every Chianti Classico producer is a member of the association.) Some of the most common names, such as Ruffino and Antinori, are consistently reliable. Good Chianti ages well.

Food matches: Pizza, for less expensive Chianti. Pasta, of course. Roasted meats and game.

Isole e Olena Chianti Classico. $17.95. DELICIOUS. Best of tasting (tie). A very serious wine that's also easy to drink, with a rich outer layer and a vibrating core of red fruit inside, like a great chocolate-covered cherry. Long, complex finish that lasts forever. (1998)

Fonterutoli Chianti Classico. $22.39. DELICIOUS. Best of tasting (tie). Serious wine. Dark as night, serious, elegant, and warming. Outrageously rich fruit and a long, lovely finish. Deceptive softness. Great with food. Could age for a very long time. Wow. (1998)

Dievole Chianti Classico. $14.95. VERY GOOD. Best value. Earthy and rich, with a hint of blackberries. A lovely core of fruit, but deep, dark, and rich. Serious stuff. A wine to enjoy in small sips, and a great deal. Tastes expensive. (1998)

Santedame Chianti Classico (Ruffino). $22.49. DELICIOUS. Classy, structured, and complete, with vibrant fruit. Soulful yet elegant. Clearly expensive, with sharp tastes and a nice balance of Sangiovese fruit and real structure. (1998)

Collelungo Chianti Classico. $19.95. VERY GOOD. Nice fruit and surprising acids. Quite young. Confidently fruity and fun, with big, plummy tastes. Soul-satisfying. (1998)

La Massa Chianti Classico. $22.95. VERY GOOD. A particularly attractive nose that transported us right to Tuscany. Effortlessly classy. Calm and easy. Nicely complex, and nothing rustic about it. (1998)

Querceto Chianti Classico. $13.89. VERY GOOD. Easy to drink and so very pleasant. Dottie was especially fond of this. She said it tasted like fruit, with no edges and just ripe friendliness. John found it pleasant but too simple. (1998)

Ruffino Riserva Ducale Chianti Classico. $19.95. VERY GOOD. Remarkably mouth-drying, with nice tannins. Lively cherrylike fruit, but tight and challenging, with plenty of edges. This is serious stuff. (1997)

Aziano (Ruffino) Chianti Classico. $8.95. GOOD/VERY GOOD. Easy to drink, with plenty of varietal fruit. Not too intense, but not too "Beaujolais-style," either. Just right. (1999)

Chapter Twenty-two

Dolcetto

One of the World's Happiest Wines

Wine should be as much fun as an antipasto. Think about this for a second: a big platter of thinly sliced Genoa salami and provolone cheese, sweet roasted peppers, black olives, very crisp lettuce, maybe some anchovies and a sprinkling of olive oil—oh, gosh. It's not just that this is a delicious dish with a kind of soul-satisfying earthiness, but it's also fun to eat. The wine should match the dish—not just the flavors of the dish, but the spirit of it. Good news: The perfect wine for that fun antipasto does exist, and it's not even expensive because so few people have heard of it. It's Dolcetto, from the Piedmont region of Italy. It's one of those wines that we work hard to get people to try because we're sure they could fall in love with it, though it can be fickle.

Dolcetto is the name of the grape, not a place (that's why you will occasionally, but not often, find a wine called Dolcetto from the United States). The wine it makes is charming, with its deep purple color, ample tannins, and vibrant, fruity tastes that sometimes remind us of blackberries, black cherries, and even plums with a dash of lemon. Occasionally, we'll pick up some sultry creaminess in the taste. The wine's aggressive fruitiness often gives the impression of sweetness, but it's actually quite dry, so dry in fact that the wine occasionally seems to have a dusty finish. The same glass of Dolcetto (dol-CHEH-toh) can be coquettish, very serious, and easily drinkable before it's empty.

Many wines taste better with food, and Dolcetto is definitely one of them. Food gives its flavors some grounding, while the wine gives any meal more life. Did we say "life"? If you've never had a Dolcetto, it's hard to describe just what we mean by this. This wine seems to leap out of the glass. It's alive, it's fresh, it's fruity, and it's meant to be drunk young.

Few wine stores carry more than two or three Dolcettos. The ones that you're most likely to see on shelves are Dolcetto d'Alba, but we've often had luck with Dolcetto di Dogliani, from a town called Dogliani, just a stone's throw from Alba. We had the best sandwich of our lives at a street fair in Dogliani years ago, a freshly carved pork sandwich on bread that had been slathered with a soft and sweet garlic clove. We can't look at a bottle of Dolcetto di Dogliani without smiling at that delicious memory.

We conduct a large tasting of Dolcetto every year because—well, frankly, because we really enjoy it, though we find this wine is particularly ill suited to "tasting," as opposed to drinking. Choosing one over another is like choosing one beautiful flower over another. Who can choose among a bouquet of gloriously colored, fragrant blossoms? Because these wines don't show well without food, we customarily take the winners of our blind flights to the dinner table to really enjoy them.

In our first tasting, back in 1998, our best of tasting was Alario Claudio e Matteo Dolcetto di Diano d'Alba (Costa Fiore) and our best value was G. D. Vajra Dolcetto d'Alba. Both were then under $10. In a later tasting, two stood out. One had cream, depth, and soulful fruit. It was oh so easy to drink. This is the one we ended up drinking for dinner one night with Dottie's spaghetti with sausage and shrimp in anchovy butter sauce. It was Giuseppe Cortese Dolcetto d'Alba. At $10.99, we promise you that this is far more interesting, lively, and life-fulfilling than what you're used to buying for $10. Our best of tasting, in a flight a couple of days later, was pretty well perfect. Here are our notes, taken over about an hour, before dinner and then with Dottie's famous chicken with mushroom sauce. "Interesting. Cream. Lots of fruity fruit. Jammy. Long, cream-fruit finish and some menthol! 'This could hurt you,' Dottie says. 'It's intoxicating, heady stuff.' Seductive. Lively, yet deep." This was Elio Altare Dolcetto d'Alba, for $18.99.

In our most recent tasting, we once again craved food to have with this great food wine, so we twice ordered in Brazilian chicken from the place down the street ($8 for a whole chicken, roasted with the most delicious herbs and spices). There's something about the wine's cool, fruity creaminess that makes it a good match with piquant dishes. That's why we often order a Dolcetto at Indian restaurants.

All of the wines were dark, but some were seriously dark, almost black. A few were so simple that we said they were like red Pinot Grigio. Most were extremely pleasant and easy to drink, with a complex combination of soft round fruit and spirited, mouth-drying tannins. Some, to our surprise, were quite serious, with edges, elegance, and structure that we don't usually associate with Dolcetto. The Ceretto, for instance, was extremely classy, with ripe, dark, brooding fruit, plenty of lemon, some soil, and real structure. Not surprisingly, it was more charming and lighter on its feet with food, but, geez, what a wine. This could age, which we wouldn't usually say about a Dolcetto. (Whenever you are looking for Italian wine, Ceretto is a good name to remember.)

Both our best of tasting and our best value, as it happened, were from Dogliani. The Patrizi ($9.99) was a makes-you-smile wine, lovely, charming, and pleasant, with approachable fruit. "Who wouldn't like this?" Dottie said as we drank it. The best of tasting was the most expensive wine we bought. We hate it when that happens, but it does happen. We had it toward the end of our tasting. Until then, we'd enjoyed quite a few of the wines, but hadn't had one yet that rang all of our bells. This did. "Just what you'd want," we wrote. "Lots of fruit, with some cream and softness. Crisp, lovely, and nicely fruity, with real edges and very ripe berries." This was Luigi Einaudi "I Filari," which cost $26.99. Luigi Einaudi also produced the best value of our Barolo tasting (see Chapter Twenty), so this is a good name to look for, too.

These are fun wines, but they're not frivolous. Next time you make an Italian meal at home, pick one up. Better yet, pick one up tonight and then shop for an Italian meal. When you're at a nice Italian restaurant and you're handed a wine list filled with unrecognizable words, look for Dolcetto. It tends to be less expensive than the more serious stuff from Italy, like Barolo, and even the better-known stuff, like Chianti. Better still, good restaurants often have outstanding, small-production, young Dolcettos that you may never find in stores.

$$\mathcal{W}ine\ \mathcal{N}otes$$

General advice: Buy the most recent vintage you can find. If you happen to see "Dolcetto di Dogliani" on the label, that's often a good sign. Repeat favorites in our tastings over the years include Elio Altare, Francesco Boschis, and Parusso. The list below includes our most recent tasting and also an earlier tasting, to give you a broader idea of some of the good names in Dolcetto. We have updated the prices of the wines in the earlier tasting to reflect more recent vintages, if more recent vintages are available; the vintage we tasted is included in parentheses.
Food pairings: Antipasto and other Italian dishes. Sausage. We like Dolcetto with Indian food, though that's a controversial choice.

Luigi Einaudi Dolcetto di Dogliani "I Filari." $26.99. DELICIOUS. Best of tasting. Just what we look for in a Dolcetto. Plenty of fruit, with a little cream and softness, yet crisp and ripe at the same time. (1998)

Elio Altare Dolcetto d'Alba. $16.99. DELICIOUS. Best value. Rich, with a core of ripe fruit. Lively yet deep, with real spirit. (1998)

Giuseppe Cortese Dolcetto d'Alba. $10.99. VERY GOOD/DELICIOUS. Cream, depth, and soulful fruit. Lovely. Perfect with dinner. (1998)

Mauro Veglio Dolcetto d'Alba. $13.99. VERY GOOD/DELICIOUS. Pleasant and fruity with a dose of real "stuff" that gives it nice body. (1998)

Patrizi Dolcetto di Dogliani. $9.99. VERY GOOD. Makes you smile. Lively fruit, lemon, and soul. Oh-so-pleasant and approachable. Who wouldn't like this? (1999)

Ceretto Dolcetto d'Alba "Rossana." $23.99. VERY GOOD. Classy, serious, and surprisingly well structured. Dark, with lemon, ripe fruit, and some soil. Bing cherries, almost brooding. Surprising. Could age. Great with food. (1999)

Chionetti Dolcetto di Dogliani "Briccolero." $18.99. VERY GOOD. Rich, with blackberries and a little cream. Lovely, and it has substance, too. (1998)

Seghesio Dolcetto d'Alba "Vigneto Della Chiesa." $14.99. VERY GOOD. Aggressive blackberry fruit, with a combination of intensity and easy drinkability that's quite special. A wine of real backbone, earth, and seriousness that's pleasant at the same time—a neat trick. (1999)

Parusso Dolcetto d'Alba "Piani Noce." $15.99. VERY GOOD. Deep, dark, and ripe, serious yet charming, with nice acids and some edges. Needs food. (1998; we also liked the 1999)

Paolo Scavino Dolcetto d'Alba. $19.99. VERY GOOD. Big and plump, yet with some real class. (1998)

Corino Dolcetto d'Alba. $14.99. VERY GOOD. Candylike fruit, "sweet" with cherries, and fun. (1998)

Sandrone Dolcetto d'Alba. $23.99. GOOD/VERY GOOD. Creamy, fruity, and a bit rich. Grapey and charming, though maybe a bit too acidic. (1999)

Francesco Boschis "Sorì San Martino" Dolcetto di Dogliani. $15.99. GOOD/VERY GOOD. Nice, dry, dusty taste underneath sweet fruit. There's real stuff in there. (1998)

Francesco Boschis "Pianezzo" Dolcetto di Dogliani. $10.99. GOOD/VERY GOOD. Heavier than most and aggressively fruity, with some soil and mineral tastes. (1998)

Clerico "Visadi" Langhe Dolcetto. $13.99. GOOD/VERY GOOD. A bit hard, but with a combination of fruit, soil, and depth that's attractive. (1998)

Pio Cesare Dolcetto d'Alba. $22.00. GOOD/VERY GOOD. The fruit is all up front, and there's a lot of it. (1998)

Shiraz

Rhymes with Razzmatazz

We first wrote about Shiraz from Australia, a big red wine of real character, back in 1998. As we said then, Shiraz is the same grape as Syrah, which makes full-bodied wines in France and, increasingly, in the United States. We predicted then that Shiraz was about to be a big deal—the headline in the newspaper was "From Down Under, the Next Merlot"—and, fortunately, we were right, at least to a point (it's nice when that happens). In fact, one of our readers, Dr. Frank Stefanec, a pediatrician from Poland, Ohio, told us that he ordered a Merlot at a restaurant and the waiter suggested that he try a Shiraz instead. "I really enjoyed it," he added. When we were visiting Dottie's mother in northern Florida and dropped into a modest waterfront restaurant in Eastpoint called That Place on 98, we couldn't help but notice this on the wine list:

"Rosemount Estate. Shiraz (Australian Merlot). Bottle $23."

While Shiraz and Merlot grapes actually have little in common, they're both showing up everywhere these days, and Shiraz, like Merlot, is being used more and more in blends. We see Shiraz/Grenache and Shiraz/Cabernet Sauvignon and even Shiraz/Malbec. While Shiraz can be very expensive, it can also be one of the best bargains around—and, in fact, this is a case where cheaper is sometimes better. Let us explain that.

Australians call this she-RAZZ. Going back to the point we made in the chapter on Viognier, we used to say she-RAHZ, but then we heard someone from an Australian wine group talk about the wine and she said she-

RAZZ. Who knew? In any event, it can be an awesome wine, huge, aggressive, and warming. It has tastes of blackberries and raspberries, with maybe a little bit of chocolate and spice. At its best, it can be so intense that it tastes a little like fermented black pepper, with a long, memorable, rich, berry finish that leaves your whole body feeling red. A very good Shiraz seems alive in your glass the way few wines do. In fact, Australia's most famous wine—and one of the most famous wines in the world—is a Shiraz, and we'll never forget our first taste of it. It was during a rare romantic week together.

We hadn't spent much time alone together since we had kids. But when we finally figured Media and Zoë could do without us for a few days, we asked our nanny to stay with them for a week so we could have a getaway and do what an old married couple like us loves best: eat, drink wine, and sleep without interruption. We checked into the Mayflower Inn in Washington, Connecticut, which had a fireplace in the bedroom that breathed flames at the flip of a switch, a mattress that was about six feet high, snow on its rolling hills, and an elegant little restaurant. There on the wine list was something extraordinary and rare: a 1986 Penfolds Grange Hermitage, Australia's most famous red wine, which is made from the Shiraz grape. It was $100, which was actually a bargain. On some lists, it can cost several times as much. We didn't order the wine the first night, but on the second day we told the innkeepers to plan our whole evening around it.

First, at six, with Dottie resplendent in a green crushed-velvet gown, we sat by a fireplace in a cozy sitting room and drank the first sips of the wine. Holy cow! It was huge and mouth-filling, but with a brawny elegance that made it unique. After an hour, we moved into the dining room, where for hours over squab and other dishes we continued to sip—and we do mean sip. This is a wine that, like a martini, cannot be gulped. The wine was delicious throughout, and never lost that massive, fruity, blackberry intensity. By the fire, at an elegant inn, in the middle of winter, with snow on the ground, alone together—well, a big, red wine just doesn't get much better than that.

More and more California wineries are making Syrah-based wines, too (see Chapter Twenty-seven). While we haven't had one yet that's really great, the appearance of these new California wines is an indication that this grape is coming on strong. Here's another: John had to fly to Chicago to visit the *Wall Street Journal* bureau there and figured he'd drop in (anonymously, of course) on Charlie Trotter's, the restaurant famous for both its food and wine. He asked the waiter to pair each course with a different glass of wine—always a good idea at fancy restaurants—and the sommelier brought out some treasures from France: a grand cru Chablis, an old Meursault-Genevrières, a Vosne-Romanée from Burgundy. He also brought out an Elderton "Command" Shiraz, from Australia, and you know what? It was John's best of tasting. Even without the inn, the fireplace, the snow—and, alas, Dottie who was minding the kids back home—the rich, ripe, forward tastes of the Shiraz, especially with an outstanding autumn dinner, were simply delicious.

For our first blind tasting of Shiraz, we bought every one we could find, regardless of price. What a tasting. The E&E Barossa Valley Estates Black Pepper Shiraz, then $60, was like a kick in the stomach. Back in the '70s, California winemakers experimented with late-harvest Zinfandel. It was overwhelming, alcoholic, and sometimes finished a little sweet. Few were great, but they were always an amazing experience. The E&E reminded us of those days—massive, unyielding, proud to be utterly outsized. Like many Shirazes, it will be better in a few years. In fact, we have a bottle of the E&E in our personal cellar and we've written on it, "Open when Zoë graduates from Harvard." That will be in 2011.

We were sure the best of our tasting would be the Pikes, which we had in one of the first flights. It had the deep, dark fruit of a Shiraz, but the class and complexity of a fine Bordeaux. What a combination! It was delicious, and good right now. But the Pikes turned out not to be best. The Wynns Michael Shiraz was huge, fruity, and dark, but, at the same time, remarkably crisp and clean. As we said in our notes: "Huge but not heavy. Beautifully made. Everything you'd want in a wine. Minerals, fruit, restraint. It's beautiful." It even earned our highest rating, Delicious! But here's the rub: A Shiraz of that intensity would be too big for us to handle most days, especially summer days, when we want a nice red wine with a Flintstone-sized steak from the grill. What to do? Good news: We find that less expensive Shiraz still has that great Shiraz character, but it's more restrained and easier to drink.

For a more recent tasting, we gathered every Australian Shiraz we could find under $20. There are far more Shiraz wines around for that price now than when we conducted our first tasting back in 1998. While there are some small boutique wineries producing Shiraz, there are a few big producers that seem to dominate the market, and their wines are widely available. We found some of the wines way too simple. They tasted like blackberry or raspberry fruit wine, and seemed sweet. Others were simply uninteresting. But most were at least charming, and some were much more than that. There also were some great deals, as little as $5.99 for wines we described variously as "lovely, soft, and easy to drink" (Banrock Station, $5.99), "pleasant and summery—great with a grilled burger" (Rosemount, $10.99) and "approachable, with no rough edges" (Tyrrell's, $7.99).

Our best of tasting didn't turn out to be one of the least expensive, but, at $11.99, it was still a great deal. "Intense and peppery," we wrote. "Easy to drink even though it's big. Warm fruit! Undercurrent of pepper. Fine wine. Soulful, satisfying, comfortable fruit." We also found that this wine, like most of our favorites, got even better as it opened and softened in the glass. This was Seppelt "Terrain Series."

So run out and get an inexpensive Shiraz to have with your hamburgers or steak. If you like it, plan to move up to a slightly more expensive Shiraz with a fine meal during cool weather. In fact, if you ever do get a chance to drink a well-aged Australian red, don't miss it. Back in the mid-'70s, when we'd barely heard of Australian wines, we ran across a 1970 Cabernet Sauvignon with a label that simply said, "Mildara Wines Limited, Coonawarra." It was such a keepsake—a 1970 Cab from Australia—that we couldn't stand to open it until June 22, 1996. Here's what we wrote about this twenty-six-year-old wine:

"Delicious! Wow! Thick, rich, and fiery. *Classic.* Lots of Cab character with classy age and no hint of decay. A real mouthful. Like a classic, old claret. Long finish. Lush, velvety, and sensuous in mouth."

This is what the wines from Down Under can be. Australian wine, and especially Shiraz, is different from anything else. You should get to know it.

Wine Notes

General advice: Big producers of Shiraz, such as Penfolds and the names below, tend to make reliably drinkable, inexpensive wines of character. The first

*notes are from a tasting of Shiraz under $20. The second group of notes are from
an earlier tasting of more expensive Shiraz. We list them to give you some idea of
the remarkable tastes of expensive Shiraz, and to provide a few names to look for.
The prices have been updated to reflect more recent vintages. Expensive Shiraz
could age just about forever, while less expensive Shiraz is good to drink now.*
*Food pairings: Expensive Shiraz: hearty winter foods, roast beef, venison.
Less expensive Shiraz: good with winter food, but also excellent in the summer with
grilled hamburgers and steaks.*

$20 and Under

Seppelt "Terrain Series." $11.99. VERY GOOD. Best of tasting. A sur-
prising combination of intensity and easy drinking. It's like warm fruit,
with an undercurrent of black pepper, all rolled into a soulful, comforting
glass of wine. Give it some time to smooth out in the glass. (1997)

Banrock Station Wines. $7.99. VERY GOOD. Best value. Lovely, soft, and
easy to drink. It doesn't have the class and character of some, but it's a perfect drink-now wine. Great with grilled hamburgers. (1999)

Wolf Blass Wines. $13.00. VERY GOOD. Peppery and interesting, with
really good fruit and some hard edges that make it more challenging than
some, but more interesting, too. (1998)

Tyrrell's Wines Long Flat Shiraz. $10.50. VERY GOOD. Round and
berrylike, with plenty of fruit and a very appealing roasted taste. Quite approachable, with no rough edges. Easy to like. (1998)

Rosemount Estate. $12.99. GOOD/VERY GOOD. Soft, simple, and a bit
grapey, with a little bit of cream and a lot of charm. A slight bit of pepper
gives it extra character. Good for summer cookouts. (1999)

Over $20

Wynns Michael Coonawarra. $21.00. DELICIOUS! Best of tasting. Dark
and rich, with a great nose. Ripe fruit on the nose, like a late-harvest Zin.

Intense, clean, and crisp, yet huge—what a combination: huge but not heavy. Minerals, fruit, and restraint. Beautifully made. Everything you'd want in a wine. Simply beautiful. (1993)

Pikes Clare Valley. $24.99. DELICIOUS. Best value. Dark, rich, and classy, with a long, sweet finish that lasts forever. Tastes fabulously expensive. (1996)

Leasingham Clare Valley. $20.00. VERY GOOD/DELICIOUS. Bright red color—looks just-made. Red, rich, and chewy. Quite young, but it's got everything going for it: blackberry sweetness, taste of the earth, and a long, plump finish. (1995)

Ebenezer Barossa Valley. $23.99. VERY GOOD/DELICIOUS. Dark, rich, sweet with fruit. More forward fruit than some, not as deep. Still, it's better after it has been open for three hours. (1994)

Frankland Estate "Isolation Ridge." $22.99. VERY GOOD. Not as powerful as some others, but classier, with more complexity. There's some real elegance here. Dottie described it as "a little black dress." (1995)

E&E Barossa Valley Black Pepper. $63.00. GOOD. Holy cow, what a wine: Massive, overpowering, remarkable. This is a wine that will blow your head off—and is proud of it. Portlike and simply massive. Have it, in small sips, on a cold night. (1994)

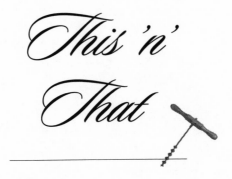

This 'n' That

Chapter Twenty-four

White Zinfandel

How Sweet It Is

Dan Berger is a widely respected wine columnist and a savvy observer of the industry, but he enjoys telling a story about the time he was very, very wrong. It concerns his early experiences with a new wine called White Zinfandel produced by a little Napa Valley winery named Sutter Home. The winery made White Zinfandel for the first time in 1972, and Dan fell in love with it. "It was always released in the summertime and we would just wait for it because it was such a perfect wine for sipping by the pool," he told us. "I'd buy cases of it and we'd have a party that weekend." He remembers the wine as dry, crisp, and delightful. In 1976, Dan was "keen to get details on this wine" so he went to a trade tasting where he knew company officials would be. "I tasted it and it was *sweet!*" he told us with horror. Roger Trinchero, the company's president, was pouring the wine. A disappointed Dan confronted Roger about the change from dry to sweet. "I told him, 'You'll never sell this stuff!'" The rest, of course, is history. Sutter Home's slightly sweet White Zinfandel went on to become a national sensation. "Obviously, my marketing skills left something to be desired," Dan told us with a laugh. "I guess we should never underestimate the American public's desire for sugar."

White Zinfandel was the top varietal wine in America throughout the early 1990s, until it was overtaken by Chardonnay, and it's still the second-most-popular varietal wine. Americans drink about 22 million cases of it every year. White Zinfandel continues to be enormously popular as a simple wine you can drink and not have to think about. It's inexpensive, fun, easy to keep in the refrigerator, and utterly lacking in pretension. People don't sniff and swirl White Zinfandel and rhapsodize about its bouquet, and that's a relief for a wine snob-weary nation. When you're sitting in an inflatable chair in the middle of the pool on a hot day with a plastic cup full of wine, an icy White Zin can be lovely. Still, those who drink it must suffer some indignities. "White Zinfandel is not held in high esteem by wine connoisseurs, but I would like to offer a word in its defense," Tom Kintigh of Tucson, Arizona, wrote us. "My wife suffers from very severe migraine headaches. One glass of most whites or any red puts her in bed for two days. White Zinfandel is the only wine she can drink and enjoy without dreading the next day. One learns to ignore the sommelier's disapproving looks."

Sutter Home was the winery that put White Zin on the map. We were skeptical when we first saw it, way back in the late 1970s. To us, God meant for Zinfandel to be red, bold, and distinctive, though, of course, just about any red grape can be made into blush wine. Almost all grapes are white inside. Contact with the grape skins gives wine its color. If you leave the wine on the skins for a short time, you get a pink, or rosé, or blush, wine. Leave the wine on its skins for a longer time and you get red wine. When we first tasted Sutter Home's White Zinfandel, we were impressed. It was crisp, refreshing, and delightful. On its Web page, Sutter Home recounts the history of White Zinfandel:

> In 1972, Sutter Home winemaker Bob Trinchero was experimenting with ways to make his acclaimed Amador County Reserve Zinfandel more robust. Finally, he drained some free-run juice from the skins before fermentation to increase the ratio of skins to juice. . . . Emulating the French rosés he so admired, Bob fermented the juice to dryness and barrel-aged it before bottling the pale pink elixir as a curiosity item for his tasting room clientele.
>
> Although Bob's customers liked this novel "blanc de noir" table wine, many felt it was too dry. So Bob began leaving a small amount of residual sugar in his "white" Zinfandel—an adjustment which pleased not only the palates of his tasting room

customers, but, as it turned out, millions of American wine consumers. During the 1980s, Sutter Home White Zinfandel was the single most popular premium wine in the United States, with sales growing exponentially from 25,000 cases in 1981 to three million in 1990.

Sutter Home now sells 4 million cases of White Zinfandel a year, and it's one of the biggest wineries in the country. Its White Zinfandel is now 3 percent sugar. Many of us wine lovers have always hoped that people who started drinking White Zinfandel might then try other wines and become wine lovers themselves. After one of our tastings, for instance, we received this letter from Kim Thornton of Lake Forest, California: "I have a soft spot for Beringer White Zinfandel because it helped me start to develop a taste for wine, about a decade ago. I don't buy much White Zinfandel anymore, but I was glad to see that Beringer made your list."

The problem, though, is that the simplicity and sweetness of White Zinfandel allow it to be made cheaply, and badly, in awesome bulk. This has resulted in a great deal of yucky wines that, in the long run, seem to be turning off possible converts to better wines. At the end of the '90s, White Zinfandel sales appeared to be slowing, apparently replaced by low-alcohol fruit-flavored "wine products," such as Canandaigua's Arbor Mist. The company said it shipped 2 million cases of Arbor Mist, such as "tropical fruits Chardonnay," in the first nine months following the launch of the beverage. Amazing. Still, White Zin continues to be a cash cow for wineries. Not only is it inexpensive to produce, but it can be sold quickly, unlike wines that need to be aged at the winery before release. We were once told of a top-notch winemaker who started a tasting event with his White Zinfandel. He put his nose in the glass, took a deep breath, and said, "I smell oak." The crowd was stunned. Oak for White Zin? Finally, someone in the audience nervously raised his hand and said, "I didn't realize your White Zinfandel got any oak."

"Of course not!" replied the winemaker. "But when I smell this White Zin, I can smell all the great oak barrels that it buys for our other wines."

All of this obscures a truth: Some White Zinfandels are better than others, and they don't have to be more expensive. If you're going to drink

White Zinfandel, and a heck of a lot of people are, you should drink a good one. That's why we conduct tastings of White Zinfandel. You can't believe the grief we get from wine aficionados for doing that. After one tasting, we received this note signed by "the dejected staff" of an Illinois wine store. "The dubious distinction 'not all White Zinfandels are alike' is like having the luxury of choosing your preferred method of execution. Alas, all the good work we've done selling rosé this summer flushed down the proverbial toilet like so much sugar and enzyme." Ouch! Our feeling, though, is that winemakers who care about quality even in low-priced wines like White Zinfandel deserve to be applauded—not to mention that we feel we have a responsibility to point our readers to the best of whatever kind of wine they prefer. There's a time and a place, after all, for every wine.

But for a wine that's so popular, it's amazing how few brands we see on shelves in most stores. Walk into any wine store and you're assaulted by scores of Chardonnays, but we've found that many stores have only two White Zinfandels: Sutter Home and one other, usually Beringer. So, for our most recent tasting, we went from store to store. We ultimately found an excellent variety, which looked very pretty in our wine closet. "Pink wine!" enthused Media and Zoë. The colors were variable, like a bouquet of tea roses, some pink, some a little orange, and some pink-gold, like a pale sunset. (Although none, of course, was actually white.) The tastes were very different, too. A couple smelled and tasted like asparagus—yech! Others were so sweet they made our teeth hurt. Still others had so little fruit they tasted like sugar water. Many of these wines had nothing to them. They were simple, sugary sweet, and watery. Media and Zoë drink Kool-Aid, and some of these wines—including, we're sad to say, the Sutter Home—tasted as if they'd been concocted from a powder. At the same time, some would be just fine, deeply chilled, by the pool or at the beach—and the fact that their alcohol content is generally 9 to 10 percent, compared with about 12 percent for many other wines, is a plus in the hot sun.

In tasting after tasting, our favorite has been from De Loach Vineyards. We first tasted De Loach White Zinfandel twenty years ago. We were impressed then and we still are. It tastes like real fruit, with some red tannins for backbone. It has a crisp, steely character and a touch of sweetness and, in general, tastes like a delightful white wine with some blush, as opposed to a pink wine. We've found several others charming, too, and just right for hot weather. One favorite in our most recent tasting (in which we "retired" De Loach after so many victories) was from The Monterey Vineyard. It had the light, fruity pleasantness of a White Zin, but also the "stuff"—the presence—that reminded us that this is, after all, made from the great Zinfandel grape. In other words, as we said in our tasting notes, "this is real wine," as opposed to many others. We also thought this White Zinfandel would be quite nice with light, summery foods.

After the tasting, we talked with Ken Greene, director of winemaking and operations at the winery, which makes about 44,000 cases of White Zin a year. He said the wine contained 2.2 percent residual sugar, higher than we would have guessed. But he said the residual sugar isn't really important, that the sugar-acid balance is the key. He said Monterey aims for a White Zin that is "sweet on entry, but dry and bright at the end." We think their aim was dead on.

We don't know how much good press has to do with the quality of wines, but Cecil De Loach told us that in the late '80s many wine writers stopped reviewing White Zinfandel and he wonders if that removed the incentive for some winemakers to make a good wine. "They said it wasn't a serious wine. A serious wine!" De Loach said, still incredulous. "Why does a wine have to be serious? It's just something you drink."

Wine Notes

General advice: De Loach Vineyards makes the best White Zinfandel. Listed below are some other wineries that have done well in our tastings over the years, listed in order of preference, with general comments about their wines through various vintages and cumulative ratings. These are all names worth looking for. The prices reflect recent vintages. White Zinfandel should be bought as young as possible and be served very well chilled.

Food pairings: Summer foods, such as barbecued chicken and cold salads.

De Loach Vineyards. $8.99. VERY GOOD. Real wine, but still great fun. Highly drinkable, perfect with barbecue.

The Monterey Vineyard. $5.99. GOOD/VERY GOOD. This has enough "stuff" that it tastes something like a flavorful red wine, with nice weight and presence. Unlike almost all others, this could be quite good with food.

Kenwood Vineyards. $8.75. GOOD. Unusual, with some mouthfeel and even a little hint of cream. Substantial, which makes it charming in its own way.

Weinstock Cellars 1999. $7.50. GOOD. Sweet, but with a nice, lemony finish and some real fruit.

Baron Herzog Wine Cellars. $6.99. GOOD. A little bit of steeliness gives it a nice fresh taste, and even a little structure, though it's pretty sweet.

Beringer Vineyards. $6.50. GOOD. Soft and quite sweet, but pleasant, well chilled. Serve with aperitifs or after the barbeque.

What to Do with
Those Leftovers
(Don't Pour Them Out!)

We're often asked two questions that have a related answer: (1) I can't finish a whole bottle of wine. How long will the leftovers keep? And (2) I only like red wine and my wife only likes white. What do I do? These needn't be major obstacles. The answers: pumps and halves.

When we think about half bottles, we think about bad wine on airplanes, cheap stuff, and maybe "splits" of Champagne and dessert wines. In fact, though, there has been a quiet little revolution in half bottles. More and more fine wines are being bottled in halves, wines from all over the world. Not only that, but more and more restaurants are offering a good selection of them, even great restaurants like the French Laundry in Yountville, California. Laura Cunningham, general manager of the French Laundry, told us the restaurant started highlighting half bottles with its tasting menu because it was wasting expensive wine with its wines-by-the-glass program. "We would open up wonderful bottles sometimes just to pour one glass a night," she said. So several years ago, she sent letters to more than 200 wineries, telling them the restaurant wanted to start emphasizing half bottles and asking if they'd like to participate. "Now, several produce half bottles exclusively for us. Some we buy in bulk, fifty cases of them, wine that no one would think would be put in half bottles because it's too good," she said.

Ms. Cunningham told us "there are a lot of people who would never have the opportunity at $100 a bottle to try a wine, but will pay $42 to try 2½ glasses of it. And you don't have this obligatory idea of ordering a whole bottle and feeling guilty about having too much." Still, diners are sometimes reluctant to consider a half bottle, she said, "because for a long time, it was the lesser wines that you used to see."

Not anymore. We went shopping for half bottles and were

pleased by what we found. We could have a great first growth from Bordeaux (Château Haut-Brion) or a fine white from Burgundy (Louis Latour Corton-Charlemagne). We could do some simple tastings—say, a Louis Martini Chardonnay against an Acacia Chardonnay. We could try a real Chablis or a Gewürztraminer from Alsace. The possibilities are almost limitless.

Keep in mind that the smaller the bottle, the faster the wine will age—because more of the wine in a small bottle is exposed to air and light—so be careful with older stuff. But if you and your better half have different tastes in wines, or if you can't finish a whole bottle, the halves are one possibility. Another is just to save the opened bottle for a while. Yes, we know. There's a lot of angst about doing this, but it's generally misplaced angst.

It's impossible to say, of course, how long any specific bottle will last once it's opened. It depends on the kind of wine, how old it is, how it was kept even before it was opened. It depends on how much you drank (how low the "fill" is now). If it's a white and it's kept, with the cork back in it, in the refrigerator, how pleasant it is the next day might depend in part on how the other things in your refrigerator smell. If it's a red and it's kept on the counter, it depends on the temperature in your kitchen. And that's just for starters. In other words, no one can predict how well any bottle will keep after it's opened. What's more, we're always hesitant to tell anyone that any opened bottle will keep because we don't want to be blamed if it goes bad. That said, it's also important to note this: Wine is tougher than you think. Because we taste six to eight wines every night for this column, we often have a bottle or two sitting around (because we didn't get around to pouring the wine out or just couldn't stand to). And we're often amazed how well the opened wine, with just the cork pushed back in, stands up.

We decided to have some fun and experiment. Our plan: to compare (1) wine that we recorked by just putting the cork back in the bottle, against (2) wine we pumped and recorked using one of those manual vacuum pumps found in wine stores that pumps the air out of a bottle, against (3) a newly opened bottle of wine. It was a complex experiment, using all sorts of bags and labels, so we wouldn't know what was what. When we tasted the wines a week after opening them, the wines simply recorked with a cork were the worst of the three, time and again. They hadn't "gone over" or even become bad. It's just that they seemed less fruity and intense, almost like a little water had been added every day. Dottie likened it to a balloon that slowly loses its air. To our surprise, it was difficult to discern much of a difference between the other two. In the long run, we chose the newly opened "fresh" bottle as the best in most cases, but the differences were small. We've used the pump for years because it's easy, but we never knew if it actually worked. Now we're going to pump and feel good about it.

This was hardly scientific. We could have conducted this experiment in so many ways that it could be a doctoral thesis instead of a column. We could have tried other whites, tried reds, put nitrogen into the bottle (there are canisters at many wine stores) or done a trick recommended by many of our readers: Pour a half-drunk full-sized bottle into a half bottle to keep air from getting to the wine. Air, of course, is the issue here. The more air a wine gets, the more quickly it blossoms and dies. Some people whose opinions we respect put opened reds as well as whites into the refrigerator, though we think they lose fruit more quickly that way. In the long run, you need to decide for yourself what's best and easiest for you. If you're thinking about keeping half-consumed bottles around, just make some common-sense calculations. Light, flowery whites obviously aren't going to keep nearly as well as heavier, more intense Chardonnays. Light reds like Beaujolais aren't going to keep as well as big wines like Barolo, which sometimes actually become more approachable after being open a day. Older wines usually won't keep as well as younger wines. Sweet wines will keep much better in the refrigerator than dry wines. And when you take an opened white out of the refrigerator (not to mention a red), let it warm up for a little while, since it has been chilled into a deep sleep after all that time.

The most important common-sense advice is this: No matter how long you've kept an open bottle around, don't pour it down the drain until you've at least tried it.

Chapter Twenty-five

Rosé Wines

With and Without Clothes

To us, so much of the enjoyment of wine is about history—world history, wine-growing history, and, above all, our own history. Certain wines remind us of certain moments in time. There's something about rosé, for instance, that makes us smile, and not just because pink wines themselves are often charming. We think back to our first years of wine discovery together, when California wineries were trying to figure out how to appeal to American wine drinkers. Rosé seemed like a good bet, so they tried to make rosé from just about every grape they could get their hands on. We tried rosés made from Pinot Noir and Cabernet Sauvignon and a rosé from Bully Hill winery in New York made from—get this—Chelois Noir, Rougeon Noir, Cascade Noir, Seyval Blanc, Aurora Blanc, and Delaware. That's right. All of those. More than twenty years ago, we tried a wine from David Bruce in California called "Rosé of Zinfandel." Others later came up with a catchier name for the same wine: White Zinfandel.

One of the most unusual rosés we ever had was a pink Gewürztraminer called Rosa made by Sebastiani Winery in 1977. Since Gewürztraminer is usually a white wine, this seemed odd indeed, but Sam Sebastiani, one of the grand old men of California winemaking, explained this on the back label:

> It has long been my belief that the natural pinkish hue of the
> Gewürz Traminer grape traditionally lost during the winemak-

ing process could be preserved. The result, in essence, would be a rosé (pink) Gewürz Traminer—a wine that paid a visual tribute to its original. The last year of our recent drought, 1977, gave me a clue as to how such an unusual wine might be created. The severe drought gave us smaller berries and a greater amount of color in the juice. Allowing this juice to remain on the skins for an extended period after crushing further enhanced the body with additional character. Even with the traditional color drop during fermentation and aging, a distinctive blush and character remained. I now present to you our first offering of this truly unique wine.

This makes us smile because it reminds us of our very first trip to San Francisco, on our way to Napa Valley. It was during that same drought and our hotel left a note in the room suggesting that we shower together. Eager to save the earth, we complied. It's fun when a wine brings back such memories.

Rosé wine also triggers memories of our first months of writing our column for the *Wall Street Journal*. After "Tastings" first appeared, many people we know suggested topics based on their own passions. How about great wines under $10? How about the wines of Spain? But the most curious thing was the number of people who would walk up to us, stand really close, look around furtively, and whisper, "Could you write something about rosés?" We realized then that rosés are a popular guilty pleasure. Many people enjoy them as their everyday summer wine. And why not? A good rosé is special—not red, not white, but something wholly different, a wine that, at best, has more character than a simple white but isn't as heavy as a light red. To us, a fine rosé has to be so easy to drink that we can enjoy it effortlessly on the hottest day, yet it still must have enough character that we know we're drinking wine and not Kool-Aid.

Rosés haven't been a big part of our wine drinking over the years. Whenever we felt like a white, we had a white; and whenever we felt like a red, we had a red. Beyond that, though, we never had that Great Experience with a rosé, or an American "pink" or "blush" wine, that set us off on a quest to broaden our experience with them. The highest compliment Dottie can give a rosé is: "It tastes pink." But most rosés, to us, seemed to be red or white wanna-bes. Many were too sweet, or too simple, or too lacking in fruit. So many people love rosé, though, that we went on a worldwide search for some good ones. We ultimately conducted three big rosé tastings.

In the first, a world-wide tasting in 1998, we found few good pink wines from the United States. Our best of tasting was Château Grande Cassagne, from Costières de Nimes, in the Languedoc region of France. After that column, we received several letters from readers who said: Whoa! You didn't try the best stuff from the United States. Give Americans another chance. So for two months, we bought every American rosé we could find (excluding White Zinfandel, which we've covered separately. See the previous chapter.) Finding American rosés was difficult. When we asked merchants why, they cited this cycle: There are few good American rosés, they said, so people tend not to buy them. Since people tend not to buy them, the stores don't carry many, so people don't buy them. The merchants said they steer customers toward French rosés because they're better, and often less expensive, than American rosés.

What we found in our American tasting was that while there are obviously some good pinks from the United States, they tend to be made by small producers who see rosé as something special, something more than a cash cow. In the United States, winemakers base their reputations on great Chardonnays, Cabernet Sauvignons, or Pinot Noirs. They might make some pink wine, too, because it can be produced and sold quickly from whatever grapes happen to be around. But pink wine isn't what their winery is about. We liked the rosés from Wolffer Estate and Macari in Long Island, New York, and from Swanson Vineyards in California. The Swanson, interestingly, was made from Sangiovese, the grape used to make Chianti in Italy. Our favorite was from a small California winery called Hart Winery. It was a Grenache Rosé, from the Cucamonga Valley of California. Grenache, one of the best-known grapes for making rosé, is used extensively to make the fine pink wines of southern France and, as Garnacha, the rosé wines of Spain. The Hart rosé was pretty, with some tannins that gave it a little edge, and had a pleasant, light sweetness—it had 1 percent residual sugar. Owner Joe Hart told us: "There's no magic in the way I make it. I just have a source of great fruit: old vines that are fairly low-yielding for Grenache."

For our third, most recent tasting, we bought every rosé we could find, from any country, at any price. We were in for a surprise.

The wines came in all colors, from very light pink to near-red. Many reminded us of watermelons or strawberries. Once again, none of our favorites were American (and, once again, this doesn't mean that there are no good American rosés, but that the best ones are small-production wines that are hard to find). Our best of tasting, again, was the Château Grande Cassagne, which then cost $8.99. Dottie described its color as "a cranberry sunset." It was crisp and classy and quite elegant, with nice, lemony acids that would make it good with food.

But here was the surprise: Many of our favorites, and our near-favorites, were from Spain. In general, like many of our French favorites and like the Hart from California, they were made at least partly from the Grenache/Garnacha grape. We found the Spanish rosés, in fact, more consistently good than those from France, Italy, or the United States—and excellent buys, too. Two of our favorites were $7.99. So our advice to you? If you walked into a wine store and happened to see the Grande Cassagne, our favorite in tastings three years apart, grab it. If not, pick up a rosé from Spain.

We still hold out hope for American rosés, and we'll certainly keep looking. Mr. Hart has a couple of theories about the problems facing American rosés. "We destroyed rosé in California by bottling it in those cheap jugs, the $2 rosés. Some of it was even called Grenache. People didn't take it seriously." His other theory he wears on a coral-colored T-shirt: "Rosé has gotten a bad rap because too many people drink it with their clothes on."

Wine Notes

General advice: Look for a rosé from Spain. Buy it as young as possible. Chill well. If you happen to see Grenache or Garnacha on the label, that's a good sign because it's the grape responsible for many excellent rosés around the world.
Food pairings: Good sipped alone. Fried chicken. Poached salmon and other cold-salad dishes during hot weather.

Château Grande Cassagne (Costières de Nîmes, France). $8.99. VERY GOOD/DELICIOUS. Best of tasting. Tastes pink. Dry, classy, and crisp. Vibrant, in both color and taste, and quite elegant. A beautiful balance of fruit and acids, with some nice citrus flavors, maybe even some pineapple. Proof that a rosé can be a substantial wine. (2000)

Vega Sindoa (Bodegas Nekeas; Navarra, Spain). $7.99. VERY GOOD. Best value. Fun and filled with nice, pink fruit. Bright, with a bit of a bite. Clean and fresh, with some mouthfeel. Delightful, with nice watermelon character. A complete wine. (2000)

Gran Feudo (Bodegas Julian Chivite; Navarra, Spain). $7.99. VERY GOOD. Nicely austere, with ripe fruit and a bit of steely backbone. "This could only be pink," Dottie says. Ripe fruit. It reminds us of a very fresh shrimp cocktail. (1999)

Roigenc (Tarragona–Falset, Spain). $8.95. VERY GOOD. Dark raspberry color prepared us for a heavy wine, but it's surprisingly light on its feet. Imagine pomegranates with a hint of cream. (1999)

Château Penin (Bordeaux, France). $8.99. VERY GOOD. Gorgeous color. Light, lovely, and very drinkable. Crisp and refreshing, yet with nice minerals and some steeliness. Passionfruit. (2000)

Château Mourgues du Gres "Les Galets Rosés" (Costières de Nîmes, France). $12.99. VERY GOOD. Strawberries. Piquant, but with the weight and guts of a red wine. More guts than most, more "stuff." (2000)

Bodegas Muga (Rioja, Spain). $9.99. GOOD/VERY GOOD. Very light color. Fruity and tart, with nice acids. Easy to drink, with light, watermelon tastes. (1999)

Bodegas Castaño "Monastrell" (Yecla, Spain). $7.95. GOOD/VERY GOOD. Dark color, lovely, and rich. It's a bigger rosé than we're used to, but is so well made that it works. It might even have a hint of cream. (2000)

Domaine Chupin Rosé d'Anjou (Anjou, France). $8.99. GOOD. Pretty raspberry color, with lovely vibrant fruit flavors and good balancing acids. A makes-you-smile wine. Refreshing and friendly. (1999)

Château d'Oupia (Minervois, France). $8.99. GOOD. A real wine, crisp and nicely austere. This would be good with food—not just for sipping. Nice acids and no "sweet" strawberry tastes that might get in the way of food. (2000)

Rosé di Regaleali (Sicily, Italy). $9.95. GOOD. One of our perennial favorites, fresh and a little bit chewy. Interesting and somewhat different. (1999)

Chapter Twenty-six

Bargain Wines

It's a Big World Out There

There are some great buys on wine today, but you'll have to leave the United States—and your comfort zone—to get them. You need to travel the world, in a sense. Sure, California produces some fine wines at good prices, and we've focused on many of them in this book, but many of the world's greatest buys are coming from elsewhere. Even the French Ministry of Agriculture, speaking about a steep drop in French wine exports, explained: "French wine producers now have to face growing competition on the world market, mainly from Australia, California, Chile, Argentina, and South Africa." Translation: It's a great time to be looking for wine values.

Why? One reason is that democracy is good for wine, too. Most countries have domestic wine industries, of course, but when there is little foreign trade, either because a nation has closed its doors or because it's shunned by the international community, the countries tend to focus on making bulk wines to be drunk within their own borders. When countries are free and trade is encouraged, the countries see wine as a good export, but the wine has to improve to compete on the world market. Not only that, but winemakers in a democracy seem more willing to take risks, to show their individuality.

Wine is available from all over now. For instance, one of California's best-known winemakers, Mike Grgich, returned to his native Croatia to help rebuild the wine industry there. One result: Grgic Posip, a lovely white wine that is increasingly available in the United States. It really is a small world. Consider this: When we took Media and Zoë on a Disney cruise, our head server was a young Croatian woman named Franka. We mentioned Mike Grgich's wine and she couldn't believe it: Her family sells some of the grapes that make that wine, she told us.

Of course, all of these rejuvenated wine industries are also competing against countries that already are free, and are producing more good wine all the time. Between 1996 and 2000, imports from Australia into the United States tripled (for more about Australia, see Chapters One and Twenty-three). Argentine imports tripled, too. Imports from Canada rose twenty fold and from New Zealand, twelvefold (for more on New Zealand, see Chapter Two). We have had some excellent wines recently from Mexico (look for Monte Xanic). There's buzz about the wines of Uruguay.

Here is a half case of value wines you should try.

CHILE: CABERNET SAUVIGNON AND MERLOT. Fine wine has been made in Chile for centuries, but the industry largely focused on the domestic market. When democracy was restored in 1989, Chileans found that they could venture out into the world and sell their wine free of the disapproval and boycotts they faced during the Pinochet dictatorship. Winemakers also felt free to experiment with international styles, leaving behind old ideas about what would sell at home. The wines that have led the comeback aren't unusual wines, but familiar kinds, like Merlot and Cabernet Sauvignon. While we have also found several Chilean whites that we like—we're especially fond of its flavorful Sauvignon Blanc—the reds seem to be where the country's heart is, and where the great bargains are.

We asked our old friend Craig Torres, who covered Latin America for the *Journal* for years and is interested in Chile's wine industry, for some insight. He helped us understand the history, and added this:

> I guess one of the features of Chilean wine is its approachability. It is friendly. It goes with pizza or pâté, and usually there is extraordinary quality for the price. Ignacio Recabarren, one of Chile's top winemakers, describes his country's red wines this way: "Intense fruit. A bit of the barrel but not too much; aromatic finesse, and a little bit of the New World. Youth."

To be sure, thousands of gallons of mediocre wine are exported from Chile each year, and it is inevitable that you open a bottle and find little more than alcoholic fruit juice. But more often than not these days, a bottle of Chilean wine, no matter how cheap, will strive to be something a little bit surprising. Chileans are as commercially minded as anybody, but they are also people of great conviction, and winemakers there are now out to prove a point. So don't be surprised if a $9 wine speaks loudly about who it is and where it came from.

In a large tasting, we found that Craig was right. One inexpensive red was more charming than the next. They were consistently filled with ripe, cherrylike fruit and hints of all sorts of spices, with more interesting tastes than many budget-priced American wines, which we often find have little personality at all. These wines were effortlessly charming. At the same time, they offered some depth and complexity that reminded us that we were drinking well-made wines.

ARGENTINA: MALBEC. The world of wine is so big and so ever-changing that hardly anyone can stay on top of it. In our case, discovering something new is fundamental to our enjoyment of wine. We were at a Cuban restaurant in New York and noticed that the wine list included a number of wines from Argentina. Remember our advice about wine lists: See where most of the wines are from and order one of those, because this is where the restaurateur's heart is. Two of the reds were made from a grape we weren't very familiar with, Malbec. We ordered them and found them excellent and quite different—slightly rustic and aggressive. We decided to find out more about Argentine Malbec by reading—and, of course, tasting.

Learning about any wine or grape is always, to some extent, a history lesson, and this was no exception. Malbec was widely planted in Bordeaux in the nineteenth century, but the phylloxera epidemic nearly wiped it out. Then the frosts of 1956 further devastated the plantings. There isn't much left in France, though it's still used as a blending grape in Bordeaux and still makes the famous "black wine" of Cahors, in southwestern France. In Argentina, meantime, Malbec became so popular that by 1968 it accounted for half of all red wine made in Argentina, according to the well-regarded

Nicolás Catena winery of Argentina. "But even in Argentina," the winery told us, "Malbec's history is not all pretty. During the country's financial crisis of the '70s and '80s, many Malbec vineyards were replanted with high-yielding varietals, and today, Malbec acreage has dropped"—from 120,000 acres to around 35,000.

We then conducted a large tasting of Argentine Malbec. Malbec doesn't taste quite like anything else. It has a dark purple color, an aggressive, earthy, blackberry nose, and a grapey, cherry, tannic, black-pepper taste. Some of the wines reminded us of herbs and spices that we couldn't quite put our finger on, but which lent the wines a rich earthiness. Most were relatively high in alcohol (13 percent and above). The best wines of our tasting had real structure, like a Bordeaux, but a certain roughness, like a Rhône. Think of it, in many ways, as the opposite of Merlot. Whereas Merlot is smooth, round, friendly, and almost flabby in your mouth, the best of these Malbecs had a crispness and sharp corners, a little like chewing on a piece of red ice.

SOUTH AFRICA: PINOTAGE. For many years, we didn't drink wines from South Africa, for obvious political reasons. When a top editor of the *Miami Herald* served a South African wine at a party in the mid-'70s, we were appalled. We didn't drink any wine from South Africa until 1994, when, for the first time, we tried South Africa's signature wine, Pinotage. It was full-bodied, vibrant, and a whole new taste for us. Still, we don't drink much wine from South Africa. It's simply that, having missed South African wines during most of our formative wine years, it's not a big part of our wine lives. It seems most people are that way—and that's why South African wines are good bargains today. Here's a fine, productive wine region that's desperate to get some market share in the United States. That's how great values come to be. In 2000, about 270,000 cases of South African wine were imported into the United States, according to the South African Consulate General. That's up from 150,000 in 1996, but still just a drop in the barrel, representing only a tiny fraction of wine shipped into the United States.

People who are familiar with South Africa and its wines tend to be passionate about both. Why? We asked our friend Ken Wells, a top editor at the *Journal,* who has been covering South Africa for years. He told us:

It isn't just an enduringly fascinating news story to me, but it's also one of the most beautiful places I've ever visited. And crowning that beauty are its stunning wine lands down in its Cape Provinces. I lived in San Francisco and often visited the Napa Valley. Well, imagine a wine-growing region four times the size of the Napa Valley, with mountains twice as high; imagine driving scenic, winding valley roads and coming upon quaint, seventeenth-century Cape Dutch farmhouses set in an endless sea of vineyards. Imagine all this suffused with exotic African rhythms. Imagine being able to stop in some lovely bistro, in a gorgeous little town with a name like Franschhoek, and being able to order a five-course Continental meal, while perusing wines from a list that includes vintages from maybe a dozen wineries in the near vicinity. How could a wine, unless it is utter plonk, taste anything but marvelous in such surroundings?

South Africa's Sauvignon Blancs are bold—proud of the grape varietal's taste and character—and its Steen, which is its name for Chenin Blanc, is crisp and delightful. But Pinotage is truly South Africa's own wine. It was developed in South Africa and is a cross between Pinot Noir and Cinsault, which is a grape from southern France. Its fruitiness and jazzy purple color remind us of Beaujolais, but it has more taste of earth, lemon, and herbs. It can be light, made for immediate drinking, or heavier, meant for a little aging. But in a blind tasting, we found this consistently: It tastes foreign. Hey, don't laugh. All of us get to a point in wine where things fit somewhere on our taste-memory map. It's unusual to find something that's truly new. Well, Pinotage can be a truly new taste. How new? After Dorothy tasted one of the wines, she thought for a minute and said, "You know, it tastes blue." And John actually knew just what she meant. Unfortunately, it's impossible for us to describe what blue tastes like, but all of these wines had a consistent taste of candylike, raspberry-cherry fruit, an interesting underlay of soil and a finish that was memorable and almost a little bitter. All had enough lemony acid to make them good with food. The ones we liked best tended to put all this together in a fascinating whole.

SPAIN: CAVA AND RIOJA. When we were young, we used to drink sparkling wines from Spain. They weren't very elegant, but they were inexpensive and perfect with Sunday brunch. We'd get lox and bagels at Zabar's, grab our Sunday *New York Times,* and spend hours reading the paper and sipping Cava.

Cava is the formal name of sparkling wines from Spain made in the traditional Champagne method—that is, with the second fermentation taking place in the bottle, creating and trapping the bubbles. The wines, Spain's finest sparklers, generally come from the Penedes region in northeastern Spain and are made from white grapes with unfamiliar names, mostly Macabeo, Parellada, and Xarel-lo, and sometimes red grape varieties like Garnacha Tinta and Monastrell. Since the late 1980s, some of the sparklers have included Pinot Noir and Chardonnay, the traditional grapes for Champagne. Like its refined French cousins, Cava ranges from dry to sweet and sometimes is made pink. Two giant producers of Cava, Freixenet and Codorníu, are ubiquitous in the United States.

In our mind, Spanish sparkling wines tended to be fat and a bit heavy-tasting, but that made them fine with smoked salmon and cream cheese. As the years went by, we had less time for Sunday brunch, and our house sparkler became Chandon, from California, which cost a few dollars more but seemed crisper and easier to drink as a come-home-to sparkler. But while we were in the Spanish aisle of wine shops, we ran across Cava, and we wondered: How are they these days? There certainly are plenty of them, and they're really inexpensive. So we bought all we could find—and we were in for a very pleasant surprise.

While sparkling wines from Spain don't have the cachet of real Champagne—which is, after all, the real thing—an amazing amount of it is sold in the United States. Good ones are marvelous to sip alone, yet they have enough fruity acid to go with many different types of foods. In Spain, they're often sipped with tapas, those incredibly varied and intriguing appetizers. The Trade Commission of Spain says about 700,000 cases of Cava were exported to the United States in 2000. Of that, about three-quarters were made by Codorníu or Freixenet, which also makes brands such as Segura Viudas. In a blind tasting, we found that Spanish sparklers, just like some of their American relatives, can indeed be fat and somewhat clumsy.

One had bubbles that were so big and aggressive they seemed to slap us around. Some were more like still wines. They had too much taste—enough to overwhelm the taste-bubble balance that makes a sparkling wine work—and some seemed to have no taste at all.

Our best of tasting in two different flights turned out to be the same wine. It was clearly the classiest, with a light elegance—the color, the taste, and the bubbles—that was special in the group. Both nights, when the tasting was finished and we turned to dinner, this was the wine we brought to the table. It was, we're happy to report, one of the most common wines around, the Freixenet Cordon Negro Brut, which then cost just $8.99, and still is remarkably affordable. This was a surprise to us, but our two flights—we had bought two bottles at two different stores by accident—confirmed to us that we had a real winner here. And what a deal.

There are other great deals coming from Spain, too. Rioja is a well-known region, of course, and it makes some fine, sometimes expensive wines. But it also makes some outstanding less expensive wines that we think of as excellent summer reds. Many people think of summertime as white-wine time because big red wines seem too heavy and serious for the steamy days of July, but you don't have to give up red wine altogether just because it's hot outside. We lived in Miami for many years, and it's pretty much always hot down there, both literally and figuratively. Not only that, but the best food in the city, which is either Cuban or Cuban-inspired, is lively with spices. So what red wine did we drink? Rioja.

Rioja has character and elegance that can enliven a wide variety of foods, but it's also light in body, easy to drink, and can be inexpensive and sometimes pleasantly simple. It's great with such picnic foods as poached salmon, chicken salad, and barbecue. We almost always have bought our old standbys, the readily available Marqués de Riscal and Marqués de Cáceres, but there are so many different Riojas out there that we thought it would be fun to do a tasting.

Rioja is made primarily from the Tempranillo and Garnacha grapes, but different wineries may bottle different blends. Sometimes even some white-wine grapes are added. (There are also white Rioja wines.) While winemakers have been making wine in the Rioja region for centuries, winemaking there got a boost in the mid-nineteenth century when phylloxera devastated the vines of Bordeaux. To keep making wine, French winemakers moved south to Rioja, bringing their expertise with them. Still, until fairly recently, Rioja wines were left so long in wood barrels that the taste of the grapes was just about wrung out, along with much of the color, too. While most of the wines still get lots of wood—that's one of the hallmarks of Rioja wines—they're not nearly as "overoaked" as they once were.

In our foraging for Rioja in wine shops, we noticed several vintages on the shelves. We had read that we shouldn't worry too much about vintages, that the inventory generally found in stores these days is ready to drink. In our blind tasting, we found that to be surprisingly true. Wine after wine was well made and delightful, and virtually none of them seemed likely to improve with age. They were ready to drink right now, regardless of the vintage or whether the wine was a Crianza, a Reserva, or a Gran Reserva (which has to do with how long they were aged before they were released). The bottles we had—all under $20—had a remarkable consistency. While each was different, of course, we were intrigued by how closely related they were. They had a fairly light color, often with a noticeable tint of gold-brown age around the edges and a touch of dust on the nose. They were fairly light in body, with enjoyable hints of earth and cherries and a little bit of pepper. Most surprising to us—we had never found this before when we drank these casually—was a noticeable tartness and tang, especially in the finish. Time and again, there was a definite taste of lemony acid.

Many people say they like smooth wines—and Rioja is not. It tends to be leathery and somewhat austere, and many in our tasting lacked the rich, ripe fruit that many people enjoy. But that distinctive taste is the charm of Rioja—and many of the wines we tasted were indeed charming. One of our longtime favorites, the Marqués de Cáceres, was simple and easy to drink, but it didn't break into the top ranks. Some others that did were most notable for their delightful, fruity tastes and lightweight bodies.

In two different flights, we were impressed with a wine that we found had real "stuff" in it—a little bit more weight and depth than most, with some aging potential. These wines seemed to have an extra element underneath, giving them more structure. As it turned out, both of these wines were the Marqués de Riscal Reserva, which we'd picked up twice as we scooped up every Rioja we could find. We were delighted by this turn of events, since this wine is almost always available, and a great bargain at around $12.99.

People are always asking us what to take to a friend's house for barbecues in July and August. Next time, surprise them: Take a Rioja. In a universe of White Zinfandels and jug wines at the barbecue, your wine is sure to stand out.

Wine Notes

General advice: Following are a few of our favorite wines from tastings of value-priced wines from Chile, Argentina, South Africa, and Spain. These are the prices we paid at the time of the tastings. Prices have risen as these have become better known, but they remain quite reasonable. Because many different kinds of wine are listed, they are not rated. Don't be afraid of wines from unfamiliar places—embrace the bargains.

Chile

Dallas-Conté Cabernet Sauvignon (Rapel Valley). $8.99. Creamy and rich, but with that distinctive earthiness. Fine enough to serve to guests, but don't tell them the price. We also liked the Dallas-Conté Merlot, at the same price. (1998)

Concha y Toro Casillero del Diablo Cabernet Sauvignon (Maipo Valley). $8.99. Crisp, with class, breeding, and some interesting edges, yet approachable and easy to drink. (1999)

Santa Rita "Medalla Real" Special Reserve Cabernet Sauvignon (Maipo Valley). $11.99. Soulful, deep, and lovely, with rich, ripe fruit. A little herbaceousness made us think it would be super with lamb. (1998)

Santa Alicia Merlot Reserve (Maipo Valley). $9.99. Easy to drink, with nice, round fruit. (1997)

South Africa

Thelema Mountain Vineyards Sauvignon Blanc (Stellenbosch). $18.99. Lots of lemon-lime taste, but plenty of minerals and soil give it grounding. Juicy. (2000)

Jardin (Gary & Kathy Jordan) Blanc Fumé (Stellenbosch). $13.99. A real favorite. Very floral nose, with a Riesling-like delicacy combined with plenty of oak. Fascinating, excellent, and wonderfully different. (1999)

Clos Malverne Sauvignon Blanc (Stellenbosch). $13.99. Elegant and shy, with lots of green pepper, nice structure, and mouthfeel. Some "stuff" in the back. (1999)

Bateleur Chardonnay (Danie de Wet, De Wetshof Estate; Robertson). $32.99. Luscious and Burgundy-like. A complex taste that's both big and re-strained. So rich that Dottie tried it and said, "This tastes like money." (1998)

Backsberg Cabernet Sauvignon (Paarl). $18.79. Tobacco and plums on the nose. Plump, with cedar and cream. Real breeding. Some bite. We'd serve this to guests in a minute, especially with steaks or game. Still young. (1997)

Simonsig Wine Estate Pinotage (Stellenbosch). $14.99. Herbal and slightly roasted, a bit chewy. Plenty of bitter herbs and soil, but good, sweet fruit. Charming. (1998)

Zonnebloem Wines Limited Pinotage (Stellenbosch). $13.69. Simple and big, great with burgers and spaghetti. Nice acids, good fruit. Fun, approachable. Like so many South African wines, it has soil, earth, herbs, and a little bit of mint. A benign introduction to this unique South African grape. (1998)

Hamilton Russell Vineyards Pinot Noir (Walker Bay). $23.99. We loved the 1998—rich, creamy, and elegant. The 1999 is still quite young, but has more structure and herbal tastes. A beautiful wine for the cellar. (1999)

Argentina

Nicolás Catena Malbec (Lunlunta Vineyards, Mendoza). $18.99. Lots of sweet fruit and lots of edges. Real Bordeaux structure and "brightness," but with interesting, herbal notes. Classy and age-worthy. (1996)

Mariposa Malbec (Mendoza). $8.99. Peppery and yet easy to drink. Lots of soil, earth, and dark, sweet fruit—and a whole spice chest full of flavors. (1997)

Rafael Estate Malbec-Tempranillo (Mendoza). $13.99. Black as night and very serious. Plenty of plummy fruit, but tightly wound and way too young. Heady and big. (1997)

Spain

Freixenet Cordon Negro Brut Cava. $8.99. Classy, nutty, and a bit rich. Clean, crisp, vibrant, and fine. (Nonvintage)

Marqués de Gelida Gran Seleccio Brut Cava. $7.99. There's some real style here, some real winemaking, with a weight and body that are special. (Nonvintage)

Paul Cheneau Brut Blanc de Blancs Cava. $6.99. A bit heavy, but still pleasant and easy to drink. (Nonvintage)

Loriñon Rioja Crianza (Bodegas Bréton). $11.99. Creamy, fruity, and classy, like raspberries and cream, but with a light body and good acids that make it easy to drink with just about any food. (1996)

Marqués de Riscal Rioja Reserva. $10.99. A great deal of character, with more structure than most. Might even age. Always available, always good. (1995)

Solabal Rioja Crianza. $11.99. Sweet with fruit, with some hints of blackberries. Heavier and more "serious" than most. Plenty of lemony acid. (1995)

Conde de Valdemar Rioja Reserva. $12.99. This is the real thing, dark, rich, zesty, and beautifully made. (1994)

How to Remember That
Wine You Liked,
with the Green Label

People are always saying to us, "I had a wine I really loved at a restaurant, but when I woke up the next day I couldn't remember what it was." Wine merchants tell us, in fact, that they're constantly frustrated by people who come in and say, "I had a really good wine last night. It was a white wine, with a green label. Do you have it?"

So here's an easy way to remember your wines: Save labels. It's easier than you think.

Readers often ask us how in the world we remember that the 1976 Firestone cost $5.99 and was "dark and pretty." The answer is that, for a quarter century, we've been taking notes and saving labels. Now, if we heard that someone did that, we'd probably say, "Whoa! Those folks are way more organized and prissy than I would ever be." The fact is, our lives are a mess, our desks are a mess, our house is a mess. But for some odd reason, way back in the '70s, we started saving labels of every new wine we tried, even ones we didn't like. We don't know why we did this except that every wine, for us, was paired with a memory, and by saving labels we were saving our past together.

Then, for Christmas 1979—the year we got married—John's parents gave us The Cellar Key Wine Diary & Catalog, a loose-leaf binder for keeping notes about wine. We have no idea why they gave us this. We can't imagine that they thought we would ever be organized enough to keep notes. But we did. Some readers ask us how to keep notes—what words to use, how to rate the wines. Don't worry about this. Just write notes to yourself any way that comes naturally to you. "This was really good" seems like a pretty cogent description. As time goes by, you might find yourself writing more complex descriptions, but remember that the only person you're writing these notes for is yourself. As long as they make sense to you, that's all that matters.

Even if you'll never keep notes on wines, at least you can keep labels. Here's how:

• When you have a good wine at a restaurant, just tell the waiter, "This was so good, I'd like to take the bottle home. I save labels." Don't be embarrassed. The restaurant will be flattered. Chances are the restaurant will offer to take the label off for you. If it doesn't, and sometimes this is a blessing because some kitchens aren't competent to do this, at least they'll give you a nice bag for your wine so you don't have to walk down the street swinging a wine bottle. (By the way, readers sometimes tell us about a wine they had at a restaurant the night before and ask us what it was. We have no idea if they didn't take the label. Call the restaurant. It'll be pleased that you enjoyed the wine so much.)

• Once you get the bottle home, fill your kitchen sink with hot water and put the bottle in. After a few minutes, see if the label is loose. German labels tend to float right off. Australian labels are impossible. Burgundy labels are easier than Bordeaux labels. Why there are regional and national differences, we don't know. In any event, if the label doesn't float off, put the empty bottle on its side on a towel and, starting with a corner, work a knife under the label. Sometimes after a couple of edges are lifted, the rest of the label comes off easily. This is how Dottie does it. John's method is as follows: Boil a pot of water and gently lower the bottle into it for a few minutes. Maybe then the label will float off. If not, take the bottle out—very carefully, because it's hot—and start lifting it off with a fingernail or a knife. If that doesn't work, John calls Dottie.

• When the label finally comes off, place it on some plastic wrap until it dries.

• Get a simple photo album, the kind with loose-leaf transparent pages that lift off and then stick back down. Put the labels into the album.

Recently, someone introduced a label-removal system that is essentially a big strip of very strong adhesive. You press the adhesive strip onto the wine label and then pull it off. It took us some practice, and this is certainly more expensive than soaking, but these work well with difficult-to-remove labels.

All of this is much easier than it sounds. In our case, we put empty bottles on the windowsill until we have a dozen or so, then plop them all into water. We now have labels organized by year going back a quarter century. We can tell our whole life story through those labels. We've affixed little notes reminding us of where we had the wine, but you don't have to get that complex. All you're trying to do is save labels so you can have the same wine again. But before you know it, you'll have a diary of some of your best times.

Chapter Twenty-seven

Unusual Stuff

Relax, They're American

We're realists. We know that no matter what we say about great bargains coming from countries all over the world, most people will continue to drink wine primarily from California. Guess what percentage of all wine consumed by Americans is made in California:

(a) 70 percent
(b) 50 percent
(c) 40 percent

If you answered 70 percent, you move to the next round. But here's something important to keep in mind: Even if you are most comfortable with California wine, you can still take your taste buds to new and different places far beyond Merlot and Chardonnay. American vintners are rediscovering old favorites and experimenting with new wines all the time. Here are some off-the-beaten-track California wines you might want to look for next time you're in the mood for something a little different. Unusual wines like these aren't going to make wineries rich and famous, so they're often produced only because winemakers are passionate about them. That's often a recipe for a memorable wine.

Petite Sirah: You probably know someone a little like John's uncle Leroy. Leroy was a big man—in height, in weight, and in personality. Yet in any room, he was also the most elegant—worldly, comfortable in any environment, and always impeccably dressed. Petite Sirah is like that. It tends to be a very big, very dark red wine, densely packed with taste, with hints of tar and maybe a little mint. Yet, at the same time, it is—like Uncle Leroy—elegant and classy.

When we were wine kids, Petite Sirah was a hot wine in California. It had been used as a blending grape for years, often to make generic California Burgundy. In a charming old book called *Great Winemakers of California,* Louis P. Martini of Louis M. Martini Winery tells the author, Robert Benson, that his Burgundy is generally a blend of Petite Sirah, Gamay, and Pinot Noir, but mostly Petite Sirah. "Why not call that Petite Sirah?" asks the author, and Martini answers: "The distributors wouldn't let us do that, we're selling too much of it as Burgundy. They'd scream."

Ah, how things change. By the late 1970s, Petite Sirah had become a remarkable stand-alone varietal. Cult wines back then weren't what they are now, but the Stags' Leap Winery Petite came pretty close. At a time when the motto of California wineries seemed to be the bigger the better, the Stags' Leap was big, bigger, and best. Then Petite Sirah kind of disappeared. Maybe it was just too aggressive. Or maybe it was just too confusing. There is nothing petite about Petite Sirah. And it's different from Syrah, the great red wine of the Rhône Valley of France, which is also coming on strong in California (see below). Nevertheless, it's sometimes called Petite Syrah. Yikes. Despite all that, Petite Sirah has been making a little comeback, which makes us happy because we love its big, red, American tastes.

One of America's cult wineries, Turley Wine Cellars, makes a remarkable Petite Sirah that's so expensive we were able to drink it only because the stock market fell sharply. A restaurant near us had a gimmick: 50 cents off any wine for every point that the Dow Jones Industrial Average dropped in a day. We'd seen this rare Turley on the wine list once and waited for the market to drop. When it did, we had a great experience— the wine seemed to leap out of the glass—for just $15. It would have been delicious anyway, but it was even more awesome at that price.

To see how the more generally available Petite Sirah wines were, we conducted a tasting. We didn't set any price limit, so our Petite Sirahs ranged from $10.99 to $55. One after another, we're happy to say, was great fun to drink. Just imagine this: You pick, right off the vine, the freshest, plumpest blackberry, blueberry, and raspberry you have ever seen and plop all three in your mouth. Imagine that explosion of fruit. That's what many of these Petite Sirahs were like. Our best of tasting was clear: "Big, almost 'sweet,' with round fruit," we wrote in our notes during the blind tasting. "A complete wine. Big, yet extremely drinkable. A liveliness about the varietal that some others iron out. An Uncle Leroy kind of wine, big, yet light on its feet. Earthy, yet bursting with fruit." When we tore off the bags, our winner was from Stags' Leap Winery. We were so pleased to find that something from our youth is just as good as ever.

Chenin Blanc: We know what you're thinking. Chenin Blanc is cheap white wine. It comes in jugs, tastes a little sweet, and is inoffensive at best. It doesn't have to be that way. In fact, the Chenin Blanc grape makes some of the loveliest white wines of France, from dry to sweet. It makes fine, fruity wines with excellent acidity, such as Vouvray, in the Loire Valley (see Chapter Seven). It makes a delightful sparkling wine. In South Africa, where it's called Steen, it accounts for a large percentage of all vineyard plantings. It's frequently used as a simple blending grape, and that's how it's often used in California. Like Chablis, which saw its name and reputation appropriated by bottlers of cheap jug wines, Chenin Blanc became synonymous with generic white wine.

The result: While fads have brought wines like Merlot and Viognier to the fore, poor Chenin Blanc is the other side of the coin. Few consumers want to spend real money on Chenin Blanc, so it doesn't pay grape growers to grow it, winemakers to produce it, or retailers to stock it. In 2000, according to the Wine Institute, the average price for a ton of Chenin Blanc grapes was $216, compared with $895 for a ton of Chardonnay. If you were a farmer, what would you do? Yep, that's what the farmers did, too. The institute says production of Chenin Blanc fell to 700,000 cases in 1999, the most recent figures, from 2.2 million in 1990.

When we were younger, we, too, thought little of American Chenin Blanc. Then, one day, we saw one from a Sonoma County winery called White Oak. Surprised that such a fine winery would make Chenin Blanc, we decided maybe it was worth a try. Was it ever. It was crisp, flavorful, and excellent with food. Unfortunately, White Oak, which started making

Chenin Blanc in 1986, stopped making it after the 1993 vintage. In fact, winery after winery has given up on Chenin Blanc. Charles Krug Winery, which twenty years ago made 125,000 cases a year and was well known for its Chenin Blanc, stopped making it in 1996.

When we were in Napa Valley in 1999, we dropped by a winery called Folie à Deux, and were thrilled to see a Chenin Blanc. The back label even said: "Folie à Deux is proud to continue producing this . . ." We bought a bottle, and it was fresh, fruity, and charming. But guess what? When we called later to talk about it, the winery told us that the 1997 we tasted would be their last. "Vineyards can make so much more money growing Chardonnay," Scott Harvey, the winemaker, told us then. "Chenin Blanc has basically been forgotten," as consumers moved from it to White Zinfandel and then on to simple Chardonnays. "We are still proud to make it," Mr. Harvey told us, "but it's too hard to sell."

We decided then that we had to start a crusade to save Chenin Blanc as a fine wine in California. We were sure some was still being made, so we searched far and wide to gather enough for a tasting. We discovered that there are still lonely winemakers committed to this grape, from Paumanok Vineyards in Long Island, New York, to Biltmore Estate in Asheville, North Carolina. In our tasting, some, like Callaway, were crisp, light, and great food wines. Others, such as Chappellet, had medium body and just the right balance of weight and acidity. One, from Chalone, left us agape—and earned a rare Delicious! on our rating scale. We were unprepared for what this wine could be—rich and serious, yet clean, with all the flavors of a fruit basket. Chalone says it has made this wine since 1960, though it makes just about 400 cases of it.

This Chalone wasn't the only excellent Chenin Blanc we tried. The Foxen, for instance, was classy, with intense fruit and a flinty-oaky taste. Bill Wathen and Dick Dore, co-owners and co-winemakers, have been making Chenin Blanc since 1987. "We're sort of attached to it," Mr. Wathen, who used to be at Chalone, told us. They make 600 to 800 cases each year. They buy superripe grapes, then put them in oak—heresy to some who consider Chenin Blanc's fruitiness inappropriate to wood—and run them through a full malolactic fermentation, which adds to the creaminess of the taste. Mr. Wathen said they've tasted bottles going back eight to ten years and they age more gracefully than many Chardonnays. Still, every day they come up against the grape's harsh reputation. "We have a tasting room," Mr. Wathen told us, "and we try to start with the Chenin Blanc. People say, 'No, no, I don't want that.' And once they try it, they go, 'Wow.'"

By the way, this story has a little bit of a happy ending. Folie à Deux didn't stop making Chenin Blanc after all because so many people asked for it. They're making only about 200 cases of it, but they have no plans to stop.

Barbera: One of the hottest trends in California is the rediscovery of grapes usually associated with Italy. So many of the seminal figures in California wine were Italian, but grapes like Barbera were cast off at some point as too rustic and old-fashioned compared to classy grapes like Chardonnay and Cabernet Sauvignon. Well, they're back. We once had an excellent Dolcetto from a California winery called Scotland Craig. There are whites, too, such as Arneis. Robert Mondavi even started a separate operation called La Famiglia di Robert Mondavi, which makes only Italian varietals.

One of the hottest Italian varietals in the United States is Sangiovese, the vibrant grape that's used to make Chianti (see Chapter Twenty-one). We found in a blind tasting, however, that Sangiovese remains a noble experiment with a long way to go. Most were pleasant enough, but too "sweet" with fruit. They lacked charm, on the one hand, and enough depth, on the other. Some were quite good, but we were far more impressed later when we conducted a tasting of Barbera wines.

Barbera can be a cheap, and bad, red wine. It's fruity and acidic and easy to make into a simple, yucky jug wine, in America and in Italy. But it can also be a very pleasant, fruity, almost exuberant wine. A Barbera d'Alba from a good producer in Italy's Piedmont region can offer the kind of dark, rich, "flat" fruit that makes you lust for chocolate or ripe figs or oil-drenched roasted eggplant, or, if you will, a juicy hamburger, all the way. Louis Martini's Barbera was the first Italian varietal wine we had from California. It was inexpensive, soul-satisfying, dark, and unpretentious.

In two tastings, we found that today's Barberas—many of them limited-production wines and hard to find (ironic considering its humble history)—were almost uniformly well made. They were rich in dark, blackberry-like fruit, without a great deal of complexity, and relatively high in alcohol. Some, in fact, were so plump with fruit that we doubted we could drink a whole bottle or find a food match. The best, though, had more restrained fruit. The Louis Martini, after all these years, continued to be fun and easy, especially after a little air. But it was overshadowed by some others, including a classy wine from Seghesio Winery, the back label of which read: "When our great grandfather, Edoardo Seghesio, immigrated to California in 1886, he brought with him Barbera cuttings to plant in his new homeland." We also liked the Barbera from Renwood, a reliable name in big, red wines, and from Ca' del Solo (Bonny Doon Vineyard).

The best of our tastings was an outstanding wine from—guess what?—Folie à Deux, the same people who make the fine Chenin Blanc. It had the deep, rich fruit of the others but also a real taste of the earth and a complexity most lacked. Not much is made—about 600 cases a year—but that goes back to our point: Wines like these are made in small quantities by committed winemakers. They're worth a special search.

Cabernet Franc: We'd always thought of "Cab Franc" primarily as a blending grape. While it's the predominant grape in some fine French wines, such as the famous Château Cheval Blanc, and is widely planted in Italy, we always thought of it simply as one of the minor grapes in fine Bordeaux wines. We remember the first "varietal" Cabernet Franc we had from California. It was a 1989 Cabernet Franc from Robert Keenan Winery, and it was delicious. But the rest of that story says a lot about the ups and downs of Cab Franc in America. When we called the winery in late 1999 to talk about its Cabernet Franc, the winery's general manager, Matt Gardner, told us that the winery's previous owners bottled Cabernet Franc as a varietal only in 1989 and 1990. Several things worked against it, he said: "It ran into market resistance. It was a different type of wine, and it didn't sell well on wine lists. It would be lumped into the 'other' wine categories and sometimes get lost." Then deadly phylloxera hit the vineyard, and the diseased plants had to be pulled out. But in 1997, the winery replanted Cabernet Franc. It bottled 100 cases of the 1999 Cabernet Franc in 2001, and plans to keep bottling it as a varietal as long as the quality is good.

To be sure, Cabernet Franc will always be a hard sell. The very things that we like so much about it—it tastes edgy, with an almost sharp structure and an aggressive taste, and it often hints of black pepper or green pepper or herbs—are the same things that might make it inappropriate as a simple glass of red wine at a bar. At its best, it demands attention—and the accompaniment of food.

We bought every American Cabernet Franc we could find for a blind tasting. There still aren't that many, and even those we found are generally small-production wines. What the best had in common was real intensity and plenty of fruit. "This is a wine that bites you back," John said, and Dottie agreed. It's hard to describe what we mean by that, but you'll know when you taste it. One of our favorites was from Ravenswood. This is a venerable name in Zinfandel, but we didn't even know it made a Cabernet Franc until we scooped up every one we could find. (The back label said that 3,456 cases were made, which is not much.) This wine was filled with "sweet," soft fruit, cream, spices, and pepper. Another hit in our blind tasting was from Cosentino Winery. In our notes, John wrote: "A glass of Merlot for people who want a real wine." It has plenty of character, but is easy to drink. We felt this could be our new house wine—the kind of wine you come home to, drink a glass of, and feel really happy to be home.

Syrah: When we spent a month in Napa and Sonoma with Media and Zoë in 1999, we stopped at dozens of wineries and tasted hundreds of wines. To our surprise, the single most exciting wine we tasted, from a winery we'd never heard of called Everett Ridge Vineyards & Winery, was a Syrah. It was a rare Delicious! on our scale. We described it as "classy, rich, and filled with plump, juicy fruit, but at base it has a great deal of soil."

Syrah is the same grape as Shiraz, the fine red wine from Australia (see Chapter Twenty-three). It's also the grape of the big, great-for-winter red wines from the Rhône Valley of France (see Chapter Nineteen). As part of California wineries' big push into "Rhône varietals" like Viognier (see Chapter Four), Syrah from the United States is beginning to show up in wine stores everywhere. Some California winemakers are even calling it Shiraz, to piggyback on the popularity of the Australian wine. We didn't know until we tasted that Everett Ridge, though, just how far California had come with this grape. So, of course, we decided it would be a good idea to conduct a tasting.

While we bought some that are made in relatively large quantities, others are small-production wines that just happened to be on the shelves when we dropped by. The good news is that some of the larger-production, less-expensive Syrahs were very good. The R. H. Phillips EXP, for instance, was vibrant and drinkable, an excellent introduction to this assertive, warming red wine. We were amazed by the Pepperwood Grove Syrah, which was a bit too fat and creamy, but still a lovely bottle of wine, and, remarkably, just $6.99 at the time. Our clear best of tasting was one of the small-production wines. We often mention wines that have a taste of the earth. That's hard to describe, but you know what dark, rich soil smells like—it's soul-satisfying, rich, and somehow touches you deeply. We find, in general, that Italian and French wines tend to have that taste, which gives them a soulful foundation, while fewer American wines have that earthy dimension. Good Rhône wines have that taste of the soil, and our favorite California Syrah from our blind tastings had it along with a deep reservoir of rich fruit. While the wine was clearly way too young—Syrah wines often age beautifully—it took us to someplace very warm, which was a good thing, since we tasted it on a very cold night. When we tore off the bag, it was from a small winery called Robert Craig Wine Cellars. Lynn Craig, Robert's wife, said they made only 283 cases of this wine, which was 97 percent Syrah and 3 percent Cabernet Franc.

One last thing: Part of the fun of drinking wine is being on the edge with a winemaker who is stretching, experimenting. One Syrah that we liked was very serious. It was dark and had intense fruit. When we tore off the bag, it was from Zaca Mesa Winery, but wait: This was 80 percent Syrah and 20 percent *Viognier*. Viognier is such a big white wine that it almost tastes red, but we never would have guessed this intense red wine was 20 percent white. What gives? Jeff Maiken, general manager and president of Zaca Mesa, told us that Viognier "softens and helps focus the fruit." That's also why it's not unusual to find it blended into red Rhône wines. Remember that good wine isn't just a beverage; it's also someone's art. While you don't have to think about what you're drinking to enjoy it, sometimes it's fun to deconstruct a wine, to savor the way the winemaker, following an inner map, pulled its components together. The Zaca Mesa Syrah wasn't our best in this blind tasting, but it's hard not to stand up and applaud the kind of thought that went into that bottle.

Wine Notes

General advice: Below are some notes from blind tastings of these unusual wines. Because they are not made in great quantities, it's impossible to know what labels you will find at any store, so—especially in this case—don't look for any specific producer. Just try something new. These notes will give you some idea what kind of experience you could be in for.

Petite Sirah

Stags' Leap Winery (Napa Valley). $28.99. DELICIOUS. Big, round, lively fruit, bursting with excitement. (1994)

Ravenswood (Sonoma Valley, Dry Creek Valley). $17.99. DELICIOUS. Black as night. Intense fruit, inky, and yet remarkably elegant and fine. (1997)

Field Stone Winery (Staten Family Reserve; Alexander Valley). $27.50. VERY GOOD/DELICIOUS. Intense and warming, with an interesting taste of the soil and, after a while, real hints of chocolate and mint. (1993)

Chenin Blanc

Chalone Vineyard. $19.00. DELICIOUS! Stunning. Big, rich, and almost chewy, yet fine, with great finesse. Pineapples, peaches, pears, vanilla, and some smoke. Marvelously clean. (1998)

Chappellet Vineyard (Napa Valley "Dry"). $10.79. VERY GOOD. Minerals, lemon, earth, and a bit tart. Lovely and drinkable. Good with food. (1997)

Girard Winery (Napa Valley "Old Vine"). $12.99. VERY GOOD. Melons, apples, and rich soil, with weight. All sorts of complexity. (1996)

Foxen Vineyard (Santa Barbara County). $16.99. VERY GOOD. Ripe and oaky and serious. Surprisingly big. (1997)

Callaway Vineyard and Winery (California). $7.99. VERY GOOD. Pure fruit, with some spice, citrus, and vanilla. Classy. (1998)

Barbera

Folie à Deux Winery (Amador County). $28.00. VERY GOOD. Vibrant, with plenty of fruit and a nice taste of the earth that others lack. Some real guts. Still young. (1997)

Seghesio Winery (Mendocino County). $21.95. VERY GOOD. Classy, lively, and beautifully made. (1997)

Renwood Winery "Linsteadt" (Amador County). $22.16. GOOD/ VERY GOOD. Nice backbone along with its sweet fruit. Interesting burnt-herb tastes. (1997)

Ca' del Solo (Bonny Doon Vineyard; Monterey). $19.99. GOOD/VERY GOOD. Very deep color. Tastes roasted and dark, yet light-bodied. Interesting and fun. (1999)

Louis M. Martini Winery (Lake County). $12.00. GOOD. After some air, this becomes classy and complex with rich fruit tastes, though a bit thin on the finish. Always reliable. (1995)

Cabernet Franc

Ravenswood (Sonoma Valley). $17.99. VERY GOOD/DELICIOUS. "Sweet," soft fruit, with a hint of green peppers. A little creamy and alto-gether quite tasty. (1997)

Cosentino Winery (Napa Valley). $22.99. VERY GOOD/DELICIOUS. What a great nose! This is easy to drink yet distinctive, with a nice spici-ness. (1996)

Richard Longoria Winery "Blues Cuvee" (Santa Ynez Valley). $20.99.

VERY GOOD. Plenty of ripe fruit and plenty of black pepper. Intense and distinctive. (1996)

Lang & Reed Wine Co. (Napa Valley). $21.99. VERY GOOD. Clean and crisp. Young, fresh, and vibrant. (1997)

Syrah

Robert Craig Wine Cellars (Paso Robles). $28.99. VERY GOOD/DE-LICIOUS. Nice taste of the earth, with plenty of deep, red fruit. Soul-satisfying, warming, and easy to drink. (1997)

Geyser Peak Winery Shiraz (Sonoma County). $15.99. VERY GOOD. Intense and peppery. What an experience! Warming, like a fireplace. Real structure. Still quite young. (1996)

Villa Mt. Eden Winery (Grand Reserve; Indian Springs Vineyard; Nevada County). $15.99. VERY GOOD. Interesting, with a taste of the soil. Inky, but easy to drink, with real character. (1996)

Pepperwood Grove Winery. $6.99. GOOD/VERY GOOD. A bit too creamy and a bit too fat, but it's still a good introduction to Syrah at a great price. (1998)

Chapter Twenty-eight

House Wines

Like Coming Home to a Puppy

Because we're journalists, we've always worked odd hours. At one point, John worked at a morning newspaper from about nine in the morning to seven at night while Dottie worked at an afternoon newspaper from midnight until nine. Sometimes one of us would want to drink a glass of wine while the other was at work, but we wouldn't want to open anything special. That's when we first started buying house wines. In restaurant parlance, the house wine is the inexpensive but (you hope) charming wine that you drink by the glass at the bar, or from a carafe with a simple meal. Our house wine at home is, in many ways, the same thing. It's a wine that's good enough to enjoy soon after we've walked in the door, but not so special that we feel guilty opening a bottle without our better half around. It has to be inexpensive, easy to drink, generally available, and simple in the best sense of the word. It should be a wine we don't have to think about to enjoy. It might be something that we sip together while preparing a dinner that will be accompanied by a finer wine. Ideally, it should also be a wine that can keep for a couple of days. Since this is a have-a-glass-when-you-come-home wine, there should always be a bottle handy, sometimes opened and recorked from the day before.

For many years when we were young—oh, at least a couple of decades ago—our house red was Premiat, from Romania. Then it was Egri Bikavér, "Bull's Blood," from Hungary. Both of these cost $1.99, which was perfect for two struggling young journalists. As the years went by, our house wine got a bit pricier. There was our Rioja period—Federico Paternina, Marqués de Riscal. Then we found a closeout on a California Cabernet Sauvignon called HMR. At some point, we got a great deal on a California Zinfandel from Amador Foothill Winery, so that became our house wine. You should always be on the lookout for a new one. Wine ruts are easy to fall into; change is good.

So we wondered: If we were looking for a house wine today, what would we choose? We conducted two large tastings to find out. We figured that $6.99 today is probably roughly equivalent to $1.99 in the mid-'70s, so we set that as our limit. Then we bought the first fifty reds and then the first fifty whites we could find for $6.99 or less. For the reds, we excluded Beaujolais. We've said many times that Beaujolais may be the greatest red-wine bargain in the world, but, despite the low price, it's so special to us that we consider it a cut above our everyday house wines. It also loses something after it's opened. Among whites, we excluded Muscadet for many of the same reasons. We also bought only regular-size bottles. Since we only drink a little of our house wine at a time, we figure that we'll end up throwing away a lot if we buy big bottles.

We included wines from just about everywhere. When you shop for a house wine, be open-minded. Don't rule out Romania or Argentina just because the wines seem unfamiliar. Some great bargains come from unfamiliar places because they're, well, unfamiliar. If you're hesitant to look outside of the United States for an inexpensive wine, you're doing yourself a disservice. We didn't conduct these tastings blind, since we were tasting so many different kinds of wines. In the end, we narrowed our list of reds to ten, and they were from seven countries and several types of grapes. Among whites, our favorites came from five countries: Australia, Chile, Spain, South Africa, and Greece. These are well-made wines with excellent fruit and a real ease, just what we're looking for in a house wine.

We also were reminded of how tastes and smells can revive memories. Our very favorite was a Chardonnay from Australia, Lindemans Bin 65, which cost $6.99. It was big, with hints of vanilla and nutmeg. We found it comforting, we think, because it reminded us a little of the huge, oaky California Chardonnays of our youth, when we were new to wine, and of the first inexpensive Australian Chardonnay we fell in love with, Jacob's Creek.

We used to meet Media and Zoë for dinner sometimes at a little Indian place near our apartment. It was a friendly place, with a little window through which Media and Zoë could watch the chef working over the tandoor oven. We'd get there first, straight from work, and sit by the window, eating appetizers and drinking a bottle of the Jacob's Creek, which was just $11. It was easy to drink, yet had enough fruit, acid, and oak tastes to stand up to, and complement, the spicy Indian food. When the girls, all dressed up, finally arrived in their double stroller, pushed by their babysitter Louise, we don't know who was more excited to see whom. A simple Australian Chardonnay always makes us think of those sweet times. That's how personal a house wine can—and really should—be.

Good news on the reds, too: While our favorite was from Portugal—the dry red wines of Portugal are often very good buys these days—we still liked our old Premiat, which gave us a smile.

Below are the wines we preferred, in our tastings, as house wines. Which house wine is for you? Let's suggest something radical: This weekend, go to your supermarket or your wine store determined to buy an entire mixed case of white or red wine. Set $6.99 per bottle as your price limit. Then buy twelve bottles, from all over the world—maybe even just the first twelve you see in that price range. At home, just put the case of red in the bottom of a closet. Or, if your case is white, put one bottle in the refrigerator. Don't worry about how long the bottle will be in the refrigerator (because it won't be there for long). Put the rest of the wines, still in the box, anywhere that it's dark and the temperature is moderate. The next time you're simply in the mood for a glass of wine—nothing special— either grab a red from the stash in your closet or that bottle of white in the fridge. Open and drink. Put a cork in it and have some more until it's gone. Then put the next bottle of white in the refrigerator. Repeat.

Remember that you're not looking for just an OK wine. You're looking for one that will be a little like a puppy you come home to every day— so very eager to please you. It took us a long time before we found Tiger, just the right dog, and it might take you some time to find just the right house wine. But we guarantee you that one of those twelve you bought will please you more than the others. Congratulations! You've found your house wine. Now, go buy a case of it.

Wine Notes

General advice: Here are some suggestions for house whites and house reds, with explanations of why we find them good enough and comforting enough to fill those important roles. You need to find your own, but, as you can see, part of the trick is to look for wines from unfamiliar countries or regions.

House Whites

Lindemans Bin 65 Chardonnay (Australia). $6.99. Oaky and rich, with nutmeg and vanilla bean. Soothing, like a really plump comforter. (1999)

Casa Lapostolle Sauvignon Blanc (Rapel Valley; Chile). $6.99. Refreshing, crisp, and a bit spritzy, with enough varietal character to show you've come home to real wine. (1999)

René Barbier Mediterranean White (Penedes; Spain). $4.49. Fresh, fruity, lemony, and pleasant. Crisp. Lifts your spirit. (Nonvintage)

Cape Indaba Sauvignon Blanc (South Africa). $6.99. Lively, flowery, and pleasant. It's bright, but subtle, perfect to get your appetite going. (1998)

Alice White Chardonnay (Australia). $6.99. Well made. Round and altogether pleasant. (1998)

Undurraga Sauvignon Blanc 1999 (Chile). $6.99. Clean and fresh, with real grassy varietal character. (1999)

Robert's Rock Chenin Blanc/Chardonnay (South Africa). $6.99. John finds it a bit too acidic, and better as a food wine, but Dorothy says it's "a nice sipping wine," pleasant and fruity. (1999)

Kourtaki Vin de Crete (Greece). $5.99. Charming and easy to drink, yet different and interesting. Probably even better with grilled fish. (1997)

House Reds

Convento da Serra Alentejo (Roquevale; Portugal). $6.99. Plump and fruity, even a bit rich, with a nice, long finish. Easy to drink. (1997)

Hardys Merlot (Australia). $6.99. Big and serious, with a nice taste of the earth and full fruit tastes. A complete wine. (1997)

Vigneti del Sole Montepulciano d'Abruzzo. (Pasqua Vigneti e Cantine; Italy). $6.99. Soft, easy and lovely. Nice, simple fruit. (1998)

Georges Duboeuf Syrah (France). $5.99. Blackberries and soil on the nose. Dark and rich and lovely. Easy as you please. (1998)

Domaine des Moulins Côtes-du-Rhône (Georges Duboeuf; France). $5.99. Flavorful and easy to drink. Better in winter. (1998)

Rosemount Estate Shiraz–Cabernet (Australia). $6.99. Aggressively fruity, with cherry-strawberry tastes. Simple in the best sense of the word. (1999)

Pepperwood Grove Syrah (California). $6.99. Deep and comforting, with plenty of dark, rich fruit. (1998)

Château Fonfroide Bordeaux (France). $6.99. Mellow and classy, very approachable. More proof that inexpensive Bordeaux can be a great buy. (1996)

Falling Star Merlot-Malbec (Trapiche; Argentina). $4.99. A lovely, simple, whet-your-appetite wine—and what a price! (1998)

Premiat Pinot Noir (Romania). $3.99. Our old favorite. Lovely, cranberry-like fruit, with some earthiness. Chill slightly. (1997)

Chapter Twenty-nine

Kosher Wines

You Don't Have to Be Jewish

Every year after we met, we traveled to Jacksonville to celebrate Passover with John's family. When John was growing up, Passover was one of the few times his family ever had wine in the house—that thick, sweet Concord-grape wine. Even Dottie's family served it in little glasses at Thanksgiving. When Dottie was converting to Judaism, and at our nephew Ben's bar mitzvah, this was the wine offered after services. It was what so many of us grew up thinking was "kosher wine." Unfortunately, some people still do. When John told a new doctor that he was a wine writer, the doctor sighed. "I really enjoy wine," he said, "but, unfortunately, because I keep kosher, my choices are limited." Are they really? We were curious, so we ended up conducting three major tastings of kosher wine.

We tried wines from all over the world—California, France, Chile, Italy, Israel, even Turkey. They were made from Cabernet Sauvignon, Merlot, Cabernet Franc, Pinot Noir, Petite Syrah, Chenin Blanc, Zinfandel, Barbera, Sangiovese, Chardonnay, Gewürztraminer, Riesling, Muscat, and more. They were red and white, dry and sweet, sparkling and still. There were high-end red Bordeaux wines from France, crisp whites from the United States, and inexpensive, delightful Italian reds. Far more were good than bad. In other words, John's doctor, and many other people, don't realize how far kosher wines have come. This is the most important lesson of our tastings: Even if you don't care whether it's kosher, you should try some of these because they're just plain good wines.

First, though, what makes wine kosher? It starts with special treatment and attention to cleanliness. Rabbis or their designated assistants supervise the wine's production from crush to bottling. Experts such as Howard Abarbanel, president of Abarbanel Wines, tell us that wines labeled "Kosher for Passover" are made with special enzymes and yeasts and special fining agents—not animal by-products, like gelatin, for example—that clarify the wine. Often their front labels will sport an "O" with a "U" inside with a "P" near it. This, they say, is the stamp of approval of the largest kosher certification body in the world and basically means there's no need to read the label further to learn that the wine is kosher for Passover.

There is another level of kosher wine that's *mevushal,* and some wines are both kosher for Passover and *mevushal.* Baron Herzog told us its wines and other kosher wines go through this added step. Sometimes it's listed on the label. "A *mevushal* wine," Herzog's representatives said, "is one that can be handled by the general public, like a non-Jewish waiter, and still remain kosher." Wine that does not go through this *mevushal* process must be served by observant Jews to retain its kosher status. Basically, Herzog explained, a *mevushal* wine is heated in seconds by flash pasteurization, with the temperature brought down quickly so as not to harm the wine. Some wineries do this to the unfermented white and blush juice; others do it with reds after fermentation. This added step, the Herzog people said, not only does not harm the wine, but "enhances its aromatics and complexities" while "stabilizing the color and tannins." Herzog said that about 40 percent of its customers aren't Jewish.

Ultimately, though, what matters is what's in the bottle, and we were pleased with what we found in our tastings. Overall, the reds were better than the whites. Some reds, though, seemed too light, and Sauvignon Blanc was the least successful varietal. A good Sauvignon Blanc has a crisp, fresh, grassy quality that's quite distinctive and vibrant. Too many of these were dull, without much character or charm. The most successful wine type was Merlot. We're not huge fans of Merlot, but these were quite good— smooth, well made, and filled with tasty, approachable fruit. One Merlot stood out. We described it in our notes as pleasant and easy to drink but with real depth and soul. One Cabernet Sauvignon was also far and away the best. It was elegant, with a long, lovely finish. We were also fond of a Cabernet Franc, which we described as "a Cabernet Franc of real character, with the kind of sharp edges this grape can offer." All three were from Hagafen Cellars, a California winery. It's clear that reds from Hagafen are worth looking for.

But kosher wines go well beyond the well-known grapes like Cabernet Sauvignon and Merlot. In one of our tastings, we focused on the kinds of wines that would make people say, "I didn't know this wine was made kosher." We conducted this tasting with our friend Neil Brown, who was visiting from Florida. Neil doesn't keep kosher, but we wondered what he'd think. So we really laid it on thick—a Chenin Blanc, two fine Bordeaux wines, a Chianti, and a Sauternes. Yep, a kosher Sauternes, the great sweet white from France. We didn't taste these wines blind, because they were different kinds from different places. We were quite fond of the Bartenura Chianti, which was fruity and delightful. And we were very impressed with the Château Giscours 1995, a Margaux from Bordeaux. Giscours is a fine, well-known château, but we didn't know it made kosher wine until we saw it in a store. We called the importer, Royal Wine Corp., and asked about this. Royal told us it has a full-time kosher winemaker in France who travels around persuading wineries to make a small amount of kosher wine. Less than 1,000 cases of this Giscours were made, more than half of which stayed in France. It didn't go through flash pasteurization, so it's not *mevushal*, Royal said.

We also didn't know that Laurent-Perrier made a kosher Champagne, which was a pleasure, though a bit aggressive for our taste. One of the most charming wines was a Rémy-Pannier Rosé d'Anjou from France. It was a treat. Our favorite was a surprise: Chenin Blanc. This one, from Baron Herzog, was crisp and vibrant, with all sorts of fruit tastes, like peaches and pears. More than any other wine he tasted, our friend Neil said this is the one he would rush out and buy, kosher or not. So would we.

Our overall advice to you would be that, even if you don't keep kosher, don't avoid kosher wines. In fact, we now routinely include kosher wines in our general tastings, and some of them have been among our favorites, including a Beaujolais Nouveau (Abarbanel Château de la Salle) and two White Zinfandels (Baron Herzog and Weinstock).

One last thing: There's more to wine than the way it tastes. When we have old-fashioned, Concord-grape kosher wine, it takes us back to happy family times, all of us sitting around a table while John's father held up a matzo and intoned "LO! This is the bread of affliction." Tradition is important, and, for many of us, that wine is part of our traditions. If it's part of yours, too, don't be shy about it. In the long run, if a wine reminds us of melons or berries or flowers, that's great. But if it reminds us of our families and our traditions, that's even better.

Wine Notes

General advice: If you keep kosher, you can find just about any kind of wine now, from all over the world, so if your wine store doesn't have a good selection, try somewhere else. If you don't keep kosher, you should try kosher wines the same way you try any kind of wine. Here are some of our favorites from three large tastings of kosher wines. They are not rated because not all of these tastings were conducted blind. They are listed in dinner order—from Champagne to whites to rosés to reds to dessert—to give an idea of the wide variety of kosher wines now available. We have generally liked the reds from Hagafen Cellars and the whites from Weinstock, and we have found the wines from Yarden, in Israel, and Bartenura, in Italy, to be consistently well made.

Yarden Vineyards Blanc de Blancs (Israel). $20.99. Smells like real Champagne, with chalk and real acid. Lovely bubbles that, like the real thing, are central to the taste. Beautifully made. Could stand up to food. Very impressive. (Nonvintage)

Laurent-Perrier Brut L.P. Champagne (France). $49.95. A bit too aggressive for us, but the real thing, with toast and nuttiness. (Nonvintage)

Baron Herzog Chenin Blanc (United States). $8.50. Lovely fruit, with all sorts of peach and pear tastes. Crisp and delightful. (1999)

Yarden Vineyards White Riesling (Israel). $10.49. This is so charming and so very Riesling. Flowers, peaches, and dew. (1995)

Bartenura Gavi (Italy). $8.99. Kosher or not, rush out and buy this. It has so much more character than most Italian whites. Real body, real taste. This can stand up to a good meal. (Nonvintage)

Weinstock Cellars Sauvignon Blanc (United States). $6.99. Fresh, with pleasant varietal grassiness. (1997)

Abarbanel Gewürztraminer (France). $13.99. Quite nice, with pepper and spice and real Gewürz character, but just a tiny bit too sweet. (1995)

Yarden Vineyards Chardonnay (Israel). $11.99. Wow! Golden, rich, and filled with cream, oak, and vanilla. Still, there's enough acid to make it all work together. This tastes familiar, like a fine California wine. (1995)

Weinstock Cellars Chardonnay (United States). $8.99. Interesting, with woody tastes and some toasty cream. (1996)

Rémy-Pannier Rosé d'Anjou (France). $8.99. Effortless and lovely, with nice lemony tastes. A bit sweet, but charming and easy to drink. (1998)

Weinstock Cellars Gamay (United States). $6.99. Delightful, with tastes of strawberries and earth. Chill. (1997)

Bartenura Barbera d'Asti (Italy). $7.49. Nice, round, and very much an Italian wine. It has a lovely smell, enchanting tastes, and a body soft as a pillow. (1996)

Bartenura Chianti (A. Sardelli; Italy). $10.99. Nicely fruity, with lots of up-front "sweet" fruit. Light, but nice berry flavors and some spice. (1997)

Alfasi Merlot (Chile). $7.99. Pretty and crisp-looking, alive in the glass. Pleasant and gulpable with very "forward" fruit tastes. (1997)

Baron Herzog Wine Cellars Zinfandel (United States). $10.49. This is what Zinfandel is supposed to taste like, with real edge, real life, real zest. (1996)

Hagafen Cellars Cabernet Franc (United States). $14.99. If you've never had a "Cab Franc," this is a good place to start. Lots of sharp varietal character, very dry, very edgy. Would give extra texture to a heavy main course such as Grandma Helen's brisket. (1996)

Yarden Vineyards Cabernet Sauvignon (Israel). $17.99. Classy and "bright," almost thick with big fruit tastes and a long, fat finish. Intense fruit with lots of guts. This is a Cabernet lover's Cabernet. (1994)

Hagafen Cellars Cabernet Sauvignon (United States). $25.99. Classy and beautifully made. Filled with fruit, elegant and complex. Some earth and cream and a lovely, lingering finish. (1996)

Château Giscours (France). $61.00. Rich and earthy. Slightly roasted taste. We also tried the 1997, which was more charming at the moment but didn't have as much character. (1995)

Château La Gaffelière St. Émilion Grand Cru (France). $54.99. After two hours of air, it finally shows its stuff, becoming flat and peppery at the same time. Wonder what a really good Merlot tastes like? This is it. (1993)

Carmel Vineyards Emerald Riesling Semi-Dry (Israel). $6.99. Clean, fresh, and not nearly as sweet as "semi-dry" would imply. Nice varietal character, with some earthy backbone that gives it real character. Excellent as a sipping wine. (1997)

Gan Eden Late-Harvest Gewürztraminer (United States). $11.99. Absolutely lovely. Pretty, floral nose and a taste full of charm. A tiny bit spritzy, and completely winning. (1996)

Kaizer Franz Josef Tokaji Furmint (Hungary). $9.99 (500 ml). Peaches, pears, and lots of apples. Lacks intensity, but its lightness would be good after a big meal. Excellent with fruit. (1997)

Sparkling Wine

American Sparklers

Making Life a Celebration

Champagne is for celebrations, but many people get it backward. They think that when they have a celebration, they should drink Champagne. It's just the opposite: They should drink Champagne to *make* a celebration. And it doesn't have to be Champagne with a capital C, either—and we mean that quite literally. If you asked us about the best sparkling wines we'd ever had, we'd tell you about some of the greatest wines of France (see Chapter Thirty-two), but we'd also tell you this:

We always wanted to live in New York, and we finally got our chance in 1980. We lived in a one-bedroom off Central Park West, with a little balcony overlooking the spot where John Lennon was shot. Columbus Avenue was the center of our universe. We were young, with no kids, and we sat at outdoor cafés for hours watching beautiful Manhattanites go by. Back then, there was a restaurant on Columbus called the Rocking Horse that served huge portions of heavy, stick-to-your-ribs Mexican food and an even heavier, delicious sangria. One beautiful spring night, we sat at the Rocking Horse for hours, drinking sangria and generally feeling very lucky to be together in Manhattan. Across the street was—and still is—a little wine and liquor shop. That night it had a big sign in the window: "André Champagne. 2 for $3.99!" All night, we talked, we watched—and we saw that sign. So when we finally left the Rocking Horse, we couldn't resist: We bought a bottle of André, chilled.

Sparkling wine can be made many ways, from very inexpensively to very expensively. Real Champagne is made in the bottle, one bottle at a time, with the second fermentation—the one that makes the bubbles—taking place inside the bottle under tremendous pressure. This is called *"méthode champenoise."* There's another way sparkling wine can be made. It's called the Charmat bulk process (named for its inventor, Eugene Charmat), and it's just what it sounds like: fermenting in great big tanks, then pumped into bottles. This is why sparkling wines like André can be so inexpensive—cheap, bulk grapes made into cheap, bulk wine. However, on that perfect spring night, we took our bottle of André back to our apartment. There, on our balcony, seven stories up, we popped it open and drank it, watching the world go by. The wine was cold and fresh after the heavy Mexican food. The bubbles, forceful as they were, were comforting going down, and the weather was perfect. That night, no sparkling wine could possibly have been more delicious.

That's what we mean about Champagne making a celebration. You can make that kind of celebration any night, and you don't have to spend a fortune or settle for André. Here's why. Until about thirty years ago, there were generally two kinds of sparkling wine: cheap stuff from the United States and expensive stuff from France. When we were growing up, there was Korbel, of course, but it wasn't that fine. Schramsberg had been making fine sparkling wine since 1966, but not in large enough quantities that it was widely distributed. In 1973, the Moët & Chandon people changed the world of American bubbly by opening Domaine Chandon in California. They began producing massive quantities of outstanding sparkling wine for a reasonable price—still usually between $13 and $17. Like a flash, others jumped in, from France and Spain, and home-grown wineries joined the rush. Now, you can find several excellent sparkling wines from California just about everywhere and most will cost you about what you'd pay for a decent bottle of Chardonnay or Merlot.

Let's get this out of the way, OK? There is no American Champagne. Real Champagne is made only in the Champagne region of France, and it's special for many reasons, including tradition and soil. All of the other stuff, from wherever, is sparkling wine. Most California winemakers don't use "Champagne" on their labels anymore. What they make should be called "sparkling wine." Is that clear? OK, now that you know it, don't worry about it. Although this really miffs the French, it isn't something you should lose any sleep over. Life is too short. We would never call a California bubbly "Champagne" in public, but around the house, when one of us says, "Let's open a bottle of Champagne," we know that could mean a sparkler from anywhere.

In any event, many of the best American "champagnes" have much in common with the real thing. Good American sparkling wine is made much the same way as Champagne: It's produced from Pinot Noir, Pinot Meunier and/or Chardonnay grapes, and each bottle is carefully turned, tilted in a special contraption for weeks or months as the impurities flow toward the cork, to be popped out before final corking. "Brut" means dry and "extra dry" means a little sweet (the same way a "medium" soft drink at a fast-food joint is actually the smallest). One thing that often separates Champagne from champagne is the bubbles. In real Champagne, the bubbles and the taste are inextricably bound; Champagne wouldn't be the same as a still wine. But most American sparklers seem to have a taste aside from the bubbles. The bubbles are lovely to have, but they aren't as much a part of the wine's soul as they are in the real thing. That said, though, America is producing some really fine stuff, in large quantities and at great prices. Two blind tastings, in which we sampled most of the widely available American sparklers under $20, proved our point. The overall quality was high. The wines were well made, fun, and tremendously drinkable. And later, tasted alone, not head to head, each was enjoyable.

In our earlier tasting, our favorite made us smile when we took the bag off and saw what it was. One of the greatest pleasures of New York is Bobby Short, the elegant pianist who has entertained for years at the Cafe Carlyle. We first went to see Bobby Short in 1983, and the occasion seemed to call for bubbly. On the wine list was something we'd never seen before: a Scharffenberger Brut 1981, from California. It was $30, and we still remember it as having class, charm, and real body. It turns out it wasn't just the mood talking. The best of our first blind tasting was a Scharffenberger, a vintage Blanc de Blancs. The real surprise came next. Another bottle was a close second. "Nice, classy bubbles. Nutty, like the real thing. Some chalk, a little lemon on the finish. A glass of class. There's a real winemaker here." When we unveiled that bottle it was the regular bottling of Scharffenberger, the brut nonvintage, which then cost just $13.99. Soon after that tasting,

Scharffenberger was sold, and its name was changed to Pacific Echo. The Scharffen Berger people now make chocolate.

In our most recent tasting, we once again found the American sparklers under $20 highly drinkable, well made, and great for any festive occasion. Some were too simple for our tastes, without enough fruit, and some were clumsy, with big bubbles and too much sweetness. But most were quite nice. We liked Pacific Echo's Brut once again and two of the bubblies from Mumm Napa Valley, both the Brut Prestige and the Blanc de Blancs, as well as the Piper Sonoma Blanc de Noir.

Blanc de Blancs means the wine was made primarily from Chardonnay. Blanc de Noir means it was made primarily from Pinot Noir, and maybe some Pinot Meunier. Most bubblies are blends of those grapes. As it happens, five of our six favorites were made primarily from Pinot Noir, which might mean that our palates prefer the structure of Pinot Noir to the elegance of Chardonnay, or might mean nothing at all.

We very much liked the Chandon Brut Classic, which was fairly aggressive and, we wrote in our notes, "not as elegant as it is fun." Chandon, which is sometimes available for as little as $11.99, was our house bubbly for years. It has always been a Halloween tradition to sip it as we trail our little trick-or-treaters. Our favorite was classy, with a depth and richness that we associate with age. It seemed different than the others, both more "serious" and eminently drinkable. It was Domaine Carneros Brut, which is widely available and an excellent buy.

Don't wait for a special occasion to buy a bottle of bubbly. Buy one now and put it in the refrigerator. You'll be surprised how many things you'll find to celebrate.

Wine Notes

General advice: The most widely available American bubblies are remarkably reliable and good bargains. Nonvintage bubbly is designed to offer a consistent taste, so it's easy to find a house bubbly. Chandon was ours for years. Keep a bottle in your refrigerator at all times. It will be fine for at least several weeks. Bubbly is always appropriate as a gift, especially when paired with a couple of nice glasses. If you're patient and look at ads, you can sometimes find great buys.

Food pairings: *Good sipped alone. Grilled seafood and vegetables, including mushrooms. Poultry folded into rich cream sauces. Sushi. Pâté. Raw oysters.*

Domaine Carneros by Taittinger Brut. $21.99. VERY GOOD. Best of tasting. Nice, yeasty nose. Lovely and crisp, with nice acids for food and a classy richness that makes it special. Elegant, with a certain seriousness that makes it different.

Chandon Brut Classic. $14.99. VERY GOOD. Best value. Lovely nose, lovely straw color and some very aggressive bubbles. Not as elegant as it is fun. (Tip: We have kept bottles of this in our closet for a while and they have improved with age, getting richer and more complex.)

Pacific Echo Brut. $16.99. VERY GOOD. Clean and crisp, with a nice touch of chalky soil and some real soul. Real character, with a pleasant, lemony finish. Easy to drink and nice to come home to.

Piper Sonoma Blanc de Noir. $14.99. GOOD/VERY GOOD. The nose alone is worth the price. Crisp, tingly, and mouth-watering. Quite dry, and a bit tight. It whet our appetite for food.

Mumm Cuvée Napa Brut Prestige. $16.99. GOOD/VERY GOOD. Lovely "Champagne" nose, with plenty of yeast and tickly bubbles. Simpler than some, but it's so pleasant and drinkable.

Mumm Cuvée Napa Blanc de Blancs. $19.99 GOOD/VERY GOOD. Clean, classy, and crisp, with nice tastes of lemon and tropical citrus flavors.

Gruet Brut. $13.99. GOOD. This bubbly from New Mexico always makes us smile. It has real taste and fruit, even a little bit of chalk, though it does tend to be overly big.

How to Open
Champagne Without
Killing Anybody

Opening a bottle of Champagne the right way is important. Sure, it might be fun to pop it open and let the Champagne spray everywhere. This is especially good fun if you've just won the World Series. But experts say that's bad idea for the wine. It lets the bubbles escape, they say, leaving you with a flatter wine. That may be true, but we think it's a bad idea for another reason: We're sure the cork will smack one of us in the eye and blind us. Remember that the wine in that bottle is under tremendous pressure. That's why it has been capped so carefully and why it's bottled in such heavy glass.

It really can explode. The day we bought our country cabin, we put a bottle of Champagne in the spare refrigerator to chill. Later, when we went back to get the bottle, we discovered for the first time that the extra "refrigerator" was actually a freezer. The bottle had exploded, and frozen Champagne was everywhere. It was very depressing, but quite memorable.

We saw a movie once in which one of those very sauve '30s characters in a tuxedo—probably William Powell—was explaining how to open a bottle of bubbly. "It shouldn't pop," he explained. "It should cough, apologetically." Always remember that: It should cough, apologetically.

This is how we do it. It might not be as elegant as some methods, but it always works and it's safe:

• Take off the foil wrapping. This is just decorative, so there's nothing to be concerned about.

• Get a kitchen towel, maybe one that's especially pretty, like Dottie's antique linens.

• Drape the towel over the top of the bottle.

• Put your hand under the towel and unscrew that metal retainer that holds down the cork. Lift it off. Be careful. This is when the cork could pop out on its own. This is why you have the towel draped over the bottle: The cork has nowhere to go.

• If the cork hasn't popped out, remove your hand from under the towel and place it on top of the shrouded cork. Hold the cork firmly and slowly turn the bottle. Keep holding the cork, with steady pressure. Remember that you don't want it to pop out.

• When you start to feel the cork giving, let up the pressure just slightly to allow the cork to slowly push its way out. When you feel the cork just about ready to come out altogether, tilt it sideways slightly.

Right then, it will cough, apologetically. All of the bubbles will be saved, as will your eyes. And you can pretend you're William Powell.

Chapter Thirty-one

How to Travel by Train

(This Is the Champagne Chapter)

People say the romance of the rails is dead. They're wrong. You can still have a remarkably romantic little vacation aboard an Amtrak train, although, as with all true romance, it's your responsibility to make the magic—and to bring the Champagne. We honeymooned on a train in 1979 with Taittinger Champagne and have been second-honeymooning on trains ever since. While many people think of trains, in principle, as romantic—remember Cary Grant and Eva Marie Saint in *North by Northwest*? (we would rank that steamy scene a Delicious!)—many people are convinced they need to pay a fortune for an Orient Express–type experience to travel back to the good old days of train travel. They don't.

We're not rough-it types, and we're here to tell you how to have a romantic getaway on Amtrak, in nine easy steps:

1. Get a route map. Don't let anyone plan your trip for you; travel agents generally don't know much about trains. Ditto for Amtrak's own agents. Besides, looking through the route map and deciphering the timetables, which are still nicely old-fashioned, is fun.

2. Decide where you want to go—not where you need to be. If you need to go to a wedding or to a business conference, take a plane. Trains can be unreliable. If you're going to worry about a schedule, this won't work for you. Part of the romance is that you don't have to be anywhere at any particular time. Best advice: Choose a route, not a destination. If this is your first time on a long-distance train, find a route that will keep you—allll aboarddd—for at least twenty-four hours, but not too much longer.

3. Get a deluxe bedroom—and get it well in advance. Make sure you ask for a "deluxe bedroom," and do not settle for anything less, when you make reservations. These go fast, so nail down your reservation a.s.a.p.

4. Take four parcels on board with you. One should be a large suitcase filled with items that will be unnecessary aboard the train, like clothes. Store this in your room. The second bag should be a small suitcase with necessities: Champagne, glasses, two table settings, toiletries, and nighties modest enough to be seen by the porter, whom you'll tip when he brings you ice. Take 50 percent more Champagne than you can possibly imagine drinking. The third thing you must bring is an ice bucket, already packed with a bottle of Champagne on ice so that as soon as the train gets under way, you'll be ready. And the fourth should be the greatest picnic you can arrange.

Finally, you're ready to board the train.

5. Tell the porter to put down the lower bed and leave it down throughout the trip. Your room will be small, but it has the essentials: Two beds (upper and lower), a toilet with a shower, a sink, and, in some newer trains, a video screen that shows current movies.

6. Close the door. Put on your pajamas. Sit on the bed and gaze out the large window that runs the length of your compartment. Get your glasses. Open the Champagne. Drink it. Think about the fact that, from this moment until the trip is over, *you never have to get out of bed*. You have your Champagne, your ice bucket (the porter will bring more ice when you ring), and you already have your first meal. If you ask and tip nicely, the porter will usually bring all of your meals to your bedroom.

7. Don't worry about delays or other glitches on the trains. Just look out the window. Sitting there, glass in hand, consider some important questions: Is the trip nicer during the day, when you can see America spread out before you, or during darkness, when the most humble home seems warm with its windows golden and bright?

8. Drift off to sleep together in the lower bed. The beds are about the size of a twin. Normally, that would be too small for two people, but the clickety-clack of the rails—honest, the train really goes clickety-clack—

is hypnotic. Let the room get a little bit cold, bundle up, and watch things go by. Sunrise aboard a train is a wondrous event you don't really have to wake up to enjoy; just try to open your eyes long enough to see it. Then go back to sleep.

9. Don't let the porter put up the bed. He'll likely want to do that in the morning. Don't let him. About a half hour before you reach your destination, it'll be time to get dressed.

All of this, of course, begs the big question: What Champagne do you take with you? We decided to conduct a tasting to see what we would recommend.

In the previous chapter, we talked about "everyday" American sparklers. In the next chapter, we discuss those once-a-year, very expensive Champagnes. For a train trip, we would recommend the classic in-between bubbly: the widely available French nonvintage brut Champagnes, like Moët, Mumm, and Piper-Heidsieck, that usually cost around $18 to $30.

Ultimately, your favorite Champagne may have everything to do with the memories associated with it, and less to do with how it actually tastes. Taittinger is "our" Champagne because we served it at our wedding and drank it on our honeymoon train. Nothing will ever change that. Maybe Moët is "your" Champagne. But, if you put our Taittinger and your Moët and all of the other well-known Champagne names against each other, what would you find?

For starters, Champagnes, like all wines, have their own style. Some are heavy, some are light, and some are in between. This is a function of the winemaker's taste, the blend (or "cuvée") of grapes selected (is there more Chardonnay, Pinot Noir, or Pinot Meunier in the blend?) and how long the wine sits on its sediment, or lees, before it is "disgorged." Disgorging is the process by which the sediment is removed and the bottle topped off with a sugary mixture called the "dosage," then finally sealed for sale. The amount of sugar in the dosage determines the Champagne's sweetness or dryness. Champagnes with no sugar added in the dosage are rare and expensive. You'll sometimes see them called something like "Brut Nature."

Nonvintage Champagne is blended year after year to ensure a consistent style, so any opinion about which is the "best" Champagne is inevitably also a statement about the style you prefer. There are some more-or-less objective benchmarks: tiny bubbles and many of them; a complete bond between the taste of the bubbles and the taste of the wine (it shouldn't taste like a still wine with bubbles added later); enough acidity to make the wine come alive; and at least a little taste of chalky soil.

One of the fun things about tasting wines in flights of several bottles is that both flaws and perfection are more obvious in comparative tastings. These are all fine wines, but in our blind tasting we were surprised that some of our long-time favorites seemed clunky and simple. Our beloved Taittinger rated just OK/Good. "Very simple. Not a lot there. Pleasant, but seems inexpensive," we wrote, even though, going back to our point, we're sure that if we tasted this by itself, we would have liked it more.

Some of the best-known names went the way of the Taittinger, but many were much better and memorable, including our three favorites—a threesome that provided a bizarre footnote to our tasting. About our third favorite, we wrote: "Lots of class, lots of taste. Cream, nuts, and yeast. Lovely and very much a winemaker's wine. For those who like 'heavier' Champagne." This tasted very expensive to us. We were shocked to discover it was plain old Piper-Heidsieck, available everywhere, and just $19.99 at that. This is a great deal.

We couldn't decide which we liked better among our two remaining favorites so we decided to declare them our co-favorites. Were we ever surprised when we took the bags off them. Both were classy and excellent, but very different. One was bold and approachable, with a great deal of fruit and depth. It had an element of weight that made it feel good in our mouths. The other was the most beautiful to look at—perfect pale straw color, perfect bubbles, classy. The taste was restrained, austere, and chalky, the essence of what we think of when we think of really good Champagne. One approachable and rich, the other austere and classy. Both excellent. What were they? The first was Charles Heidsieck. The second was Heidsieck & Co. Monopole Blue Top. That's right: Our top three all had Heidsieck in the name. We told you the outcome was bizarre.

We looked up these wines and this is what we found: Florenz-Louis Heidsieck founded a great Champagne house, Heidsieck & Co., in Reims in 1785, with three nephews. After Florenz's death, one nephew stayed with the company. The other two nephews started their own separate

Heidsieck houses. Today, Rémy-Cointreau owns Piper-Heidsieck and Charles Heidsieck, which share a winemaker, and Vranken Monopole owns the original company, now called Heidsieck & Co. Monopole.

Now, all that said, we can't emphasize this too strongly: If you see a Champagne on the shelf that you've never seen before that's in your price range, grab it. If the bottle is from France and it says "Champagne," it has to be the real thing, under French law. There are many outstanding little Champagne houses whose bubblies rarely make it to the United States, and, if they do, there's very little of it. We've found over the years that these are usually great buys. They're well made, highly personal, and inexpensive because, after all, no one has ever heard of them.

One final tip: You can often find good buys on well-known Champagne, too, because they're so widely available that stores compete aggressively on price. Keep watching the ads, and when you see a good deal, pounce. Keep this story in mind from Jonathan Brown of Gardiner, Maine, who wrote to us: "It's been years since I've had any good French Champagne. I can't afford it and, if the truth be known, there's lots of other good bubbly stuff from other places to drink. Nonetheless, I've missed not having any of the real article with its tiny bubbles that go on forever.

"So imagine my delight when the local supermarket put out reduced-price bins of the Mumm's Cordon Rouge and Perrier-Jouët it couldn't sell for the millennial New Year. And imagine my further delight when even that maneuver failed and they were reduced to offering the Cordon Rouge for $9.99 a bottle and the P-J for $12.99! I now have a closetful thanks to all that Champagne hysteria, and I'm becoming quite popular once again."

Wine Notes

General advice: Nonvintage Champagne—the real stuff, from the Champagne district of France—is widely available at prices from $18 to $30. Most of the names are well known, like Mumm and Moët, and it's hard to go wrong. "Brut" means dry, while "extra dry" means a little sweet. All Champagnes should be well chilled. The list below includes our favorites from a tasting of well-known names, but some of the greatest bargains are Champagnes that most of us have never heard of.

Food pairings: Dishes with cream sauces and mushrooms. Sushi and grilled foods of all kinds.

Heidsieck & Co. Monopole Blue Top Brut. $27.99. VERY GOOD/DE-LICIOUS. Best of tasting (tie). Absolutely gorgeous. Austere, chalky, and classy. Plenty of lemon and yeast and a real hint of age, which gives it some bearing.

Charles Heidsieck Brut Réserve. $21.99. VERY GOOD/DELICIOUS. Best of tasting (tie). Lemony fruit, yeasty taste. A bigger, more approachable style than Heidsieck & Co., but just as classy. This is the real thing—and it tastes quite expensive.

Piper-Heidsieck Brut. $24.99. VERY GOOD. Best value. Yeast and nuttiness on the nose, like a classy, expensive Champagne. Cream, nuts, and yeast combine into a big mouthful of bubbly. Big taste, for those who prefer a bigger-style sparkler.

Laurent-Perrier Brut L.P. $29.99. VERY GOOD. On the lighter side. Lovely and flowery, like a big bouquet of very fresh roses.

Lanson Black Label Brut. $18.99. VERY GOOD. A very complex wine, with plenty going on in the glass: nuts, yeast, and flowers. This got better as it was open, making it all the more interesting. A lot of wine for the price.

A. Charbaut et Fils Brut. $19.99. GOOD/VERY GOOD. Much simpler than those above, without much taste of soil, chalk, or yeast, but so clean and crisp that it made us smile.

Visiting Wineries:
Twelve Steps to a Good Time

Visit a winery this weekend.

Me? Visit a winery? you may be thinking. But I live in Missouri—or Texas or Florida or Georgia. Truth is, there are wineries all over the country, and they're dying to greet you. How do you find them? Look in the Yellow Pages, under "Wineries." You'll be surprised how many are listed.

Some people think wineries are intimidating, the kind of place where John Beresford Tipton, the stuffy gent in the '50s TV series *The Millionaire,* greets you with a bow tie, a vest, and an attitude. But we've visited hundreds of wineries—the last decade with kids in tow—and we've almost always had a great time. You wouldn't be nervous about visiting a pumpkin farm, right? Well, just think of a winery as a grape farm—and a grape farm that often gives away samples of its products, at that.

Be sure to hire a car or have a designated driver. Here are twelve tips to make your visit more enjoyable:

(1) Go early. It might seem odd to start drinking wine before noon, but the real point of your visit is to talk to the folks who make the stuff. That might not be possible later in the day when the place gets crowded.

(2) Plan a picnic. Many wineries have picnic tables. Having lunch surrounded by vines that produced the wine you've just bought is marvelous. (Wines, especially light whites, never taste better than they do straight from the cellar of the winery. Buy it, open it to have with your sandwiches, and—we guarantee this—the wine will be great.)

(3) Don't be shy. If you drive up and there's no one else there, that's not a problem, it's an opportunity. You'll have a much better

time. Many wineries have special bottles under the counter they don't pour for everybody. If it's crowded, they stay under the counter. If you're there all alone, you may get a sip.

(4) Avoid crowds. If the parking lot is crowded or there's a bus outside, go to another winery nearby if you can. A crowded tasting room is no fun, trust us.

(5) Keep an open mind. Too many people walk into wineries and say, "I'd like to try your sweet wine," or "I only like Chardonnay." Relax. Experiment. When the person at the counter asks, "What would you like to try?" ask, "What do you recommend?" The person doing the pouring will likely suggest starting with dry whites and moving to reds, or say, "We're particularly proud of our . . ."

(6) Do comparative tastings. This is a terrific opportunity to taste wines against one another. Tasting rooms often have, say, the regular Chardonnay and a special-reserve Chardonnay (usually the first is simpler, the second more complex because of more care and barrel aging). If there are two of you, ask to have a taste of each, and take a sip of each other's. You'll enjoy discovering the difference.

(7) Be respectful. You wouldn't walk into an artist's studio and say, "I don't like that painting." Think of a winery as an artist's studio. The person behind the counter could well be the winemaker, the owner, or a member of the owner's family. If you don't like a wine, just pour it discreetly into the bucket on the counter. It's OK—that's what it's there for. You should still be able to find something nice to say about at least one of the wines.

(8) Show interest. Listen to what the pourer is saying and ask questions. If a wine smells like melons to you, say, "This has a really interesting melon nose." There's no right or wrong here. Just the fact that you smell or taste something interesting will likely be enough to get the pourer's attention, which might lead to a taste of that wine

under the counter. Ask common-sense questions like the ones you would ask a strawberry farmer: "Where are you in the production cycle?" or "How many acres do you have?"

(9) Don't pretend you're an expert. There are few things more obnoxious in a tasting room—in fact, anywhere—than a wine showoff. You're there to learn and have fun. If you do know something about wine, it will be clear from your enthusiasm.

(10) Ask about wines sold only at the winery. Sometimes wineries make small amounts of special stuff they sell only in their tasting room. It'll be all the more special when you open it because it'll remind you of your visit. At a California winery called Gundlach Bundschu, for instance, we found a wine called Kleinberger that, we were told, is a German grape that isn't even used much in Germany anymore. We bought a bottle and drank it right there, with lunch. No surprise: We found it delightful.

(11) Buy a bottle. You don't have to. We have left wineries without buying and have never gotten a dirty look. But it's a sweet gesture. If you've had a nice talk with the winemaker or owner, ask him or her to sign the bottle. Signed bottles always taste especially good.

(12) Finally, about kids: You really should think about taking your kids along, especially if the alternative is not to go at all. Children love farms, and wineries are grape farms. In all of our years, we've only run across one winery that said kids weren't welcome, and its wines weren't anything to write home about. Many more are smart enough to keep toys, books, or candy around, figuring that parents will stay longer—and buy more—if the kids are happy. But keep a close eye on your children. Farms can be dangerous places, and wineries are filled with breakables.

Many people ask us specifically what wineries to visit when they visit wine regions around the world, especially Napa and

Sonoma. First, let's say this: You don't really want to visit anyplace we'd recommend. We're not being flippant. The wineries that are most fun to visit are the undiscovered ones, the little places that most people—including us—have never heard of. Not only that, but the winery you'll remember most is the winery you discover yourself, like that little hole-in-the-wall restaurant that only you know about. We almost never make plans when we visit wine regions. We just knock on doors of anyplace that looks like a winery and ask if we can taste. Some wineries charge a small tasting fee that they usually apply to the purchase of a bottle; others are free.

But if you absolutely insist on specifics, in Napa we always drop in on Sullivan, Milat, Louis Martini, V. Sattui (for sandwiches), Stonegate, and Regusci. Other good stops are Dutch Henry, Rutherford Grove, and Pine Ridge. In Sonoma, look for Christopher Creek and Limerick Lane (they're right down the street from each other), Wellington, Family Wineries of Sonoma Valley (where you can taste the wines of several different small-production wineries) and Kunde. Things change all the time, though—owners, tasting room personnel, moods—so it really is important to find your own way.

Chapter Thirty-two

Expensive Champagne

A Bargain at $119.95?

A friend of ours who's an editor at the *Journal* messaged us a while back with a question. "Some 20 years ago, I jokingly offered to buy a woman a magnum of Dom Pérignon," the famous Champagne named for the monk who was involved in early Champagne making. "We've now been married for 19 years, and she's reminding me of the promise. Where would I go, how much would that cost, and what do you think?" We told him we thought that was a charming idea and that he could buy a magnum—a double bottle—for about $300. Our friend wrote back this three-word e-mail:

Oh.

My.

God.

But you know what? He bought the bottle anyway. And that's our point: Few people drink $100 bottles of Champagne every day, but many people buy a bottle at least once to celebrate a very special occasion. A hundred dollars is a lot of money for a bottle of Champagne, but it is, after all, an experience you'll remember forever. When you celebrate something truly special—a new baby, say, or a new job or a romantic promise kept—it's time to live out loud, and that's what "superpremium" Champagne is all about. When you spend that kind of money, though, you sure as heck want to make sure you get your money's worth.

There are several very expensive Champagnes out there, many in only limited supply. The most famous, of course, is Moët & Chandon's Dom Pérignon. Perrier-Jouët's "flower bottle" and Louis Roederer Cristal are popular, too. We decided it would be fun—and maybe even useful—to taste all of the best-known, special Champagnes against each other. There are some times when it's especially nice to have the *Journal* pay for all of our wine, and this was certainly one of them.

All of these wines are terrific, and most of them are special to us in their own way. There's the rare Salon le Mesnil that touched our daughter Media's lips seconds after she was born, and the Taittinger, from our wedding, that touched Zoë's. There's the Cristal John proposed over and the Dom Pérignon with which we celebrated the twenty-fifth anniversary of the day we met. In today's world, when so many things are expensive because of their cachet, these Champagnes are expensive, at least partly, for good reasons. They're made only in the Champagne region of France from only the best grapes (mostly Chardonnay and Pinot Noir) in the finest years. They require a great deal of personal attention for years because the Champagne-making process itself is very intensive. Fine Champagnes also generally are aged at the winery for a long time before being released, and keeping inventory around, in any business, is expensive. These are, after all, the prestige wines of great Champagne houses. It's important they be outstanding, and they are. They're also expensive, though, simply because there's a great deal of demand for them, and many people are willing to pay whatever it takes to own them. There's no question that their special cachet adds to the price—and that's where our surprising "bargain" comes into play.

One thing to keep in mind with all of these superpremium Champagnes is that, even in different vintages, each has its own style, so personal preference has a great deal to do with which Champagne anyone prefers. Bollinger R.D., for instance, has always been one of the most interesting of the high-end stuff. The "R.D." stands for "recently disgorged," which means the wine was kept on its sediment for many years, longer than most Champagnes. This gives the Bollinger a heavy, very serious taste that's like a drum roll. We consider it a connoisseur's wine, something that engages the intellect.

We conducted our first tasting of high-end Champagne in time for the millennium celebration, and we were joined by our friends Joanne

Lipman and Tom Distler. We bought every one of the best-known expensive Champagnes and tasted them blind, against one another. Average price: exactly $99.99. The surprise winner was Pol Roger Cuvée Sir Winston Churchill 1986, which cost $89.99 at the time. We found it a remarkably balanced wine, serious enough for a special occasion yet light enough to drink well past midnight.

Balance is one of the hallmarks of a good wine. In the case of outstanding Champagne, there should be smells and tastes of chalk, yeast, lemon, nuts, and fruit that all mesh into a seamless taste in your mouth. Beyond that, the taste should be inextricably bound to the bubbles, which should be like sparkling little pinpricks. A good Champagne shouldn't just be wine with bubbles, but a wine in which the bubbles themselves are part of the taste. It should be impossible to know where the wine leaves off and the bubbles begin, or vice versa. We know this sounds like a bunch of romantic mishmash, but that's what good Champagne does to us. It encourages flights of fancy.

We thought the Pol Roger was a bargain compared to the better-known expensive Champagnes. We think this has something to do with fashion and America's fascination with status. On those rare occasions when people spend this much for a wine, they want not just a good wine, but one that will immediately impress their friends and loved ones. So they go with names their friends are sure to know, like Dom Pérignon. By contrast, most people have probably never heard of Pol Roger Cuvée Sir Winston Churchill. In fact, we had never had it. The result, we figure, is that it doesn't command as much of a premium, which makes it, as these things go, a good deal.

We let a couple of vintages go by and tried again. Once again we invited Joanne and Tom over to taste with us. Once again, we bought all of the best-known "prestige cuvées." Average price this time: $116.75. Keep in mind that there are often two or three vintages of a good Champagne on the market (probably because they don't sell that quickly) and it's impossible to know what you'll find. In fact, sometimes Champagne houses release a newer wine before an older wine because they feel, given the vagaries of the vintage, that the older wine needs more time to develop before release. In any event, we picked up the vintages we saw. Other vintages might taste somewhat different, though the style should be consistent.

We came down to some decisive favorites, for very different reasons. There was one, for instance, that we didn't really love that much compared to the others. It was light and flowery and kind of "feminine," and we felt others eclipsed it. But then a funny thing happened: All of us kept coming back to it. Somehow, we found it charming in a way we couldn't quite put our finger on. We all agreed in the end that it would be the perfect wine for a summer wedding—airy, romantic, and a bit prim. It was Veuve Clicquot La Grande Dame 1990.

We liked another because it was remarkably complex. It had a lovely, bubbly nose with lots of lemon, but changed as it traveled through our mouths, from a very slightly bitter taste at the front to a little bit of sweetness at the back. It had nice body, but seemed to disappear into pure taste once swallowed. It was some mouthful of wine. This was the Louis Roederer Cristal 1994. Much as we've loved this wine over the years, we were surprised by it this time. It seemed more challenging, and we liked that.

Another old favorite also showed well. It was the Bollinger R.D. 1988. We've often found this so heavy in taste that it seems inappropriate to a celebration. This one, though, was quite lovely, with livelier, more approachable tastes than usual. It still tasted very serious and quite expensive, but it was easy to drink and memorable.

Our best of tasting was absolutely clear. "Elegant and classy. Lovely balance," we wrote in our notes. "Bigness on the palate. Beautiful. Nice acids but not too much. A little toast. Nice fruit. Everything in proportion. Lovely." Guess what? It was the Pol Roger Sir Winston Churchill again, this time the 1988. Compared with many of these famous wines, it was a bargain at "just" $119.95 (it's now higher; the prices in the Wine Notes below have been adjusted to reflect prices of more recent vintages). Bottom line: Your friends might be impressed with the label of the best-known expensive Champagnes, but they'll be impressed with the taste of the Pol Roger—and with your taste, too.

One more thing: We consider rosé Champagne especially romantic. There's something about that blushing color that makes it special. Unfortunately, good rosé Champagne is rare and expensive. How are they, for all that money? We lined them all up in bags to find out.

First, some background. Almost all grapes, even dark grapes, have colorless juice. The skins give wine its color. Most rosé wine is made by leaving the skins in contact with the juice for a short time. Some rosé Champagnes are made that way, too, but it's more common for rosé Champagnes to get their color from the addition of a small amount of red wine from the Champagne region. The Champagne Wines Information Bureau, a trade group, told us that less than 5 percent of Champagne production is rosé. The bureau also said that rosé comes in many colors—"salmon pink, gooseberry pink, pale pink, topaz-colored, old pink, orangey pink, or can draw its pinky color from that of the 'thigh of a blushing nymph.' " Hmm. Anyway, we decided we'd conduct a tasting of every high-end rosé we could find with Joanne and Tom. And we took an extra step: In the week leading up to the grand tasting, the two of us conducted blind tastings of every midrange rosé Champagne we could find. Our thought was that if some of these could run with the big boys, it would be a good idea to "promote" them to the finals. In the long run, we felt that three of the midrange rosés deserved to be promoted: the Pommery non-vintage, Charles Heidsieck 1985, and Laurent-Perrier nonvintage. We added them to our blind tasting of every top-end rosé we found, including famous names such as Dom Pérignon, Taittinger, and Laurent-Perrier Grand Siècle.

We were surprised how different each bubbly was. Their colors went from pale brick to bright pink, their bubbles from aggressive to shy, their taste from powerful to almost nonexistent. We tasted and tasted, trying to come up with a best, and ultimately narrowed the field down to No. 1, No. 4, and No. 8. We went back and forth among them. No. 1 was beautifully made, different and interesting, with a hint of tutti-frutti. No. 4 was elegant, lovely, and a bit creamy. And No. 8, from the first sip, was simply stunning—big, bold, confident.

When we finally eliminated No. 1, the tasting became a head-to-head battle. We went back and forth. "No. 4 is so elegant," John said. "You could just sip it on its own." "No. 8 is perfect," said Tom. "It has every-thing." "No. 4 suffers from being delicate," said Dottie. "It has elegance and restraint." "But No. 8 is perfect," said Joanne. "It's got everything right."

As time went by and the fill of the two bottles got lower, each of us changed our minds any number of times. In the long run, we decided that

No. 8 was the best of tasting, closely followed by No. 4. We couldn't wait to tear off the bags. No. 1 was first unveiled. It was Krug, which cost $179.95. Now we were down to the final two favorites. We tore the bag off our best of tasting. Ta-da! It was the 1989 Louis Roederer Cristal, the most expensive wine of our tasting at $299.95. So what was the very close runner-up? To our amazement, it was the nonvintage Pommery. It then cost just $34.99, which was not much more than the New York sales tax on the Cristal. What a bargain.

Would we buy rosé Champagne instead of the regular stuff? Joanne said she'd buy one for an "intimate occasion, one where Champagne is more of a focus: to toast the new year, or to give to my parents for a major wedding anniversary." As for Tom, he said he'd buy the Pommery—and by the case.

Wine Notes

General advice: *Individually, all of the following Champagnes would be terrific and almost every one is, in its own way, special to us. Don't worry about vintages. These wines aren't even produced in bad years, so it's hard to go wrong. These bubblies should be chilled well to bring all of their tastes into focus. The notes below are from our most recent tastings. All of the prices have been updated to reflect more recent vintages. In some cases the prices are higher now than they were at the time of tasting. In some cases they are the same or even lower.*
Food match: *We drink these alone.*

Expensive Champagne

Pol Roger Cuvée Sir Winston Churchill. $134.00. DELICIOUS. Best of tasting and best value. Elegant and classy, with everything in perfect proportion and a taste that lingers in your mouth forever. (1988)

Bollinger R.D. $154.59. DELICIOUS. A wine of real weight and lovely fruit, yet also with nice acids that make it good with food. Tastes expensive. A bigger wine than most, so be prepared. (1988)

Louis Roederer Cristal. $179.95. VERY GOOD. A wonderful, bubbly nose and an edgy, fascinating taste, almost a bit bitter at the front, nicely yeasty in the middle, and a little sweet at the end, with an ephemeral finish. (1994)

Billecart-Salmon Grand Cuvée. $125.00. VERY GOOD. It looks so elegant, with those gorgeous little bubbles. Quite shy. Give it time to open up and to grow on you. (1989)

Veuve Clicquot Ponsardin La Grande Dame. $109.95. VERY GOOD. Flowery, light, and "feminine." This is the Champagne we'd recommend for a summer wedding. (1990)

Rosé Champagne

Louis Roederer Cristal Brut Rosé. $299.95. DELICIOUS. Best of tasting. Creamy, toasty, and lovely, with real body. Robust, vibrant, and strong. Starts great, finishes great. (1989)

Pommery Brut Rosé. $34.99. DELICIOUS. Best value. Perfect on its own, without food. Just a little bit of shy, lovely taste. Totally elegant and "feminine." (Nonvintage)

Krug Brut Rosé. $190.00. VERY GOOD. Deeply golden, not really pink, and simply beautiful. Fruity and a bit nutty. Different and interesting, with real character. Beautifully made. (Nonvintage)

Veuve Clicquot Ponsardin La Grande Dame Brut Rosé. $199.95. GOOD/VERY GOOD. Salmon color with plenty of aggressive bubbles. Quite stark, almost a bit bitter on the finish. A bubbly with real attitude. (1989)

Dessert Wine

Chapter Thirty-three

Dessert Wine

Wait, Do NOT Turn the Page!

We were staying at the New Otani Hotel in Los Angeles in 1986 and walked a few blocks to check out a Japanese market. There, just sitting on the shelf, was a remarkable bottle of California wine: Chateau St. Jean Sauvignon d'Or 1982, Select Late Harvest. Chateau St. Jean is a fine name in California wine—it was one of our favorites when we were first learning about wine—but we'd never even heard of this wine. It said on the label that it was 59 percent Sauvignon Blanc and 41 percent Sémillon, that the grapes were picked at 35.3 percent sugar and the wine was bottled with 12.8 percent residual sugar. It was bottle No. 112. And it was just $14.98. We schlepped it all the way home on Amtrak.

Over the years, we desperately tried to find out something, anything, about this wine. We dropped into Chateau St. Jean once, where they told us we'd confused this with a simple Sauvignon Blanc and we should drink up. We even once met the winemaker whose signature was on the label, the famous Richard Arrowood, at a tasting in Miami, and he told us we couldn't possibly have a bottle of 1982 Sauvignon d'Or. And through it all, the wine, which started out golden in a clear bottle, got darker and darker, just like a Château d'Yquem, the greatest sweet wine in the world (see the following chapter). Several times a year, we took it out and just stared at it as the wine got deeper, darker, more concentrated.

We finally opened it. We are drinking it now, as we write this. Oh, gosh. It is deep brown, with a nose like burnt sugar. The taste is indescribable, like sugar-cane syrup and peaches, still surrounded by dark, fertile soil—yet with no real mouthfeel and no real weight. It's just pure, sweet taste. A little like prune juice in the intensity of its mineral tastes, layered with flavors you would get from the juices of stewed peaches and plums. Smoky, frothy nectars. Nirvana.

Now, c'mon, you'd like a taste of that even though it's a dreaded *sweet wine,* wouldn't you?

We realize most people think they don't like dessert wine, and they offer plenty of reasons: (1) they're expensive; (2) they're so sweet they make my teeth hurt; (3) I don't have time to savor a wine after dinner; hell, I don't even have time to savor dinner; and (4) I can drink only a tiny bit of sweet wine and then what am I supposed to do with the rest of the bottle? Stick with us here and we'll try to convince you at least to try a dessert wine, because (1) they don't have to be expensive; (2) good dessert wines can be light even though they're sweet; (3) a special dessert wine will make you feel you're savoring life even while doing the dishes; and (4) you can have a little glass every night for days, and the wine will keep just fine. In the long run, though, we believe one taste of a good dessert wine will do more to convince you than any number of reasoned arguments.

One problem, of course, is that any sweet wine can be called a "dessert wine" (not even to mention other fine things, like Port and Sherry). Some are made from superripe grapes, while others are "fortified" with sugar or spirits. Some are made from Sauvignon Blanc grapes, others from Chenin Blanc or Sémillon, Riesling or even Chardonnay. And they're made all over the world. We've seen more and more sweet red dessert wines from Eastern Europe on the market recently. For years, our house dessert wine was Muscat de Beaumes-de-Venise, Muscat des Papes, from France, which was nonvintage and cost about $8 for a full-size, strangely shaped bottle. This is the bottle we usually served to skeptical guests after dinner—which they drained after we finally got them to taste it. We haven't seen that particular Muscat de Beaumes-de-Venise, which is from the Rhône Valley, in years, but there are many others.

The great sweet wines of Sauternes and Barsac, in France, are in a special category (and in their own chapter, which follows), but they tend to be expensive and special. How to choose? Four words of advice: Muscat,

Ice Wine, and Tokaji (actually, just three words if you're in Canada, but we'll get to that).

When grapes are picked, the sugar breaks down about half and half into alcohol (55 to 60 percent) and carbon dioxide (40 to 45 percent). So—and this is very simplified—if you pick a grape at about 24 percent sugar and ferment the wine until it's dry, you'll get a dry wine of maybe 12 percent alcohol. If you stop the fermentation before the wine is completely dry, you'll be left with more sugar and less alcohol. If you want a sweeter wine, you must wait until the grapes get plumper, riper, and sweeter (although there are less natural ways to do this, such as adding some sugar to the fermentation, which is common and called chaptalization, or adding some alcohol to stop the fermentation, which leaves the wine sweeter and higher in alcohol). Leaving grapes on the vine until they are ripe enough to make sweet wine is fraught with risk, because the longer you wait to pick your grapes, the greater chance they'll be destroyed by a freeze, or by insects and birds, who know a good thing when they see it.

Under certain, very special conditions, grapes are attacked by a naturally occurring fortuitous mold called *Botrytis cinerea,* or noble rot, that shrivels the grapes, making them truly ugly, but concentrating their sugar. From this concentrated juice, a small amount of luscious, rich wine is made.

In terms of what advice we'd give friends on the way to the wine store, we wouldn't just say, "Pick up a dessert wine." That's why we've narrowed our advice to Muscat, Ice Wine, and Tokaji, which still covers a lot of territory.

Let's start with Muscat, because that's where we started, many years ago, with our house dessert wine, the Muscat de Beaumes-de-Venise, which even had a screwtop, so we could have a small glass before bed and put it right back into the refrigerator. Muscat is a lovely, fragrant grape that tastes of orange blossoms and honey, but Muscat encompasses far too much ever to compare them all. Muscat-based wines are sometimes dry and often sweet, sometimes low in alcohol and sometimes quite high, sometimes light and sometimes heavy. A California winery named Quady makes one dessert wine called Essensia from Orange Muscat and another called Elysium from Black Muscat. For a wide-ranging tasting of sweet Muscat wines, we tried Muscat Beaumes-de-Venise from several producers, but we found them all too heavy and alcoholic (they were all about 15 percent alcohol, and tasted as if they were, with the hot, aggressive alcohol tastes overwhelming the fruit). All of our favorites except one were quite airy and light, with alcohol below 10.5 percent (the exception was from Beaulieu Vineyard, an excellent, round wine in which the alcohol seemed well integrated, offering depth and mouthfeel).

Our favorite California Muscat for years has been the Moscato d'Andrea from Robert Pecota Winery. Not only do the color, the nose, and the taste please, but it feels good in our mouths. Seductive. It commands attention. In our most recent tasting, we were also impressed with a Moscato from St. Supéry and a Moscato Bianco from La Famiglia di Robert Mondavi, Mondavi's winery that makes wines only from Italian varietals. These were all delightful, light, and very easy to drink.

To us, though, the happiest light Muscat wine in the world is Moscato d'Asti from northern Italy, such as our all-time favorite, the La Spinetta from Rivetti. Moscato d'Asti is spritzy, sunny, and simply fun to drink. Low in alcohol, these are wines you could almost gulp, but then you'd miss the playful way the wines burst in your mouth. They make us smile. Moscato d'Asti wines are generally very, very pleasant and not expensive. Whenever we serve this to people, they love it.

We'd tell friends to look for the youngest, freshest Muscat-based wine they can find with an alcohol level under 11 percent. That's no magic formula for success, but we find that wines fitting that description can be lovely both before and after dinner.

Ice Wine is becoming pretty chic at the moment, especially from Canada, where it's called Icewine (one word). This really is wine made from grapes that have frozen on the vine. As the label of an Icewine from Paradise Ranch Wines in Canada put it: "On January 19, 2000, an Arctic front settled over the vineyards of Paradise Ranch and drove temperatures down to below -10°C. Under the light of the moon, the grapes were hand picked and pressed while frozen." That freezing leaves a tiny amount of nectar that's sweet, concentrated, and, as you can imagine, quite expensive.

Ice Wine is made all over—some is made in the United States, and the granddaddy is *Eiswein*, from Germany—but not all of it is genuine Ice Wine. Juice can simply be frozen in tanks to make a kind of Ice Wine, which creates a wine without the intensity of the real thing but without the price tag, either. In a tasting of some Ice Wines, a Selaks from New Zealand made this way was delightful. But the real thing is more than delightful, it's a unique experience. One of the best-known names in the burgeoning Canadian wine industry is Inniskillin, which is famous for its Icewine. In our most recent tasting, we had its 1998 Icewine made from Vidal grapes. (Icewines from other wineries that we tried were made from Riesling and Chardonnay.) The grapes were harvested from January 1 to January 12, the label says, and the wine was extraordinary, an impossible-to-describe combination of rich, intense, tongue-coating, concentrated fruit and exuberance. The residual sugar in the wine was—get this—27 percent. Now, we know that's making you shudder, but wait. The key to a successful sweet wine is a balance of sweetness and acids; without that, a wine can just taste like syrup. The balance here was right on the money.

Finally, we'd be remiss if we didn't mention our current very favorite dessert wine, Tokaji Aszú, from Hungary: (The region is Tokaj, which is pronounced tok-EYE, while the wine from the region is pronounced tok-eye-EE, but most people call the wine tok-EYE, too.) The wine industry of Hungary is still in the process of being rejuvenated, so these wines are not widely available. But if you see one—well, consider the Tokaji Aszú, 6 Puttonyos, Disznókö, from Hungary. "Wow! It's full-throated and confident. Everything is accentuated—the nectar nose, the earth and spice, even the artful restraint that keeps it from going over the top. You know how good chocolate dissipates in your mouth? This is like that. A creamy fullness that finishes like an orange soufflé."

What in the world does "6 puttonyos" mean? The great wine writer Hugh Johnson, in his *Modern Encyclopedia of Wine,* says Tokaji is made by adding botrytis-affected or raisined grapes to the already fermented base wine. The mixture is then refermented, incorporating the shriveled grapes' sweetness. The amount of raisined grapes added to each barrel, and therefore the sweetness, "is conventionally measured in puttonyos—a puttonyo being a grape-carrying hod containing 20–25 kilograms. 3-, 4- and 5-puttonyos wines are the most usual; 6 is exceptional." Pretty cool, huh? Wine experts are increasingly excited about the great Tokaji wines coming out of Hungary. They are expensive, but worth every penny—and more. It's only a matter of time before they regain their long-ago fame, when they were a favorite of kings and czars. Move fast!

Many dessert wines, especially heavier dessert wines, age beautifully. In fact, some are legendary for their long lives. The Moulin Touchais Anjou, a famous sweet wine made from Chenin Blanc grapes in the Loire Valley of France, is said to last forever. We remembered that when we saw the 1964 in a wine store in Dallas during a visit there in 1986. We paid $15 for it and let it sit for years. When we finally drank it, it was thirty-five years old. Our notes: "Brown, gold, red, looks like Scotch. Sherry-like on the nose, with earth and alcohol. Rich, earthy, hot on the finish, with sweetness yet lightness. Easy to drink. Baked peaches. So pretty and clean and crisp. Still vibrant, with many years ahead of it. The sugar is fundamental to the taste, like bubbles in Champagne. No harshness. Looks like liquid gold, the perfect weight and the nicest finish. A perfect mouthful. Delicious."

Wine Notes

General advice: Moscato d'Asti from Italy is a special treat; be sure to buy it young. Any young Muscat wine under 11 percent alcohol has a good chance of being a delightful apéritif or dessert wine. If you're willing to splurge, look for an Icewine from Canada. Inniskillin is always a good name to look for. If you see something on a dessert-wine label about the sugar, or Brix, at harvest, that's usually a good sign, because the winery is telling you this is a wine made from superripe grapes. The Inniskillin below, for instance, was picked at 43 percent Brix, which is extraordinary. The label might also say something about residual sugar. Buy lighter dessert wines, such as the Robert Pecota Muscat, as young as possible, but heavier dessert wines can last for many, many years. Chill all of these well. Don't worry about drinking one glass and leaving the rest corked in the refrigerator—the wine will be fine. Most good dessert wine is made in small quantities, so it's impossible to know which you will find.

Food pairings: Fruit and nuts and simple pastries.

La Spinetta "Bricco Quaglia" Moscato d'Asti (Rivetti) (Italy). $14.99.

One of our all-time favorites, a fruit bowl immersed in a lightly sparkling nectar. Clean and light as an orange blossom. Great after dinner. (2000)

Robert Pecota Winery Moscato d'Andrea Muscat Canelli (Napa Valley). $12.00 (375 ml). Like flowers and honey and the lightest of fruit nectars. Taste is light and a little spritzy, like just-picked grapes. So easy to drink, almost ephemeral. (2000)

St. Supéry Vineyards & Winery Moscato (California). $15.99. Peaches and oranges. Clean, light, and refreshing, with acids that give it a nice crispness. The sweetness tastes like fruit, not sugar. (2000)

Daltôn Muscat (Israel). $9.99 (500 ml). Highly drinkable and crisp, like biting into a ripe piece of citrus. Lovely, and kosher, too. (2000)

La Famiglia di Robert Mondavi Moscato Bianco (California). $15.99 (500 ml). Quite simple, but also very pleasant, with a long finish of honey, oranges, and peaches. (1999)

Beaulieu Vineyard Muscat de Beaulieu (California). $7.79 (375 ml). Complete, whole, round, and well integrated. Oranges and earth. Quite luscious and warming. Good after dinner on a cool night. (Nonvintage)

Inniskillin Wines Vidal Icewine (Niagara Peninsula; Canada). $53.99 (375 ml). One of Canada's most famous wines for a reason. Stunning. A remarkable combination of tongue-coating richness and exuberance. (1998)

Selaks Riesling/Gewürztraminer Ice Wine (New Zealand). $13.99 (375 ml). It's not genuine Ice Wine and lacks the intensity of the real thing, but it's still a delightful bottle of wine, with good balance and lovely fruit. (2000)

Baron Bornemisza Tokaji Aszú (6 Puttonyos) (Hungary). $34.25 (500 ml). Majestic, with sweet, stewed fruit, plenty of rich earth, nice acids, and rich layers of taste—and, despite all that, a surprising soufflé lightness. Like nothing else. (1993)

Disznókö Tokaji Aszú 1993 (6 Puttonyos) (Hungary). $45.00 (500 ml). Smells like nectar. Thick and spicy, sweet yet a bit light, with plenty going on—earth and oranges, apples and pears. Long, sweet-earth finish makes everything come together.

How the Internet
Will Change the Wine World

We're certainly not the savviest high-tech couple around, and we're real rookies when it comes to the Internet. Our twelve-year-old, Zoë, is much more competent than we are in this realm. But it's clear, even to us, that the Web is going to have a major impact on wine in the years to come. Consider this:

The only problem with a great wine list is that there's never enough time to study it so you can find the real hidden treasures. Diners who are going to Le Cirque in New York City tonight can sign onto the restaurant's Web site (www.lecirque.com) and look at the entire wine list. Then they can link to www.winedirector.com, the site of the restaurant's sommelier, Ralph Hersom, where they can ask Ralph about some of the wines and what might be good with dinner that night. By the time they show up, their wine can be on the table. How easy is that?

More and more restaurants are putting their wine lists on the Web. Not only does this make dining more fun—peeking at the wine list during the day at work sure makes the day go faster—but it means you can compare wine lists, and, most important, you can compare prices. Why does one restaurant have Sonoma-Cutrer for $58 when another has it for $38? Is every wine considerably higher at that restaurant? Why might that be? You already know some restaurant wine lists are rip-offs. This way, you can tell, before wasting your money, which restaurants offer good values—and which don't. You also can scout rare wines that are rationed to restaurants and the few lucky souls on wineries' mailing lists, wines you would never find in stores. So before you take that trip to Chicago in two weeks, you can use what you've gleaned from lists on the Web to help you plan your meals (and, perhaps, impress your colleagues). Some restaurants let you call ahead and reserve the wine, along with the table. Be sure to confirm the wine's availability the day before.

Wine shopping is getting easier, too. Some outfits are trying to sell wine on the Web nationally, but it's difficult because of crazy-quilt state and local laws. More important, scores of good local wine shops are putting their entire inventories on-line. They can often ship to people within their own states, and can sometimes ship to other states, as well. Does wine shopping make you nervous? Go on-line, where you can spend all the time you want with no pushy salesmen. Not only that, but even if your state doesn't allow you to buy wines from out of state, you can now see what's available elsewhere, and at what prices. Maybe you got a bargain. That's always good to know.

There's a remarkable amount of information available on-line about specific wines. Hundreds of wineries have their own Web sites. Did you enjoy that Chardonnay last night? Then sign onto thenameofthatwinery.com and read the winemaker's notes on that very wine. It's fun, and it's easy.

Most wine regions have Web sites now, too, so you can find out more about wines from Germany, or France, or even Cyprus. There are also all sorts of small sites run by wine clubs and hobbyists where regular people just talk about the wines they enjoy.

We know that wine intimidates many people. Now, you don't have to study the wine list at the restaurant, suffer through an annoying wine salesman, or wonder if you can order more of that great wine from the winery. It's all on-line. It seems to us that, in the long run, that has to make people more comfortable with and confident about wine, and that's a very good thing indeed.

Sauternes

Because—Well, Because You Only Live Once

This is not only the last chapter of this book. It's also the chapter we researched and wrote last. What could we possibly drink to celebrate our last chapter? We thought long and hard about that, and we finally made the tough call: It was time to open the 1971 Château d'Yquem.

Château d'Yquem is the most remarkable wine in the world. In the famous Bordeaux Classification of 1855, d'Yquem was listed *above* the first growths, as the only wine, either red or white, accorded status as "grand premier cru." There's a reason for this. Made from very carefully selected botrytis-affected grapes, and only in good years, this is as close as mortals get to a divine elixir. When we decided to have a baby, after being together for more than twelve years, we drank a bottle of Château d'Yquem 1970 to bless our first attempt. We'd had dessert wines before then, of course, but never a fine, well-aged Sauternes. It was a revelation. The wine was rich, brown, and gorgeous. It was sweet and mouth-coating—and yet it had real backbone, a significant taste of earth, and an actual lightness. As we wrote in our notes: "More like *wine* than *sweet* wine." We had never imagined Sauternes, or any wine, could have that kind of complexity: sweet yet light, rich yet restrained, bursting with ripe juice and yet full of earth.

This is what Sauternes is all about. Sauternes and Barsac, which are neighbors, make spectacular dessert wines, like no other wine on earth. In fact, earth—the soil of the region—is key. Here the soil presents itself not so much in mineral tastes, but in leavening and infusing the fruity sweetness with a firm structure. Think of toasted almonds bathed in an intensely flavored but light nectar. These wines are not sweet and flabby, with flavors spilling all over the place. The earthy core and abundant alcohol—at least 13 percent—give these sweet flavors a certain discipline and lightness that translates, in marvelous years, as perfect-pitch delicious in your mouth.

Centuries of winemaking know-how also show here in the careful management of the Sauvignon Blanc and Sémillon grapes that have been attacked by botrytis, or noble rot. Botrytis, the fungus that shrivels grapes, can be a very bad thing. In Sauternes, it's good: Because of a variety of local factors, such as climate, botrytis concentrates the sugars of the grapes there, creating nectarlike juice. There isn't much of that juice, though, and harvesting the fruit and making the wine is difficult and risky. The progression of the rot from vine to vine requires several harvesting trips as the grapes reach their optimum shriveled state at different times. The longer the grapes remain on the vines, the more vulnerable they are to destructive, nasty weather and beasties that like sweet grapes. We've read that it takes the grapes of an entire vine to produce just one glass of Yquem. In some years, some châteaux make no Sauternes at all. By all rights, these wines should be astonishingly expensive.

But sweet wines aren't very popular, and that keeps prices down, which is good for us—and you. Not only that, but since Sauternes tends to sit on store shelves, and since it tends to improve with time, you can often get a great, well-aged Sauternes for far less than it's really worth. What's more, these are also the only wines that, though very expensive, are worth the money even if you never open them. What do we mean by that? Well, consider that 1971 Château d'Yquem. We bought it in 1978 for just $30. Even in average years, Yquem can age gracefully for a long time, but in a fine year like 1971, it could last forever. So we just let it sit in our wine closet. Every couple of months, year after year, we'd take it out and look at it. At first, the wine, which comes in a clear bottle, was bright yellow-gold. With each passing year, it got darker, richer, more gorgeous, more special. We tasted that wine hundreds of times—in our heads. Finally, to toast the beginning of this chapter, we took it to one of our favorite restaurants, where they said we'd be welcome to linger over the bottle all night.

Let's start with the color. Imagine a big brick of solid gold sitting on a California beach as the sun sets over the Pacific. Imagine the interplay of the sunlight, the sand and the gold. That's what the color was like. Gold, but with fiery red-orange highlights. The nose was earthy, like sweet, damp earth. Here are our notes on the taste: "Taste is sweet yet ephemeral. A bit creamy, with nice, fluffy mouthfeel. It's perfect. Peaches, plums, almonds. Finish is so pure, so clean. There's nothing like age. Burnt oranges, stewed peaches and plums. But it's not 'sweet' the way we usually think of it. It's *very* serious. It's majestic—truly the most majestic white wine we've ever tasted. Wow. It sort of dissolves into your flesh. It evaporates and leaves the essence of itself behind. You taste fruit, not sugar."

We tasted the wine before our dinner, then put it on ice. An hour later, we came back to it—and it had not lost anything, which indicates that, indeed, this wine has years and years ahead of it. We took home enough for one last glass each and waited three days to drink it, just wondering what we'd find. It was remarkable, one of the most incredible tastes of wine we've ever had. It was as if fresh, dark, sweet, rich soil itself had somehow been fermented into wine. We cannot imagine ever again in our lifetimes experiencing such a taste.

Once in your lifetime, you should try a Yquem. But, heaven knows, you don't have to start at the top. There are a number of fine Sauternes out there, often in half bottles. Where would be a good place to start? We conducted a tasting to find out. We bought every Sauternes we found on shelves for $50 or less (or $25 or less for a half bottle, because Sauternes often comes in smaller bottles). No Sauternes is produced in mass quantities, so it's impossible to know which ones you'll find in your local wine store, but what we found in our blind tasting is that you don't need to be particular. One after another was a joy to drink. In our notes, words such as "nectar" and "sweet earth" and "lovely" came up again and again. Consider this one:

"Smoky and rich, a Lauren Bacall kind of wine. Fruit nectar, rich, and elegant. Serious wine, not just a confection, because of a serious underpinning of earth. Peaches, plums, pears. Like a fruit bowl, but distilled with a lot of mouthfeel and some earth." This was the Castelnau de Suduiraut (the second label of the well-known Château Suduiraut). This cost $16.99 for a half bottle. (Prices are all over the map on these wines.

Sometimes shops keep prices high because the wines are worth it, and other times they drop prices to get rid of them. Sometimes stores raise prices as the wines age, and sometimes they don't.)

This is how we described our favorite: "Taste of the earth. Some crispness. Baked luscious fruits like peaches and apricots, but light in body. Effortless. Still young. The contrast of the nectar and the lightness is what makes this work—along with a big dollop of soil." This was Château Coutet, which cost $41.99.

Bite the bullet. Buy a Sauternes, put it in the refrigerator, and serve it tonight after dinner, even if it's just the two of you—in fact, especially if it's just the two of you. This isn't just a good wine, but a wine that might change your mind about a whole genre of wine. Remember, too, that Sauternes makes a great gift for wine novices and wine aficionados alike. Novices will be amazed at how delicious a dessert wine can be, and even most wine lovers don't buy Sauternes that often, because it seems like such a luxury.

Value tip: If you happen to see a wine that looks just like Sauternes on the shelf but it's from Monbazillac, another area of France, grab it. Monbazillac is often excellent, and tastes a lot like Sauternes, but is much less expensive, often less than $20 for a regular-size bottle. You can have a glass of Monbazillac or Sauternes for several nights and leave the bottle corked in the refrigerator.

Here's another tip: People always ask us what wine they should "lay down" for their newborn child. Our advice is Sauternes, both because it ages so beautifully (literally and figuratively) and because it reminds us of children: Sweet and direct in youth, more textured and interesting with age. We have several bottles of 1989 d'Yquem, from Media's birth year. When our friends Paul Steiger and Wendy Brandes were over at our apartment and told us they were getting married, we thought only such a great bottle could match the occasion, so we opened one up. How was it? Although twelve years old at the time, it was still far too young to drink— lovely and complex, to be sure, but without the richness and intensity that age will bring to it.

In other words, it should be just about ready to drink at Media's graduation from Harvard.

Wine Notes

General advice: Look for Sauternes or Barsac on the label. Many good ones come in half bottles, so that might be a good place to start. If you see "Grand Cru Classé in 1855" or "1er Cru," that's a good sign but, as always, no guarantee. Sauternes gets better and better as it gets older, so if you see an older bottle, grab it. The first chart below shows the results of a recent tasting. The second chart shows some of the results from an earlier tasting to give you a few more reliable names. It wouldn't be surprising to see some of these older wines on the shelves. The prices from the earlier tasting are the prices we paid at the time. In some cases, the prices for more recent vintages of these wines are actually somewhat lower. In general, prices for Sauternes are quite variable from store to store.

Food pairings: Sauternes and foie gras is a classic combination, but we prefer to drink Sauternes with nuts or fruit. Some people like it with sweetbreads, pâté, duck, or rabbit.

Château Coutet. $43.00. VERY GOOD/DELICIOUS. Best of tasting. Luscious baked fruits—peaches and apricots—but light, with nice tastes of the earth. (1996)

Castelnau de Suduiraut. $16.99 (half bottle). VERY GOOD/DELICIOUS. Best value. Smoky, rich, and elegant, but not just a confection. It has a serious underlay of earthiness. (1997)

Clos Labère. $27.99. VERY GOOD/DELICIOUS. Soft, lovely, and effortless. Peaches and vanilla. (1996)

Château Roûmieu-Lacoste. $18.99 (375 ml). VERY GOOD/DELICIOUS. More serious and weighty than most, with good fruit and acids and plenty of backbone. (1997)

Château Lafaurie-Peyraguey. $47.59. VERY GOOD/DELICIOUS. Sweet almond-cheese pastry, wrapped in a light-as-air package. (1995)

Previous Tasting

Château Doisy-Védrines. $32.99. DELICIOUS. Best of tasting. Restrained and elegant, with all sorts of fruit flavors. Charming, clean, and lovely, with pure, sweet fruit tastes. (1995)

Château Roûmieu-Lacoste. $19.99 (375 ml). VERY GOOD/DELI-CIOUS. Best value. Rich, creamy, and sensuous, with some nutmeg, cream, and spice. Sweet with fruit. Wow. (1996)

Château Bastor-Lamontagne. $14.99 (375 ml). VERY GOOD. Burnt sugar and pine needles—yet a lovely, dry finish that leaves hints of earth and grass. Beautifully made. (1994)

Château Coutet. $27.00 (375 ml). It tastes like peaches and candy, but with some real backbone. Long, sweet-fruit—yet light—finish. (1995)

Château Rieussec. $49.95. GOOD. This seems to have obvious acids, which make it knifelike. Not as charming as some, but better with food than most. We've liked this wine better in previous years. (1995)

Château Rabaud-Promis. $30 (half bottle). GOOD. Very sweet, without a hint of age. Plenty of sugar and fruit, but it's not showing a lot—yet. (1989)

Acknowledgments

Over the years, many people have helped us learn about wine. We have mentioned a number of them throughout this book. We are in their debt. There are also people without whom this book, quite literally, never would have been written:

- Paul Steiger, the managing editor of the *Wall Street Journal,* the best boss anyone could have, who has consistently supported us;
- Joanne Lipman, the founder of *Weekend Journal* and now a deputy managing editor of the *Wall Street Journal,* who asked us to write a wine column and has been its biggest fan;
- Bill Shinker, the former president and publisher of Broadway Books, who asked us to write the first edition of this book long before most people understood our column's potential;
- Jennifer Josephy, our editor at Broadway Books, who thought it would be fun to prepare a second edition and whose enthusiasm for the project did indeed make it fun;
- Gerry Howard, editor in chief of Broadway Books, who encouraged the idea throughout;
- Our daughters, Media and Zoë, who have always been patient with us, and never more so than during the production of this book;
- And our parents, Worrell and Dorothy E. Gaiter, and Ben and Ruth Brecher, who didn't teach us anything about wine, but everything about life and passion and, by example, what marriage is all about.

$\mathcal{I}ndex$

About the Authors

DOROTHY J. GAITER has been a reporter, editor, and columnist at the *Wall Street Journal*, the *New York Times*, and the *Miami Herald*. JOHN BRECHER was Page-One editor of the *Wall Street Journal* from 1992 to 2000. They currently write the weekly "Tastings" column for the *Wall Street Journal* and are the authors of *Love by the Glass: Tasting Notes from a Marriage*. They live in New York City with their two daughters, Media and Zoë.